한국의 토익 수험자 여러분께,

토익 시험은 세계적인 직무 영어능력 평가 시험으로, 지난 40여 년간 비즈니스 현장에서 필요한 영어능력 평가의 기준을 제시해 왔습니다. 토익 시험 및 토익스피킹, 토익라이팅 시험은 세계에서 가장 널리 통용되는 영어능력 검증 시험으로, 160여 개국 14,000여 기관이 토익 성적을 의사결정에 활용하고 있습니다.

YBM은 한국의 토익 시험을 주관하는 ETS 독점 계약사입니다.

ETS는 한국 수험자들의 효과적인 토익 학습을 돕고자 YBM을 통하여 'ETS 토익 공식 교재'를 독점 출간하고 있습니다. 또한 'ETS 토익 공식 교재' 시리즈에 기출문항을 제공해 한국의 다른 교재들에 수록된 기출을 복제하거나 변형한 문항으로 인하여 발생할 수 있는 수험자들의 혼동을 방지하고 있습니다.

복제 및 변형 문항들은 토익 시험의 출제의도를 벗어날 수 있기 때문에 기출문항을 수록한 'ETS 토익 공식 교재'만큼 시험에 잘 대비할 수 없습니다.

'ETS 토익 공식 교재'를 통하여 수험자 여러분의 영어 소통을 위한 노력에 큰 성취가 있기를 바랍니다.

감사합니다.

Dear TOEIC Test Takers in Korea,

The TOEIC program is the global leader in English-language assessment for the workplace. It has set the standard for assessing English-language skills needed in the workplace for more than 40 years. The TOEIC tests are the most widely used English language assessments around the world, with 14,000+ organizations across more than 160 countries trusting TOEIC scores to make decisions.

YBM is the ETS Country Master Distributor for the TOEIC program in Korea and so is the exclusive distributor for TOEIC Korea.

To support effective learning for TOEIC test-takers in Korea, ETS has authorized YBM to publish the only Official TOEIC prep books in Korea. These books contain actual TOEIC items to help prevent confusion among Korean test-takers that might be caused by other prep book publishers' use of reproduced or paraphrased items.

Reproduced or paraphrased items may fail to reflect the intent of actual TOEIC items and so will not prepare test-takers as well as the actual items contained in the ETS TOEIC Official prep books published by YBM.

We hope that these ETS TOEIC Official prep books enable you, as test-takers, to achieve great success in your efforts to communicate effectively in English.

Thank you.

입문부터 실전까지 수준별 학습을 통해 최단기 목표점수 달성!

ETS TOEIC® 공식수험서 스마트 학습 지원

www.ybmbooks.com에서도 무료 MP3를 다운로드 받을 수 있습니다.

ETS 토익 모바일 학습 플랫폼!

ETS 토익기출 수험서 **어플**

구글플레이   앱스토어

교재 학습 지원	· 교재 해설 강의
	· LC 음원 MP3
	· 교재/부록 모의고사 채점 분석
	· 단어 암기장
부가 서비스	· 데일리 학습(토익 기출문제 풀이)
	· 토익 최신 경향 무료 특강
	· 토익 타이머
모의고사 결과 분석	· 파트별/문항별 정답률
	· 파트별/유형별 취약점 리포트
	· 전체 응시자 점수 분포도

ETS 토익 학습 전용 온라인 커뮤니티!

ETS TOEIC® Book **공식카페**

etstoeicbook.co.kr

강사진의 학습 지원	토익 대표강사들의 학습 지원과 멘토링
교재 학습관 운영	교재별 학습게시판을 통해 무료 동영상 강의 등 학습 지원
학습 콘텐츠 제공	토익 학습 콘텐츠와 정기시험 예비특강 업데이트

*toeic.
토익 단기공략
650+

LC **RC**

토익 단기공략
650+

발행인	허문호
발행처	YBM

편집	윤경림
디자인	DOTS, 이현숙
마케팅	정연철, 박천산, 고영노, 김동진, 박찬경, 김윤하

초판발행	2020년 7월 20일
11쇄 발행	2024년 12월 5일

신고일자	1964년 3월 28일
신고번호	제 1964-000003호
주소	서울시 종로구 종로 104
전화	(02) 2000-0515 [구입문의] / (02) 2000-0345 [내용문의]
팩스	(02) 2285-1523
홈페이지	www.ybmbooks.com

ISBN	978-89-17-23593-7

PREFACE

Dear test taker,

The purpose of this book is to help you succeed in using English for communication with colleagues and clients in Korea and around the world. Now more than ever, English is a tool that can yield great professional rewards.

This book provides practical steps that you can use right now in a two-week or four-week program of study for the TOEIC test. Use your TOEIC test score as a respected professional credential and a sign that you are ready to take your career to the next level. Your TOEIC score is recognized globally as evidence of your English-language proficiency.

With **<ETS 토익 단기공략 650+>**, you can make sure you have the best and most thorough preparation for the TOEIC test. This book contains key study points that will familiarize you with the test format and content, and you will be able to practice at your own pace. The test questions are created by the same test specialists who develop the TOEIC test itself, and the book contains questions taken from actual TOEIC tests.

Here are some features of **<ETS 토익 단기공략 650+>**.

- This book contains carefully selected questions taken from actual TOEIC tests.
- All TOEIC Listening and Reading test content is included in one book that is suitable for short-term study in two-week or four-week plans.
- You will hear the same ETS voice actors that you will hear in a real ETS test.
- Key study points will help you to achieve your target score with the least amount of time and effort.
- The enhanced analyses and explanations are based on the latest TOEIC test research.

In preparing for the test with **<ETS 토익 단기공략 650+>**, you can be confident that you have a solid resource at hand and are taking the best approach to maximizing your TOEIC test score. Use **<ETS 토익 단기공략 650+>** to become familiar with the test, including actual test tasks, content, and format. You will be well prepared to show the world what you know by taking the test and receiving your score report.

We hope that you will find this high-quality resource to be of the utmost use, and we wish you all the very best success.

●

출제기관이 만든
점수대별
단기 완성 전략서!

• 기출 문항으로 보강된 단기 완성 시리즈

풍부한 기출 문항뿐만 아니라 토익 출제기관인 ETS가 정기시험과 동일한 유형 및 난이도로 개발한 문제들로 구성된 고품질의 전략서이다.

• 단기 목표 달성에 최적화된 구성

LC와 RC를 한권으로 구성하고, 목표 점수 달성에 필요한 핵심 내용만 수록하여 학습 부담을 최소화하였다.

• 정기시험과 동일한 성우 음원

토익 정기시험 성우가 실제 시험과 동일한 속도와 발음으로 직접 녹음하였으므로 실전에 완벽하게 대비할 수 있다.

• ETS만이 제시할 수 있는 체계적인 공략법

토익 각 파트에 대한 이해를 높이고 원하는 점수를 달성하기 위한 체계적인 공략법을 제시하고 있다.

• 토익 최신 경향을 반영한 명쾌한 분석과 해설

최신 출제 경향을 완벽하게 분석하고 반영하여 고득점을 달성하게 해줄 해법을 낱낱이 제시하고 있다.

CONTENTS

▪ LC

■ RC

TOEIC 소개

■ **TOEIC** Test of English for international Communication(국제적 의사소통을 위한 영어 시험)의 약자로, 영어가 모국어가 아닌 사람들이 일상생활 또는 비즈니스 현장에서 꼭 필요한 실용적 영어 구사 능력을 갖추었는가를 평가하는 시험이다.

■ **시험 구성**

구성	PART	유형		문항 수	시간	배점
Listening	Part 1	사진 묘사		6	45분	495점
	Part 2	질의 응답		25		
	Part 3	짧은 대화		39		
	Part 4	짧은 담화		30		
Reading	Part 5	단문 빈칸 채우기		30	75분	495점
	Part 6	장문 빈칸 채우기		16		
	Part 7	독해	단일 지문	29		
			이중 지문	10		
			삼중 지문	15		
Total	**7 Parts**			**200문항**	**120분**	**990점**

■ **평가 항목**

LC	RC
단문을 듣고 이해하는 능력	읽은 글을 통해 추론해 생각할 수 있는 능력
짧은 대화체 문장을 듣고 이해하는 능력	장문에서 특정한 정보를 찾을 수 있는 능력
비교적 긴 대화체에서 주고받은 내용을 파악할 수 있는 능력	글의 목적, 주제, 의도 등을 파악하는 능력
장문에서 핵심이 되는 정보를 파악할 수 있는 능력	뜻이 유사한 단어들의 정확한 용례를 파악하는 능력
구나 문장에서 화자의 목적이나 함축된 의미를 이해하는 능력	문장 구조를 제대로 파악하는지, 문장에서 필요한 품사, 어구 등을 찾는 능력

※ 성적표에는 전체 수험자의 평균과 해당 수험자가 받은 성적이 백분율로 표기되어 있다.

수험 정보

■ **시험 접수 방법**

한국 토익 위원회 사이트(www.toeic.co.kr)에서 시험일 약 2개월 전부터
온라인으로 접수 가능

■ **시험장 준비물**

신분증	규정 신분증만 가능 (주민등록증, 운전면허증, 기간 만료 전의 여권, 공무원증)
필기구	연필, 지우개 (볼펜이나 사인펜은 사용 금지)

■ **시험 진행 시간**

09:20	입실 (9:50 이후 입실 불가)
09:30 ~ 09:45	답안지 작성에 관한 오리엔테이션
09:45 ~ 09:50	휴식
09:50 ~ 10:05	신분증 확인
10:05 ~ 10:10	문제지 배부 및 파본 확인
10:10 ~ 10:55	듣기 평가 (LISTENING TEST)
10:55 ~ 12:10	읽기 평가 (READING TEST)

■ **TOEIC 성적 확인**

시험일로부터 10~11일 후, 오후 12시부터 인터넷 홈페이지와 어플리케이션을 통해
성적을 확인할 수 있다. 성적표는 우편이나 온라인으로 발급 받을 수 있다.
우편으로 발급 받을 경우 성적 발표 후 대략 일주일이 소요되며, 온라인 발급을
선택하면 유효기간 내에 홈페이지에서 본인이 직접 1회에 한해 무료 출력할 수 있다.
TOEIC 성적은 시험일로부터 2년간 유효하다.

■ **토익 점수**

TOEIC 점수는 듣기 영역(LC)과 읽기 영역(RC)을 합계한 점수로 5점 단위로 구성되며
총점은 990점이다. TOEIC 성적은 각 문제 유형의 난이도에 따른 점수 환산표에 의해
결정된다.

LC 출제 경향 분석

PART 1

문제 유형 및 출제 비율 (평균 문항 수)

사람을 주어로 하는 사람 묘사 문제가 가장 많은 비중을 차지하며 사람/사물 혼합 문제, 사물/풍경 묘사 문제가 각각 그 다음을 이룬다.

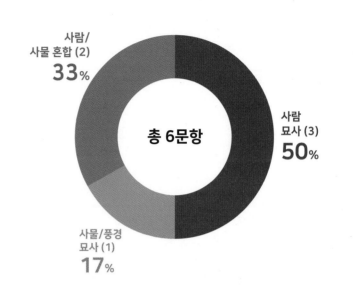

사람/사물 혼합 (2)
33%

사람 묘사 (3)
50%

사물/풍경 묘사 (1)
17%

총 6문항

PART 2

문제 유형 및 출제 비율 (평균 문항 수)

의문사 의문문이 거의 절반가량을 차지하며 일반 의문문과 평서문이 그 다음을 이룬다. 부가/부정/선택 의문문은 평균 2문항씩 출제되며 간접 의문문은 간혹 1문제 출제된다.

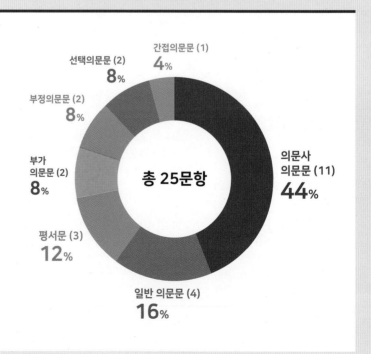

간접의문문 (1)
4%

선택의문문 (2)
8%

부정의문문 (2)
8%

부가 의문문 (2)
8%

의문사 의문문 (11)
44%

평서문 (3)
12%

일반 의문문 (4)
16%

총 25문항

PART 3

문제 유형 및
출제 비율
(평균 문항 수)

세부 사항을 묻는 문제가 가장
많은 비중을 차지하며 주제,
목적, 화자, 장소 문제, 다음에 할
일, 미래 정보 문제가 그 다음을
차지한다. 문제점 및 걱정 거리
문제는 출제 빈도가 다소 낮다.
의도 파악 문제와 시각 정보
문제는 각각 2문항, 3문항 고정
비율로 출제된다.

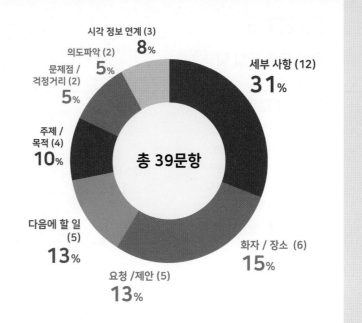

시각 정보 연계 (3) **8**%
의도파악 (2) **5**%
문제점 / 걱정거리 (2) **5**%
주제 / 목적 (4) **10**%
다음에 할 일 (5) **13**%
요청 /제안 (5) **13**%
화자 / 장소 (6) **15**%
세부 사항 (12) **31**%

총 39문항

PART 4

지문 유형 및
출제 비율
(평균 지문 수)

전화 메시지와 공지, 안내, 회의
발췌록이 가장 많이 출제된다.
광고, 방송, 보도가 그 다음을
차지하며 여행, 견학, 관람,
인물, 강연, 설명은 출제 빈도가
다소 낮다.

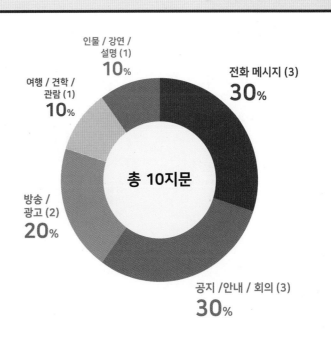

인물 / 강연 / 설명 (1) **10**%
여행 / 견학 / 관람 (1) **10**%
전화 메시지 (3) **30**%
방송 / 광고 (2) **20**%
공지 /안내 / 회의 (3) **30**%

총 10지문

RC 출제 경향 분석

PART 5

문법 문제 유형 및 출제 비율 (평균 문항 수)

전치사와 접속사를 구분하는 문제와 동사 문제, 품사 문제 출제 비중이 가장 높다. 기타 문법에서는 준동사가 1~2문항, 관계사가 매회 거의 1문항씩 출제된다.

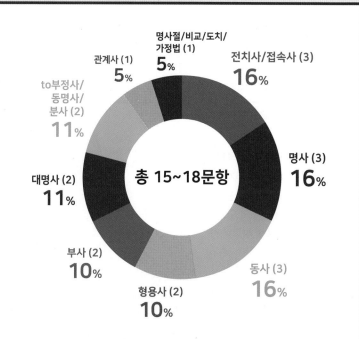

명사절/비교/도치/가정법 (1) 5%
관계사 (1) 5%
전치사/접속사 (3) 16%
to부정사/동명사/분사 (2) 11%
명사 (3) 16%
대명사 (2) 11%
동사 (3) 16%
부사 (2) 10%
형용사 (2) 10%

총 15~18문항

PART 5

어휘 문제 유형 및 출제 비율 (평균 문항 수)

전치사, 명사, 부사 어휘 문제가 가장 많이 출제되며 형용사, 동사 어휘가 그 뒤를 잇는다.

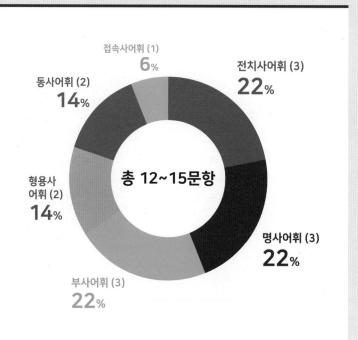

접속사어휘 (1) 6%
동사어휘 (2) 14%
전치사어휘 (3) 22%
형용사 어휘 (2) 14%
명사어휘 (3) 22%
부사어휘 (3) 22%

총 12~15문항

PART 6

문제 유형 및
출제 비율
(평균 문항 수)

문법과 어휘 비중이 비슷하게
출제되며 접속부사는 1~2문항
출제된다. 문장 삽입 문제는
4문항 고정 비율로 출제된다.

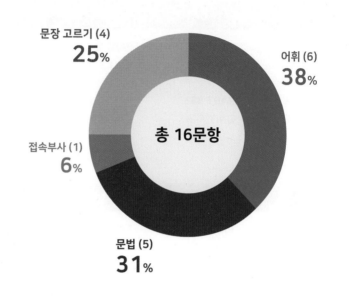

문장 고르기 (4)
25%

어휘 (6)
38%

접속부사 (1)
6%

총 16문항

문법 (5)
31%

PART 7

문제 유형 및
출제 비율
(평균 문항 수)

세부 사항 문제가 가장 높은
비율을 차지하며 추론/암시
문제와 (NOT) mention/true
문제가 그 다음으로 출제율이
높다. 주어진 문장 넣기와 의도
파악 문제는 각각 2문항씩 고정
비율로 출제된다. 이중, 삼중
지문에서는 연계 문제가 8문항
정도 출제된다.

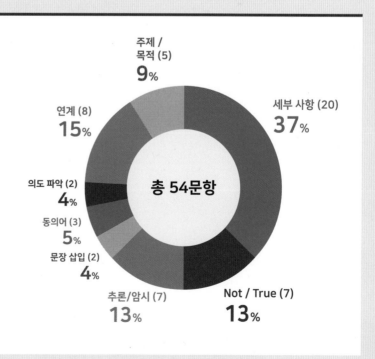

주제 /
목적 (5)
9%

연계 (8)
15%

세부 사항 (20)
37%

의도 파악 (2)
4%

동의어 (3)
5%

문장 삽입 (2)
4%

총 54문항

추론/암시 (7)
13%

Not / True (7)
13%

2주 완성 플랜

초단기에 토익 650점을 돌파하고자 하는 중급 수험생을 위한 2주 완성 플랜

	DAY 1	DAY 2	DAY 3	DAY 4	DAY 5
LC	PART 1 UNIT 1~2	PART 2 UNIT 3~4	PART 2 UNIT 5~6	PART 2 UNIT 7~8	PART 3 UNIT 9
RC	PART 5&6 UNIT 1~3	PART 5&6 UNIT 4~6	PART 5&6 UNIT 7~9	PART 5&6 UNIT 10~12	PART 5&6 UNIT 13~15

	DAY 6	DAY 7	DAY 8	DAY 9	DAY 10
LC	PART 3 UNIT 10	PART 3 UNIT 11~12	PART 4 UNIT 13	PART 4 UNIT 14~15	PART 4 UNIT 16~17
RC	PART 5&6 UNIT 16~17	PART 7 UNIT 18	PART 7 UNIT 19	PART 7 UNIT 20	PART 7 UNIT 21

4주 완성 플랜

초단기에 토익 650점을 돌파하고자 하는 중급 수험생을 위한 4주 완성 플랜

	DAY 1	DAY 2	DAY 3	DAY 4	DAY 5
LC	PART 1 UNIT 1	PART 1 UNIT 2	PART 2 UNIT 3	PART 2 UNIT 4	PART 2 UNIT 5
RC	PART 5&6 UNIT 1	PART 5&6 UNIT 2	PART 5&6 UNIT 3	PART 5&6 UNIT 4	PART 5&6 UNIT 5

	DAY 6	DAY 7	DAY 8	DAY 9	DAY 10
LC	PART 2 UNIT 6	PART 2 UNIT 7	PART 2 UNIT 8	PART 1, 2 UNIT 1~8 복습	PART 3 UNIT 9
RC	PART 5&6 UNIT 6	PART 5&6 UNIT 7	PART 5&6 UNIT 8	PART 5&6 UNIT 9	PART 5&6 UNIT 10

	DAY 11	DAY 12	DAY 13	DAY 14	DAY 15
LC	PART 3 UNIT 10	PART 3 UNIT 11	PART 3 UNIT 12	PART 3 UNIT 9~12 복습	PART 4 UNIT 13
RC	PART 5&6 UNIT 11	PART 5&6 UNIT 12	PART 5&6 UNIT 13	PART 5&6 UNIT 14	PART 5&6 UNIT 15~16

	DAY 16	DAY 17	DAY 18	DAY 19	DAY 20
LC	PART 4 UNIT 14	PART 4 UNIT 15	PART 4 UNIT 16	PART 4 UNIT 17	PART 4 UNIT 13~17 복습
RC	PART 5&6 UNIT 17	PART 7 UNIT 18	PART 7 UNIT 19	PART 7 UNIT 20	PART 7 UNIT 21

Part

사진 묘사

1

Part 1 | 사진 묘사 총 6문항

Part 1은 사진을 보면서 4개의 보기를 듣고, 그 중에서 사진을 가장 잘 묘사한 보기를 고르는 유형이에요.

■ Part 1 이렇게 풀자

1 음원을 듣기 전
사진 파악

2 음원을 들으면서 오답 보기 소거

(A) She's ~~paying at a cash register.~~
(B) She's choosing an item off a shelf.
(C) She's ~~reading a restaurant menu.~~
(D) She's ~~pouring a beverage into a glass.~~

3 음원을 듣고 난 후?
정답 선택

(B)

■ 오답을 소거하자

음원을 듣기 전에 사람의 동작이나 상태, 사물의 이름, 위치 등을 파악한 다음, 음원을 들으면서 오답을 소거하다 보면 쉽게 정답을 찾을 수 있어요. 오답 유형은 크게 두 가지로 나뉘어요.

1 사진과 다른 동작이나 상태 표현이 들리면 오답이에요.

A woman is ~~filling~~ a bucket. 여자가 양동이를 채우고 있다.
→ **A woman is carrying some buckets.** 여자가 양동이를 들고 있다.

She is ~~putting on~~ a hat. 여자가 모자를 쓰는 중이다.
→ **She is wearing a hat.** 여자가 모자를 쓰고 있다.

ⓘ 착용 중인 상태를 나타내는 wearing과 무언가를 착용하는 동작을 가리키는 putting on을 혼동하지 않도록 주의하세요.

2 사진에 없는 단어가 들리면 오답이에요.

Some ~~boats~~ are docked along the beach.
배들이 해변을 따라 정박해 있다.

Some ~~children~~ are climbing on a ~~rock~~. 어린이들이 바위를 오르고 있다.
→ **A path extends along the shore.**
길이 해안을 따라 나 있다.

■ 동작이나 상태를 묘사하는 동사의 형태에 주목하자

Part 1에서는 주어 뒤에 나오는 동사를 듣는 것이 중요해요. 동작이나 상태를 묘사하는 동사의 시제는 다음과 같습니다.

1 현재진행 시제 주로 사람의 동작을 묘사할 때 써요.

주어 + is / are + -ing	주어가 ~하고 있다

- The man is holding a basket. 남자가 바구니를 들고 있다.
- He is shopping for some food. 남자가 장을 보고 있다.

2 현재 시제 현재의 상태를 나타낼 때 써요.

주어 + is / are + 형용사	주어가 ~한 상태이다
주어 + is / are + 전치사구	주어가 ~에 있다

- Some baskets are full of fruit. 바구니에 과일이 가득하다.
- Some merchandise is on display. 상품들이 진열되어 있다.

3 현재완료 시제 행동이나 움직임이 완료되었을 때 써요.

주어 + have / has p.p.	주어가 ~했다

- A man has picked up a phone. 남자가 전화를 받았다.

4 현재 수동태 / 현재완료 수동태 주로 사물의 위치나 상태를 묘사할 때 써요.

주어 + is / are + p.p.	주어가 ~되어 있다
주어 + has / have been p.p.	

- Chairs are unoccupied. 의자들이 비어 있다.
- Chairs have been arranged in a row. 의자들이 일렬로 정렬되어 있다.

인물 등장 사진

① 1인 사진

사람이 한 명만 있는 사진으로, 주로 사람의 손동작이나 상태 등을 묘사하는 문장이 나와요.

> **출제 포인트 1** 4개의 보기가 모두 동일한 주어로 시작하면서 현재진행(is/are+-ing) 시제로 사진을 묘사하는 문제가 주로 나와요. 이런 경우 주어보다는 '-ing' 부분이나 명사에 집중해서 들으세요.
>
> **출제 포인트 2** 사람의 손이 닿아 있거나 사진에서 두드러지는 사물을 기준으로 묘사하는 문장도 나와요.

■ **기출 사진**으로 분석하는 정답 vs. 오답

동작 묘사

정답 He's **writing** on a notepad. 남자가 수첩에 뭔가를 쓰고 있다.
오답 He's ~~sharpening~~ some pencils. 남자가 연필을 깎고 있다.

정답 He is **talking** on the phone. 남자가 전화통화를 하고 있다.
오답 He is ~~dialing~~ a phone. 남자가 전화를 걸고 있다.

> [Tip] 구체적인 사물명 대신에 포괄적인 단어로 묘사하는 경우도 많아요.

사진 속 명사와 사진에 없는 명사

정답 She's examining **a vase**. 여자가 꽃병을 보고 있다.
오답 She's cutting ~~some flowers~~. 여자가 꽃을 자르고 있다.

정답 She is holding **a pottery item**. 여자가 도기 제품을 들고 있다.
오답 She is serving ~~some customers~~. 여자가 고객을 응대하고 있다.

상태 묘사와 동작 묘사

정답 A woman is **standing** in front of a cabinet.
여자가 캐비닛 앞에 서 있다.
오답 A woman is ~~wiping~~ a cabinet. 여자가 캐비닛을 닦고 있다.

정답 A woman is **wearing** glasses. 여자가 안경을 쓰고 있다.
오답 A woman is ~~putting on~~ glasses. 여자가 안경을 쓰는 중이다.

> (!) A woman is ~~putting on~~ a jacket. 여자가 재킷을 입고 있다.
> → put on/try on은 입거나 착용하는 동작을 묘사하는 표현이에요.

T **실전 도움닫기** | 음원을 듣고 사진을 가장 잘 묘사한 문장을 고르세요. 다시 듣고 빈칸을 채우세요.

650_P1_01

정답과 해설 p. 002

LC

PART 1

1.

(A) A man is _____ under a tree.

(B) A man is _____ some bushes.

(C) A man is _____ a machine.

(D) A man is _____ some tools.

2.

(A) She's _____ some books.

(B) She's _____ for a door handle.

(C) She's _____ a piece of paper.

(D) She's _____ some shelves.

3.

(A) He's _____ a computer screen.

(B) He's _____ the phone.

(C) He's _____ a lamp.

(D) He's _____ a hat.

4.

(A) A woman is _____.

(B) A woman is _____.

(C) A woman is _____.

(D) A woman is _____.

② 2인 이상 사진

사람들이 공통적으로 하고 있는 동작이나 상태가 주로 나와요. 공통점이 없는 경우, 각각의 인물들이 개별적으로 하는 동작에 주목하세요.

> **출제 포인트 1** 2인 사진: 보통 두 사람의 공통된 동작이나 상태를 먼저 파악하세요.
> **출제 포인트 2** 3인 이상 사진: 다수의 사람들이 하는 동작 → 개별 행동을 하는 사람 → 눈에 띄는 배경이나 사물 순서로 잘 나와요.

■ 기출 사진으로 분석하는 정답 vs. 오답

2인 사진 - 공통 동작

정답 The men are **seated side by side**.
남자들이 나란히 앉아 있다.

오답 The men are ~~strolling~~ past a bench.
남자들이 벤치를 지나가고 있다.

2인 사진 - 개별 동작

정답 A salesperson is **helping a customer with a necklace**.
판매원이 손님의 목걸이 착용을 돕고 있다.

오답 A salesperson is ~~reaching into a display case~~.
판매원이 진열장에 손을 뻗고 있다.

3인 이상 사진 - 공통 동작

정답 Some people are **meeting in a conference room**.
사람들이 회의실에서 만나고 있다.

오답 ~~The women are sitting~~ at a table. 여자들이 테이블에 앉아 있다.

ⓘ 일부 사람들만 하고 있는 개별 동작을 공통 동작처럼 묘사하는 오답 문장에 주의하세요.

3인 이상 사진 - 개별 동작

정답 A waiter is **taking an order**.
웨이터가 주문을 받고 있다.

오답 The man is ~~giving his menu~~ to a waiter.
남자가 웨이터에게 메뉴를 주고 있다.

1.

(A) They're _____ a photocopier.

(B) They're _____ on laptop computers.

(C) They're _____ some documents.

(D) They're _____ their jackets.

2.

(A) Two men are _____ a wall.

(B) A man is _____ in a cord.

(C) A man is _____ to his coworker.

(D) _____ are using tools.

3.

(A) Some people are _____.

(B) Some people are _____.

(C) Some people are _____.

(D) Some people are _____.

4.

(A) They're _____.

(B) They're _____ from their bags.

(C) They're _____.

(D) They're _____.

1.

(A) (B) (C) (D)

2.

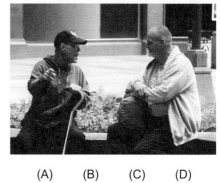

(A) (B) (C) (D)

3.

(A) (B) (C) (D)

4.

(A) (B) (C) (D)

5.

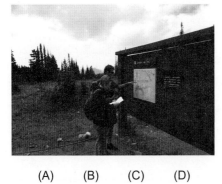

(A) (B) (C) (D)

6.

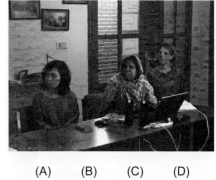

(A) (B) (C) (D)

7.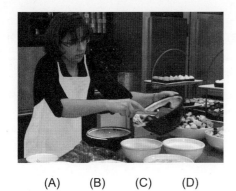

(A)　　(B)　　(C)　　(D)

8.

(A)　　(B)　　(C)　　(D)

9.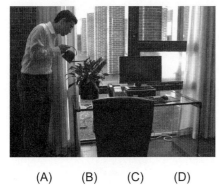

(A)　　(B)　　(C)　　(D)

10.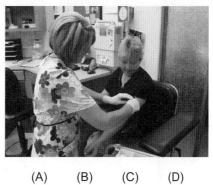

(A)　　(B)　　(C)　　(D)

11.

(A)　　(B)　　(C)　　(D)

12.

(A)　　(B)　　(C)　　(D)

사물 · 배경 사진 / 인물 · 사물 혼합 사진

① 사물 · 배경 사진

사물이나 공원, 거리, 호수 등과 같은 배경이 중심이 되는 사진으로, 사물의 위치나 상태를 묘사하는 문제가 주로 나와요.

> **출제 포인트 1** 문장 뒷부분에 나오는 전치사구를 듣고 사물의 위치를 정확히 묘사하는지 확인하세요.
> **출제 포인트 2** 동사 형태 부분을 잘 들어야 해요. be being p.p.는 '~되는 중이다'라는 의미이므로 그 동작을 행하는 사람이 있어야 해요. 사람이 없는 사진인데 be being p.p.가 들리면 오답일 확률이 높아요.

■ 기출 사진으로 분석하는 정답 vs. 오답

사물 주어

정답 Some **musical instruments** are **on display**.
악기들이 진열되어 있다.

오답 Some ~~benches~~ are lined up. 벤치 몇 개가 늘어서 있다.
ⓘ 사진에 bench가 보이지 않아요.

오답 A piano ~~is being polished~~. 피아노 한 대가 닦아지고 있다.
ⓘ polish(닦다) 동작을 하는 사람이 없어요.

② 사물 · 배경 + 인물 혼합 사진

특별히 부각되는 부분이 없는 사진에서는 인물과 사물, 배경에 대한 묘사가 모두 다뤄지기도 해요. 사진의 중심이 되는 부분뿐 아니라 주변 배경까지 놓치지 않고 파악하세요.

> **출제 포인트** 주어를 잘 듣고 인물, 사물, 배경 중 어떤 부분에 대해 언급하는지를 파악한 뒤, 제대로 묘사하는지 확인하세요.

■ 기출 사진으로 분석하는 정답 vs. 오답

인물 주어

정답 He's **holding a ladder sideways**.
남자가 사다리를 옆으로 들고 있다.

오답 He's ~~removing a box~~ from a storage unit.
남자가 창고에서 상자를 꺼내고 있다.

사물 주어

정답 **A ladder** is being **held sideways**. 사다리가 옆으로 들어지고 있다.

오답 A hose has been left ~~on the ground~~. 호스가 바닥에 놓여 있다.

T **실전 도움닫기** | 음원을 듣고 사진을 가장 잘 묘사한 문장을 고르세요.
다시 듣고 빈칸을 채우세요.

650_P1_04

정답과 해설 p.007

LC

PART 1

1.

(A) _____ are being washed.

(B) _____ has been set up outdoors.

(C) Chairs have been _____.

(D) Food is _____ at a café.

2.

(A) A mirror is _____.

(B) A drawer _____.

(C) A lamp has been turned on _____.

(D) _____ is being laid on a dresser.

3.

(A) _____ are being distributed at a meeting.

(B) _____ is being repositioned on a wall.

(C) Some men are _____.

(D) Some men are _____.

4.

(A) A man has _____ of a ladder.

(B) _____ is docked at a pier.

(C) _____ are carrying cargo up a ramp.

(D) A crowd has _____.

1.

(A)   (B)   (C)   (D)

2.

(A)   (B)   (C)   (D)

3.

(A)   (B)   (C)   (D)

4.

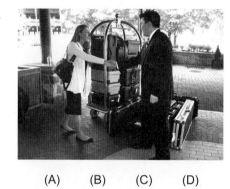

(A)   (B)   (C)   (D)

5.

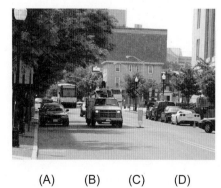

(A)   (B)   (C)   (D)

6.

(A)   (B)   (C)   (D)

7.

(A)　　　(B)　　　(C)　　　(D)

8.

(A)　　　(B)　　　(C)　　　(D)

9.

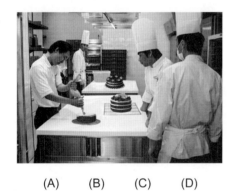

(A)　　　(B)　　　(C)　　　(D)

10.

(A)　　　(B)　　　(C)　　　(D)

11.

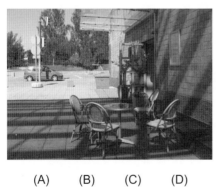

(A)　　　(B)　　　(C)　　　(D)

12.

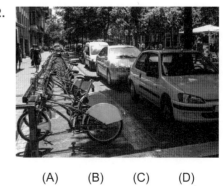

(A)　　　(B)　　　(C)　　　(D)

■ 동작 묘사

hanging up 걸고 있다

holding 들고 있다

pointing at ~을 손으로 가리키고 있다

reaching for ~로 손을 뻗고 있다

taking an order (식당에서) 주문을 받고 있다

paying for ~의 값을 지불하고 있다

climbing 올라가고 있다

lying on ~에 누워 있다

leaning against ~에 기대어 있다

riding on ~을 타고 있다

sitting at ~에 앉아 있다

standing in line 줄을 서 있다

waiting in line 줄을 서서 기다리고 있다

boarding 타고 있다

crossing 건너고 있다

exiting 빠져나가고 있다

facing 마주보고 있다, 향하고 있다

waving 손을 흔들고 있다

walking along ~을 따라 걷고 있다

talking on the telephone 전화로 대화하고 있다

trying on ~을 입어 보고 있다

relaxing 쉬고 있다

having a conversation 대화하고 있다

greeting 인사하고 있다

using 사용하고 있다

removing 치우고 있다

drinking 마시고 있다

preparing 준비하고 있다

■ 작업

adjusting 조절하고 있다

lifting 들어올리고 있다

loading (물건을) 싣고 있다

mopping 닦고 있다

mowing 잔디를 깎고 있다

carrying 나르고 있다

cleaning 청소하고 있다

filling 채우고 있다

fixing[repairing] 수리하고 있다

pouring 붓고 있다

pulling 끌고 있다

pushing 밀고 있다

stacking 쌓고 있다

operating 작동시키고 있다

wiping 닦고 있다

serving (손님을) 응대하고 있다

washing[doing] dishes 설거지를 하고 있다

painting 페인트를 칠하고 있다

taking measurements 치수를 재고 있다

■ 시선

checking 점검하고 있다

examining 살펴보고 있다

inspecting 살펴보고 [검사하고] 있다

looking at 보고 있다

peering into 안을 들여다보고 있다

reviewing 검토하고 있다

overseeing 감독하고 있다

■ 사물 설명 동사

be arranged 정돈돼 있다

be attached to ~에 부착되어 있다

be being loaded 실리고 있다 (⇔ be being unloaded)

be hanging 걸려 있다

be harvested (작물이) 수확되다

be on display 진열되어 있다 (be displayed)

be packed 포장돼 있다

be placed 놓여 있다 (be lying, be resting)

be positioned 자리잡고 있다

be propped against ~에 기대어 있다

be scattered 흩어져 있다

be secured[fastened] to ~에 묶여 있다

be stacked[piled] up 쌓여 있다

be stocked[filled] with ~로 채워져 있다

be suspended 매달려 있다

be tied to ~에 묶여 있다

be unoccupied[empty] (의자 등이) 비어 있다

be illuminated by ~에 의해 밝혀지다

be separated by 분리되어 있다

be decorated with 장식되어 있다

be exhibited 전시되어 있다

be occupied (사용하는 사람이) 있다

have been set 준비되어 있다

have been sorted into ~으로 분류되어 있다

have been turned on 켜져 있다

have been left outside 밖에 놓여 있다

■ 배경 설명 동사

border ~와 경계를 이루다

overlook 내려다보다

lead to ~로 이어지다

line ~을 따라 늘어서다

span ~에 걸쳐 펼쳐지다

stand 우뚝 서 있다

surround 둘러싸다

float 떠다니다

separate 구획을 나누다

extend 뻗어 있다

be reflected 반사되다

be under construction 공사 중이다

be crowded with ~로 붐비다

be located ~에 위치하다

be docked 부두에 대어 있다

be stationed 배치돼 있다

be covered with ~로 덮여 있다

be set 설치되어 있다

be laid out 가지런히 펼쳐져 있다

be painted 페인트칠 되어 있다

be closed 닫혀 있다

have been tiled 타일이 깔려 있다

be obscured by ~에 가려져 있다

be lined up in rows 줄지어 있다

be planted 심어져 있다

■ 상태 동사

lead 뻗어 있다

surround ~을 둘러싸다

be arranged 정렬되어 있다

be being displayed 전시되고 있다

be being removed 제거되는 중이다

be lined up 정렬되어 있다

be empty 비어 있다

be occupied 점유되다

be located 위치해 있다

be piled into ~에 쌓여 있다

be propped on[against] ~에 기대어 있다

be stopped at ~에 멈춰 있다

be tied to ~에 묶이다

be docked in ~에 정박되다

be set outside 야외에 놓여 있다

be spread out 펼쳐져 있다

be stocked with ~으로 채워져 있다

be separated with ~와 분리되어 있다

have been placed 놓여 있다

have been hung 걸려 있다

have been stacked 쌓여 있다

have been pushed 밀려(넣어)져 있다

have been set 준비되어 있다

have been set up 설치되어 있다

have been left ~인 채로 있다

have been opened 펼쳐져 있다

have been folded 접혀 있다

■ 실내 사물

closet 옷장

crate 상자

trash can 쓰레기통

light bulb 전구

flower pot 화분

rug 깔개

shelf 선반

toolbox 공구 상자

counter 진열대, 계산대

jar 병, 단지

screen 화면

cushion 쿠션

■ 실외 사물

bush 숲

field 들판

pond 연못

garage 차고

handrail (계단의) 난간

ladder 사다리

patio 옥외 테라스

pavement 인도, 포장 도로

ramp 경사로, 슬로프

doorway 출입구

platform 승강장

driveway 진입로

■ 장소

harbor 항구

dock 부두

deck 갑판

shore 물가, 해변

garage 차고, 주차장

curb 도로 경계석

intersection 교차로

construction site 공사장

archway 아치로 덮인 통로

cash register 금전 등록기

fence 울타리, 담

hallway 복도

(outdoor) market (야외) 시장

pier 부두

pillar 기둥

walkway 보도

outdoors 야외에

library 도서관

lobby 로비

balcony 발코니

counter 카운터

restaurant 식당

café 카페

ramp 경사로

■ 위치

in the middle of ~의 중간[중앙]에

on the top of ~의 꼭대기에, ~의 맨 위에

on the ground 땅 위에

at the back of ~의 뒤에

across from ~의 맞은편에

alongside ~의 옆에, 나란히

in the corner of ~의 구석에

on both sides of ~의 양쪽에

behind a vehicle 차량 뒤에

between the trees 나무 사이에

next to the mirror 거울 옆에

■ 배경

above the bridge 다리 위에

across the water 물 건너 쪽에

against the wall 벽에 기대어

along the lake 호수를 따라

from a ceiling 천장에

near the river 강 가까이에

on the platform 승강장에

toward the stream 개울 쪽으로

in the corner of the room 방의 구석에

under a counter 조리대[계산대] 아래에

Part

질의 응답

LC

2

Part 2 | 질의 응답 총 25문항

Part 2는 한 개의 질문과 세 개의 대답을 듣고 질문에 가장 적절한 대답을 고르는 유형이에요.

■ Part 2 이렇게 풀자

1 질문을 들으면서?
첫 4단어를 듣고 핵심 의도 파악

Where do we keep our office supplies?

▶

2 보기를 들으면서?
오답 보기 소거하며 듣기

(A) ~~That's a nice tie.~~
(B) In the storage cabinet.
(C) ~~Two o'clock on Thursdays.~~

▶

3 음원을 듣고 난 후?
정답 선택

(B)

■ 빈출 오답 유형을 알아두자

1 질문과 상관없는 대답 - 다른 주어, 다른 시제, 다른 개념

Q Who came up with our new slogan?
누가 새 슬로건을 생각해 냈죠?

A ~~This escalator~~ goes down. (X)
이 에스컬레이터는 내려갑니다.

→ **Someone on the marketing team. (O)**
마케팅 팀의 누군가요.

2 의문사 의문문에 Yes/No로 대답

Q When will the road works begin?
언제 도로 공사가 시작될까요?

A ~~Yes, it will.~~ (X) 네, 그럴 겁니다.

→ **In late April. (O)** 4월 말에요.

3 발음이 같거나 비슷한 단어로 대답

Q Which **supplier** do you use for fruits?
과일에는 어떤 공급업체를 쓰세요?

A In the ~~supply~~ closet. (X) 물품 창고에요.

→ **The one on Edgewood Street. (O)**
에지우드 가에 있는 곳이요.

4 연상 어휘로 대답

Q This is the best **Italian restaurant** in town.
이 곳이 마을 최고의 이탈리안 식당이에요.

A ~~Pasta and a salad.~~ (X) 파스타와 샐러드요.

→ **It's where I take all of my clients. (O)**
제가 고객들을 접대하는 곳이에요.

■ 만능 답변을 잡자

의문문에 '모른다'라고 대답하면 정답이 돼요. 비슷한 맥락의 표현들을 기억해 두세요.

Q Who will be the head of the marketing? 누가 마케팅 책임자가 될 건가요?

---

1 모르겠어요.

- I don't know. 모르겠어요.
- I'm not sure. 모르겠어요.
- I have no idea. 전혀 몰라요.

- Nobody knows. 아무도 몰라요.
- It's not certain yet. 모르겠어요.
- I wish I knew. 저도 알았으면 좋겠네요.

---

2 알아볼게요.

- I'll check. 확인해 볼게요.
- I'll find out. 알아볼게요.
- Let me check. 확인해 볼게요.
- Let me figure it out. 알아볼게요.

- I'll ask the supervisor. 상사에게 물어 볼게요.
- I'll call ~ and find out. ~에 전화해서 알아볼게요.
- Let me talk to my manager. 매니저에게 얘기해 볼게요.

---

3 나중에 알려줄게요.

- I'll let you know later. 나중에 알려 줄게요.
- It'll be announced this afternoon. 오늘 오후에 공지될 거예요.
- I'll tell you all about it when I get back. 돌아와서 전부 다 말해 줄게요.

---

4 ~에게 물어보세요. / ~가 알아요. / ~가 도와줄 거예요.

- Ask the receptionist. 안내데스크 직원에게 물어보세요.
- Oscar might know. 오스카가 알고 있을 거예요.
- Check with Mr. Carter. 카터 씨에게 확인해 보세요.
- Didn't your supervisor tell you? 상사가 말해주지 않았나요?

---

5 아직 결정되지 않았어요.

- They are still deciding. 아직 결정하지 못했어요.
- It hasn't been decided yet. 아직 결정되지 않았어요.
- The board is reviewing it. 이사회에서 검토 중이에요.
- It hasn't been announced. 공지되지 않았어요.

---

6 상황에 따라 달라요.

- It depends. 상황에 따라 달라요.
- It's up to the board. 이사회에 달려 있어요.

① Who 의문문

Who로 시작하면서 특정 행위의 주체나 대상을 묻는 질문으로, 매회 1~3문제 출제됩니다.

■ 빈출 질문 & 응답 패턴

사람 이름   Mr. / Ms. / Dr. 등의 호칭이나 낯선 단어가 들리면 사람 이름일 확률이 높아요.

Q Who approved the budget estimate?   누가 예산안을 승인했나요?
A Mr. Allawi did.   알라위 씨가 했어요.

직업 / 직책 / 부서명 / 회사명   이름 대신 그 사람이 소속된 곳으로 답할 수 있어요.

Q Who's in charge of scheduling employees' work shifts?   직원 업무 교대 일정은 누가 짜나요?
A The factory supervisor.   공장 감독관이요.

부정 대명사   특정 인물을 구체적으로 언급하지 않고 someone, no one 등으로 답할 수 있어요.

Q Who authorized that purchase?   그 구매건은 누가 승인했나요?
A Someone in the accounting department.   회계부 사람이요.

1인칭 대명사 I / We   해당하는 사람이 누구인지 묻는 질문에 본인이라고 또는 본인이 아니라고 말하는 것은 자연스러운
응답이에요.

Q Whose turn is it to buy lunch?   누가 점심을 살 차례인가요?
A I already bought it.   전 이미 샀어요.

우회적 응답   장소나 정보의 출처를 알려 주는 식의 답변도 정답이 될 수 있어요.

Q Who should I call to set up my printer?   프린터 설치는 누구한테 전화해야 해요?
A The phone number's on your desk.   당신 책상 위에 번호가 있어요.

ETS 유형 연습 ....   650_P2_01 🎧

다음 질문을 먼저 읽고 음원을 들은 후 적절한 응답을 고르세요.   정답과 해설 p. 011

1	Who's ordering supplies for the laboratory?	(A)	(B)	(C)
2	Who's getting the lunch order today?	(A)	(B)	(C)
3	Who came up with our new slogan?	(A)	(B)	(C)
4	Who's in this photo with you?	(A)	(B)	(C)
5	Who's managing the bookstore tomorrow?	(A)	(B)	(C)

② What / Which 의문문

What/Which(+명사)로 시작하는 의문문으로 매회 2~3문제 정도 출제됩니다. 의문사 뒤에 오는 명사를 들어야 정답을 선택할 수 있어요

■ 빈출 질문 & 응답 패턴

명사구 답변 대상을 묻는 What 의문문은 명사구를 이용한 단답형 정답이 자주 나와요.

Q **What's the price** of this item? **(가격)** 이 물건은 얼마인가요?
A **Five euros.** 5유로요.

Q **What time are we meeting** with the architect? **(시간)** 건축가와 몇 시에 만나나요?
A **Right after lunch.** 점심 직후요.

Q **What floor** is the workshop on? **(층수)** 워크숍은 몇 층에서 하나요?
A **The sixth.** 6층요.

대명사 one 어떤 '것/사람'을 묻는 Which 의문문은 대명사 one을 이용한 정답이 가장 흔해요.

Q **Which shoes are on sale** this weekend? 이번 주말에는 어떤 신발들이 할인되나요?
A The **ones** on this table. 이 탁자 위에 있는 것들이요.

Q **Which event space** would you like to use? 어떤 행사 장소를 이용하고 싶으세요?
A I like the **one** we used last year. 작년에 우리가 썼던 곳이 좋아요.

의견 'What do you think of/about ~?'은 의견을 묻는 질문이므로 호불호를 표현하는 응답이 가장 자연스러워요.

Q **What do you think** of the new floor plan? 새 평면도 어떻게 생각하세요?
A It's **a good design**. 디자인이 근사하네요.

Q **What did you think** of the training video? 교육 영상 어땠어요?
A I thought it was **very helpful**. 매우 유익했던 것 같아요.

ETS 유형 연습

650_P2_02 🎧

다음 질문을 먼저 읽고 음원을 들은 후 적절한 응답을 고르세요. 정답과 해설 p.011

1	What happens at the weekly meetings?	(A)	(B)	(C)
2	Which of these notebooks is yours?	(A)	(B)	(C)
3	What time does the restaurant close?	(A)	(B)	(C)
4	Which company developed this software?	(A)	(B)	(C)
5	What do you think of this month's budget?	(A)	(B)	(C)

1. Mark your answer.

(A)   (B)   (C)

_____ the floor plan?

(A) They're _____.

(B) Only _____.

(C) Mr. Bryson _____.

2. Mark your answer.

(A)   (B)   (C)

What's _____?

(A) _____ and water.

(B) On Atlantic _____.

(C) She _____ her bicycle.

3. Mark your answer.

(A)   (B)   (C)

_____ still need to be processed?

(A) _____ a new one.

(B) He _____.

(C) Those _____.

4. Mark your answer.

(A)   (B)   (C)

What's the _____?

(A) _____.

(B) I'm _____.

(C) No, _____.

5. Mark your answer.

(A)   (B)   (C)

Who will _____?

(A) A new _____.

(B) Lisa has the _____.

(C) At the _____.

1. Mark your answer on your answer sheet.

2. Mark your answer on your answer sheet.

3. Mark your answer on your answer sheet.

4. Mark your answer on your answer sheet.

5. Mark your answer on your answer sheet.

6. Mark your answer on your answer sheet.

7. Mark your answer on your answer sheet.

8. Mark your answer on your answer sheet.

9. Mark your answer on your answer sheet.

10. Mark your answer on your answer sheet.

11. Mark your answer on your answer sheet.

12. Mark your answer on your answer sheet.

13. Mark your answer on your answer sheet.

14. Mark your answer on your answer sheet.

15. Mark your answer on your answer sheet.

16. Mark your answer on your answer sheet.

17. Mark your answer on your answer sheet.

18. Mark your answer on your answer sheet.

19. Mark your answer on your answer sheet.

20. Mark your answer on your answer sheet.

21. Mark your answer on your answer sheet.

22. Mark your answer on your answer sheet.

23. Mark your answer on your answer sheet.

24. Mark your answer on your answer sheet.

25. Mark your answer on your answer sheet.

LC

PART 2

When / Where 의문문

① When 의문문

When으로 시작하면서 어떤 일이 발생하는 시점을 묻는 질문으로, 매회 2~3문제 출제됩니다.

■ 빈출 질문 & 응답 패턴

특정 시점-전치사구   전치사(at, in, by, until 등)가 들어간 구체적 시간 표현 정답이 자주 나와요.

Q **When will Mr. Ota finish** his conference call?   오타 씨는 언제 전화회의가 끝나시나요?
A **In about five minutes.**   5분 정도 후에요.

특정 시점-부사구   부사(ago, sometime, soon, earlier 등)가 들어간 구체적 시간 표현 정답도 많아요.

Q **When did you join** the company?   언제 입사했나요?
A **Three years ago.**   3년 전에요.

부사절 표현   before, after, as soon as 등의 부사절 접속사로 시작하는 표현도 있어요.

Q **When will the renovation start?**   보수공사 언제 시작되나요?
A **After** the budget is approved.   예산안이 승인되고 나서요.

정보 제공 불가 응답   원하는 정보를 답해줄 수 없다는 답변이 '통지 받지 못했다, 확인해 보겠다, (다른 이에게) 물어보라, (설명서 등을) 참고하라' 등의 여러 표현으로 등장해요.

Q **When will the conveyor belt be fixed?**   컨베이어 벨트가 언제 수리될까요?
A **Let's ask Mr. Miller.**   밀러 씨에게 물어봅시다.

우회적 응답   구체적인 시점으로 답하는 대신 시점과 관련된 단서를 우회적으로 제시하기도 해요.

Q **When will the sales report be ready?**   판매 보고서는 언제 준비되나요?
A **I just have to add** a few more tables.   표 몇 개만 더 삽입하면 돼요.

ETS 유형 연습 ....

650_P2_05 🎧

다음 질문을 먼저 읽고 음원을 들은 후 적절한 응답을 고르세요.

정답과 해설 p.018

1	When does the grocery store close?	(A) (B) (C)
2	When is someone coming to repair the roof?	(A) (B) (C)
3	When will the construction begin?	(A) (B) (C)
4	When will the camera be fixed?	(A) (B) (C)
5	When will you have the results of the customer survey?	(A) (B) (C)

② Where 의문문

Where로 시작하는 의문문으로 매회 2문제 정도 출제됩니다. 주로 장소나 위치에 대해서 묻지만, 물건이나 정보의 출처를 묻기도 해요.

■ 빈출 질문 & 응답 패턴

장소·위치 전치사(at, in, on, near, across 등)가 들어간 장소·위치 표현 정답이 가장 많아요.

Q Where did you meet with Ms. Jenkins?   젠킨스 씨와 어디에서 만났나요?

A In the cafeteria.   구내식당에서요.

사람 물건을 갖고 있거나 사용 중인 사람이 답이 되기도 해요.

Q Where can I get an ink cartridge for the printer?   이 프린터용 잉크 카트리지는 어디에 있죠?

A Jacob has the key to the supply room.   제이콥한테 비품실 열쇠가 있어요.

출처 물건의 출처로는 물건을 준 사람이나 구입처, 정보의 출처로는 웹사이트, 신문, 설명서 등이 답이 될 수 있어요.

Q Where did you get that beautiful scarf?   그 멋진 스카프는 어디에서 사셨나요?

A It was **a gift from my colleague.**   제 동료가 준 선물이에요.

정보 제공 불가 응답 원하는 정보를 답해줄 수 없다는 답변이 '통지 받지 못했다, 확인해 보겠다, (다른 이에게) 물어보라, (설명서 등을) 참고하라' 등의 여러 표현으로 등장해요.

Q Where do I board the plane to London?   런던행 비행기는 어디서 탑승하나요?

A Check your boarding pass.   탑승권을 확인해 보세요.

ETS 유형 연습

650_P2_06

다음 질문을 먼저 읽고 음원을 들은 후 적절한 응답을 고르세요.   정답과 해설 p.019

1	Where's the closest pharmacy?	(A)	(B)	(C)
2	Where can I get a pencil?	(A)	(B)	(C)
3	Where was Mr. Wagner yesterday?	(A)	(B)	(C)
4	Where can I attend an evening course?	(A)	(B)	(C)
5	Where's the library branch going to be built?	(A)	(B)	(C)

1. Mark your answer.

   (A)   (B)   (C)

When will the _____?

(A) They haven't given us _____.

(B) A new _____.

(C) Through the _____.

2. Mark your answer.

   (A)   (B)   (C)

_____ the manager's office?

(A) _____ the hall.

(B) _____ when you leave.

(C) I can _____.

3. Mark your answer.

   (A)   (B)   (C)

_____ from your trip?

(A) I'll _____ to you later.

(B) _____.

(C) To San Francisco.

4. Mark your answer.

   (A)   (B)   (C)

When will the _____?

(A) During the _____.

(B) The _____, downstairs.

(C) Yes, it's _____ now.

5. Mark your answer.

   (A)   (B)   (C)

_____ this article?

(A) In yesterday's _____.

(B) It's _____.

(C) Yes, I have a _____.

1. Mark your answer on your answer sheet.

2. Mark your answer on your answer sheet.

3. Mark your answer on your answer sheet.

4. Mark your answer on your answer sheet.

5. Mark your answer on your answer sheet.

6. Mark your answer on your answer sheet.

7. Mark your answer on your answer sheet.

8. Mark your answer on your answer sheet.

9. Mark your answer on your answer sheet.

10. Mark your answer on your answer sheet.

11. Mark your answer on your answer sheet.

12. Mark your answer on your answer sheet.

13. Mark your answer on your answer sheet.

14. Mark your answer on your answer sheet.

15. Mark your answer on your answer sheet.

16. Mark your answer on your answer sheet.

17. Mark your answer on your answer sheet.

18. Mark your answer on your answer sheet.

19. Mark your answer on your answer sheet.

20. Mark your answer on your answer sheet.

21. Mark your answer on your answer sheet.

22. Mark your answer on your answer sheet.

23. Mark your answer on your answer sheet.

24. Mark your answer on your answer sheet.

25. Mark your answer on your answer sheet.

① Why 의문문

Why로 시작하면서 어떤 일의 원인이나 이유, 목적을 묻는 질문으로, 매회 1~2문제씩 출제돼요.

■ 빈출 질문 & 응답 패턴

Because가 있는 문장   Because로 시작하면서 이유를 설명하는 문장이 정답일 수 있어요.

Q **Why has there been a delay** in shipping these orders?　왜 이 주문품의 배송이 지연됐나요?

A **Because** we ran out of packing materials.　포장재가 떨어졌거든요.

오답 함정 Because the order has arrived.　주문품이 도착했거든요.

→ Because는 함정으로 사용되기도 하므로 이유를 말하는 문장이 맞는지 끝까지 들어야 해요.

Because가 없는 문장   Because를 생략하고 이유를 설명하는 문장이 정답인 경우가 가장 많아요.

Q **Why do you want to exchange** this coat?　왜 이 코트를 교환하시려는 거죠?

A **It's the wrong size.**　사이즈가 맞지 않아요.

---

to부정사구   '~하기 위해'라는 뜻의 목적을 설명하는 to부정사구 표현도 있어요.

Q **Why is the legal department having a party**?　법무팀에서 왜 파티를 여는 거죠?

A **To welcome** some new employees.　신입 직원 몇 명을 환영하기 위해서요.

정보 제공 불가 응답   원하는 정보를 답해줄 수 없다는 답변이 '모른다, 통지 받지 못했다, 확인해 보겠다, (다른 이에게) 물어보라, (설명서 등을) 참고하라' 등의 여러 표현으로 등장해요.

Q **Why did Juan decline** the job offer?　후안은 왜 그 일자리 제안을 거절했죠?

A **I have no idea.**　모르겠어요.

부정 의문문   <Why+동사+not>의 부정 의문문 형태도 자주 출제되는데, Because 없이 이유를 설명하는 문장이 가장 흔한 정답 유형이에요.

Q **Why isn't the printer working**?　왜 프린터가 작동하지 않죠?

A **It's out of ink.**　잉크가 떨어졌어요.

ETS 유형 연습

650_P2_09

다음 질문을 먼저 읽고 음원을 들은 후 적절한 응답을 고르세요.　정답과 해설 p.025

1	Why was the schedule changed?	(A)	(B)	(C)
2	Why do we need three copies of the contract?	(A)	(B)	(C)
3	Why are the technicians here?	(A)	(B)	(C)
4	Why are the clients coming so early?	(A)	(B)	(C)
5	Why aren't these scarves included in the clearance sale?	(A)	(B)	(C)

② How 의문문

How로 시작하는 의문문으로 매회 2문제 정도 출제됩니다. 방법이나 의견을 주로 묻지만, <How+형용사/부사>의 형태로 수량, 가격, 시기 등을 묻는 문제도 나와요.

■ 빈출 질문 & 응답 패턴

방법 '어떻게'라고 묻고 그에 대한 방법 및 수단을 알려 주는 답변이 정답인 경우가 가장 많아요.

Q How will you notify the applicants? 　지원자에게 어떻게 통지할 건가요?
A I'll call them. 　전화하려고요.

의견·상태 형용사나 부사로 의견이나 상태를 표현하는 답변이 많아요.

Q How is Ivan's new job at the law firm going? 　법률회사에서 이반의 새 일은 좀 어떤가요?
A He seems to be doing quite well. 　꽤 잘 하고 있는 것 같아요.

수량 How many 질문에는 수량, How much 질문에는 가격을 나타내는 수 표현이 정답이에요.

Q How many people are there in the art department? 　예술부서에는 사람이 몇 명 있나요?
A Around twenty. 　20명 가량이요.

빈도 How often 질문에는 빈도를 나타내는 수 관련 표현(once, twice, every 등)이 정답이에요.

Q How often is the hotel swimming pool cleaned? 　호텔 수영장은 얼마나 자주 청소하나요?
A Every morning. 　매일 아침마다요.

시간·기간 How long 질문에는 기간, How soon/late 질문에는 시간 관련 수 표현이 정답이에요.

Q How late does the store stay open? 　그 가게는 얼마나 늦게까지 문을 여나요?
A It closes at nine. 　9시에 문을 닫아요.

ETS 유형 연습 .... 650_P2_10 🎧

다음 질문을 먼저 읽고 음원을 들은 후 적절한 응답을 고르세요. 　　정답과 해설 p.026

1	How do I get to the doctor's office?	(A)	(B)	(C)
2	How was your stay at the hotel?	(A)	(B)	(C)
3	How long can you park here?	(A)	(B)	(C)
4	How much is this umbrella?	(A)	(B)	(C)
5	How often do you visit your family?	(A)	(B)	(C)

1. Mark your answer.

(A)   (B)   (C)

_____ for the meeting?

(A) My car _____.

(B) It was _____ you too.

(C) Yes, she _____.

2. Mark your answer.

(A)   (B)   (C)

_____ for the conference?

(A) _____ our new model.

(B) Just _____.

(C) I'd _____.

3. Mark your answer.

(A)   (B)   (C)

_____ do you need?

(A) That really _____.

(B) Twelve should _____.

(C) _____, thanks.

4. Mark your answer.

(A)   (B)   (C)

Why is the store _____ today?

(A) No, it isn't _____.

(B) Yes, I _____ today.

(C) It's a _____.

5. Mark your answer.

(A)   (B)   (C)

_____ does this tea kettle _____?

(A) With _____, please.

(B) Oh, you should _____.

(C) I _____.

1. Mark your answer on your answer sheet.

2. Mark your answer on your answer sheet.

3. Mark your answer on your answer sheet.

4. Mark your answer on your answer sheet.

5. Mark your answer on your answer sheet.

6. Mark your answer on your answer sheet.

7. Mark your answer on your answer sheet.

8. Mark your answer on your answer sheet.

9. Mark your answer on your answer sheet.

10. Mark your answer on your answer sheet.

11. Mark your answer on your answer sheet.

12. Mark your answer on your answer sheet.

13. Mark your answer on your answer sheet.

14. Mark your answer on your answer sheet.

15. Mark your answer on your answer sheet.

16. Mark your answer on your answer sheet.

17. Mark your answer on your answer sheet.

18. Mark your answer on your answer sheet.

19. Mark your answer on your answer sheet.

20. Mark your answer on your answer sheet.

21. Mark your answer on your answer sheet.

22. Mark your answer on your answer sheet.

23. Mark your answer on your answer sheet.

24. Mark your answer on your answer sheet.

25. Mark your answer on your answer sheet.

일반 / 선택 의문문

① 일반 의문문

의문사 없이 Be동사/Do동사/조동사/Have동사로 시작하는 의문문으로 매회 4문제 정도 나와요. 의문사 의문문과는 달리 Yes/No로 응답할 수 있으며 다양한 내용이 출제돼요.

■ 빈출 질문 & 응답 패턴

Yes / No 응답   <Yes + 긍정 내용>과 <No + 부정 내용>으로 구성된 응답이 출제돼요.

Q **Was that the last bus** to the airport?   저 버스가 공항행 마지막 버스인가요?
A **No, there's another one soon.**   아니요, 곧 또 한 대가 올 거예요.

Yes / No 대체 표현   Yes는 Sure, Okay, No는 Unfortunately, Not yet 등으로 대체되기도 해요.

Q **Are you going to join** that new fitness center?   새로 생긴 헬스클럽에 등록할 건가요?
A **I don't think so.**   아니요.

Yes / No가 빠진 응답   Yes/No를 생략한 채 Yes/No의 의미를 나타내는 응답이 가장 흔해요.

Q **Does your store carry** any tomato sauce?   이 가게에 토마토 소스가 있나요?
A **It's in aisle sixteen.**   16번 통로에 있어요.

되묻는 응답   질문에 답하는 데 필요한 추가 정보 등을 되묻는 답변도 정답이 될 수 있어요.

Q **Do I have to replace my car's tires?**   제 차의 타이어를 교체해야 할까요?
A **When did you buy the car?**   언제 차를 사셨는데요?

간접 의문문 응답   일반 의문문에서 중간에 의문사가 들리면 간접 의문문이에요. 간접 의문문에는 Yes/No 답변이 가능하고, 의문사에 해당하는 내용을 답하면 돼요.

Q **Do you know where** the library is?   도서관이 어디에 있는지 아시나요?
A **Yes,** it's **around the corner.**   네, 모퉁이를 돌면 있어요.

ETS 유형 연습 ....

650_P2_13 🎧

다음 질문을 먼저 읽고 음원을 들은 후 적절한 응답을 고르세요.   정답과 해설 p. 032

		(A)	(B)	(C)
1	Do you want to see a play tomorrow night?	(A)	(B)	(C)
2	Is this material water-resistant?	(A)	(B)	(C)
3	Has the gallery received our shipment of artwork?	(A)	(B)	(C)
4	Is there a manual for the new projector?	(A)	(B)	(C)
5	Do you know what kind of car you'd like to lease?	(A)	(B)	(C)

② 선택 의문문

<A or B> 형태로 or가 들어가 A와 B 중 어떤 것을 선택할지 묻는 의문문으로 매회 2문제 정도 나와요. 빈출 정답 패턴이 골고루 답으로 나오는데, 우회적 응답이 정답인 경우가 많아요.

■ 빈출 질문 & 응답 패턴

둘 중 하나 선택 질문에서 제시된 두 가지 중 하나를 선택하는 답변이 정답으로 나와요.

Q Are you going to buy **the small suitcase or the backpack?** 작은 여행가방과 배낭 중 뭘 사실 건가요?
A I decided to get **the backpack.** 배낭을 사기로 했어요.

둘 다 선택 혹은 거부 '둘 다 좋다' 혹은 '둘 다 안 하겠다'라고 답할 수 있어요.

Q Are you going to watch **the movie or the game**? 영화와 경기 중 어떤 걸 보러 갈 거예요?
A **Neither**, I'm too tired. 둘 다 안 가요, 너무 피곤하거든요.

상관 없음 '둘 중 어느 쪽이든 상관없다'는 답변이 들리면 정답일 확률이 매우 높아요.

Q Can I pay **by credit card or** do I have to pay **cash**? 신용카드와 현금 중 어떤 걸로 계산해야 하나요?
A **Either is fine.** 어느 쪽이든 상관없습니다.

제3의 선택 질문에서 주어진 두 가지가 아닌 제3의 것을 선택하는 응답도 있어요.

Q Should I turn **at this traffic light or the next one**? 이번 신호등에서 방향을 바꿔야 하나요.
  아니면 다음 번 신호등에서인가요?
A **Wait until the one at Maple Street.** 메이플 로 신호등이 나올 때까지 기다리세요.

우회적 응답 둘 중 하나를 선택할 경우, 질문에서 주어진 선택 사항을 반복하지 않고 우회적으로 돌려 답변하는 경우가 많아요.

Q Do you want to hire **one or two interns** for the summer? 올 여름에 인턴을 한 명 채용하실 건가요.
  아니면 두 명 채용하실 건가요?
A **The budget's quite small** this year. 올해 예산이 꽤 빠듯하네요.

ETS 유형 연습

650_P2_14 🎧

다음 질문을 먼저 읽고 음원을 들은 후 적절한 응답을 고르세요.

정답과 해설 p.033

1	Does Henry speak Spanish or Italian?	(A)	(B)	(C)
2	Was the order for a vanilla or chocolate cake?	(A)	(B)	(C)
3	Would you like this shirt or a smaller one?	(A)	(B)	(C)
4	Do you want my home or work phone number?	(A)	(B)	(C)
5	Has the keynote speaker for the conference been chosen, or is the committee still deciding?	(A)	(B)	(C)

1. Mark your answer.

(A)   (B)   (C)

Are these _____?
(A) No, could you _____?
(B) It's _____.
(C) He's a _____.

2. Mark your answer.

(A)   (B)   (C)

Do you want an _____?
(A) _____ is that?
(B) Yes, it's _____.
(C) I'd like _____, please.

3. Mark your answer.

(A)   (B)   (C)

Have the _____ yet?
(A) No, they _____.
(B) Yes, they're _____.
(C) I can't _____ today.

4. Mark your answer.

(A)   (B)   (C)

Should we _____ today, or
_____ OK?
(A) They got _____.
(B) Yes, I _____.
(C) It _____ to me.

5. Mark your answer.

(A)   (B)   (C)

Do your employees _____?
(A) The _____ today.
(B) Yes, _____.
(C) That job is _____.

1. Mark your answer on your answer sheet.

2. Mark your answer on your answer sheet.

3. Mark your answer on your answer sheet.

4. Mark your answer on your answer sheet.

5. Mark your answer on your answer sheet.

6. Mark your answer on your answer sheet.

7. Mark your answer on your answer sheet.

8. Mark your answer on your answer sheet.

9. Mark your answer on your answer sheet.

10. Mark your answer on your answer sheet.

11. Mark your answer on your answer sheet.

12. Mark your answer on your answer sheet.

13. Mark your answer on your answer sheet.

14. Mark your answer on your answer sheet.

15. Mark your answer on your answer sheet.

16. Mark your answer on your answer sheet.

17. Mark your answer on your answer sheet.

18. Mark your answer on your answer sheet.

19. Mark your answer on your answer sheet.

20. Mark your answer on your answer sheet.

21. Mark your answer on your answer sheet.

22. Mark your answer on your answer sheet.

23. Mark your answer on your answer sheet.

24. Mark your answer on your answer sheet.

25. Mark your answer on your answer sheet.

LC

PART 2

① 부정 의문문

부정 의문문은 대부분 사실을 확인하는 내용이지만, 제안을 하거나 동의를 구하는 경우도 있어요. 매회 2문제 정도 나오며, not을 제외한 내용에 대해 일반 의문문과 같은 방식으로 답을 찾으면 돼요.

■ 빈출 질문 & 응답 패턴

Yes / No 응답 <Yes + 긍정 내용>과 <No + 부정 내용>으로 구성된 응답이 출제돼요.

Q Aren't **you working** next week? 다음 주에 근무하시지 않나요?
A **No, I'll be on vacation.** 아니요, 저는 휴가예요.

Yes / No가 빠진 응답 Yes / No를 생략한 채 Yes / No의 의미를 나타내는 응답도 있어요.

Q Isn't **the store closed**? 그 상점은 문을 닫지 않았나요?
A **It's open 24 hours** a day. 거기는 하루 종일 영업해요.

정보 제공 불가 응답 원하는 정보를 답해줄 수 없다는 답변이 '모른다, 들은 바 없다, 확인해 보겠다, (다른 이에게) 물어보라, (설명서 등을) 참고하라' 등의 여러 표현으로 등장해요.

Q Isn't **Mr. Tao opening** a new office in town? 타오 씨가 시내에 새 사무실을 열지 않나요?
A **I haven't talked to him** lately. 최근에 그와 얘기를 나눈 적이 없어요.

우회적 응답 Yes / No에 해당하는 내용을 직접적으로 말하는 대신 참고할 수 있는 상황이나 관련 사항 등을 우회적으로 제시하는 답변도 자주 나와요.

Q Don't **I need to make another doctor's appointment**? 진료 예약을 또 해야 하지 않나요?
A **Most patients** only **come in once a year**. 환자분들 대부분이 일 년에 한 번만 오세요.

되묻는 응답 제안하거나 동의를 구하는 질문에는 직접 해달라고 요청하거나 추가 관련 정보를 되묻는 응답이 정답이 될 수 있어요.

Q Shouldn't **we update** the price list? 가격표를 수정해야 하지 않을까요?
A **Could you do it**? 직접 해 주시겠어요?

ETS 유형 연습

650_P2_17

다음 질문을 먼저 읽고 음원을 들은 후 적절한 응답을 고르세요. 정답과 해설 p. 039

1	Aren't you leaving for Santiago this evening?	(A)	(B)	(C)
2	Didn't he order the furniture yesterday?	(A)	(B)	(C)
3	Aren't we offering a free-ticket promotion next week?	(A)	(B)	(C)
4	Shouldn't the roof be inspected for potential leaks?	(A)	(B)	(C)
5	Isn't Alonso moving into an apartment in the city?	(A)	(B)	(C)

② 부가 의문문

평서문 끝에 문장의 내용을 확인하는 의문문이 붙은 형태로 매회 2문제 정도 나와요. 평서문의 내용에 대해 일반 의문문과 같은 방식으로 답을 찾으면 돼요.

■ 빈출 질문 & 응답 패턴

Yes / No 응답   <Yes + 긍정 내용>과 <No + 부정 내용>으로 구성된 응답이 출제돼요.

Q   **You have a receipt** for the purchase, don't you?   구매 영수증이 있으신 거죠?
A   **No, I left it at home.**   아니요, 집에 두고 왔어요.

Yes / No 대체 표현   Yes는 Sure, Okay, No는 Unfortunately, Not yet 등으로 대체되기도 해요.

Q   **The gymnastics class was** really **fun**, wasn't it?   체조 수업이 정말 재미 있었죠?
A   **Absolutely**—I really enjoyed myself.   그럼요, 정말 즐거웠어요.

Yes / No가 빠진 응답   Yes/No를 생략한 채 Yes/No의 의미를 나타내는 응답도 있어요.

Q   **You rescheduled my** Tuesday **appointments,** didn't **you?**   제 화요일 일정은 조정하신 거죠?
A   **All of them except** for Mr. Park's.   박 씨와의 일정만 빼고 전부요.

정보 제공 불가 응답   원하는 정보를 답해줄 수 없다는 답변이 '모른다, 들은 바 없다, 확인해 보겠다, (다른 이에게) 물어보라, (설명서 등을) 참고하라' 등의 여러 표현으로 등장해요.

Q   **Ron's last day at work is Friday,** isn't it?   론의 마지막 근무일이 금요일이죠?
A   **I don't really know.**   잘 모르겠어요.

우회적 응답   Yes/No에 해당하는 내용을 직접적으로 말하는 대신 참고할 수 있는 상황이나 관련 사항 등을 우회적으로 제시하는 답변도 자주 나와요.

Q   **I e-mailed you the presentation,** didn't I?   제가 발표자료를 이메일로 보내 드렸죠?
A   **My computer is broken.**   제 컴퓨터가 고장났어요.

ETS 유형 연습 ···　650_P2_18 🎧

다음 질문을 먼저 읽고 음원을 들은 후 적절한 응답을 고르세요.   정답과 해설 p.040

1   The new aquarium opens in June, doesn't it?   (A)   (B)   (C)
2   That photocopy machine is broken, isn't it?   (A)   (B)   (C)
3   You drive to work every day, don't you?   (A)   (B)   (C)
4   We can't use this room, can we?   (A)   (B)   (C)
5   You're meeting Monica tomorrow, aren't you?   (A)   (B)   (C)

1. Mark your answer.

(A)　　(B)　　(C)

> My car will _____, won't it?
>
> (A) I _____.
>
> (B) All _____.
>
> (C) It _____ how busy we are.

2. Mark your answer.

(A)　　(B)　　(C)

> _____ Tony Flynn's presentation?
>
> (A) It was a _____.
>
> (B) Unfortunately, I _____.
>
> (C) Try _____.

3. Mark your answer.

(A)　　(B)　　(C)

> You don't _____ now, do you?
>
> (A) Yes, this is _____.
>
> (B) I _____, thanks.
>
> (C) No, I just _____.

4. Mark your answer.

(A)　　(B)　　(C)

> Shouldn't we _____?
>
> (A) _____ fine.
>
> (B) _____ more people get here.
>
> (C) Martin _____.

5. Mark your answer.

(A)　　(B)　　(C)

> That building's still _____, isn't it?
>
> (A) Maybe the _____.
>
> (B) Yes, it's _____ in October.
>
> (C) Yes, it's _____.

1. Mark your answer on your answer sheet.

2. Mark your answer on your answer sheet.

3. Mark your answer on your answer sheet.

4. Mark your answer on your answer sheet.

5. Mark your answer on your answer sheet.

6. Mark your answer on your answer sheet.

7. Mark your answer on your answer sheet.

8. Mark your answer on your answer sheet.

9. Mark your answer on your answer sheet.

10. Mark your answer on your answer sheet.

11. Mark your answer on your answer sheet.

12. Mark your answer on your answer sheet.

13. Mark your answer on your answer sheet.

14. Mark your answer on your answer sheet.

15. Mark your answer on your answer sheet.

16. Mark your answer on your answer sheet.

17. Mark your answer on your answer sheet.

18. Mark your answer on your answer sheet.

19. Mark your answer on your answer sheet.

20. Mark your answer on your answer sheet.

21. Mark your answer on your answer sheet.

22. Mark your answer on your answer sheet.

23. Mark your answer on your answer sheet.

24. Mark your answer on your answer sheet.

25. Mark your answer on your answer sheet.

LC

PART 2

요청 · 제안 의문문 / 평서문

① 요청 · 제안 의문문

'Could / Can you ~?, Do / Would you mind ~?, Would you ~?' 등으로 시작하는 요청 의문문과 'Why don't you / we ~?, Would you like to ~? Should we / I ~?, Do you want me to ~?' 등으로 시작하는 제안 의문문이 매회 2~3문제 정도 출제돼요.

■ 빈출 질문 & 응답 패턴

수락하는 응답　수락할 때는 'That's a good idea, That sounds great, Sure, Absolutely, Of course' 등의 표현이 정답이며, 거절보다는 수락하는 응답이 훨씬 많아요.

Q **Can you help** me plant these flowers?　　　　이 꽃을 심는 걸 좀 도와 주시겠어요?
A **Sure**, let me get some gardening gloves.　　　물론이죠, 원예용 장갑을 가져올게요.

거절하는 응답　거절할 때는 'Sorry, I'm not sure ~, I don't think ~, Thanks but ~' 등의 표현이 정답이에요.

Q **Would you like help** revising the contracts?　　계약서를 수정하는 걸 도와 드릴까요?
A **Thanks, but** I'm almost done.　　　　　　　　고맙습니다만, 거의 다 했어요.

Yes / No 응답　'Why don't you / we ~?, What / How about ~?'은 의문사로 시작하지만 Yes / No 및 Yes / No 대체 표현으로 응답이 가능해요.

Q **Why don't you come** to the beach with us?　　우리와 함께 해변에 가는 게 어때요?
A **Sure.** When are you leaving?　　　　　　　　좋아요. 언제 떠날 거예요?

되묻는 응답　제안 및 요청 사항에 대해 추가 정보를 되묻는 응답이 정답이 될 수 있어요.

Q **Would you like to go** see the opera tonight?　오늘 밤에 오페라 공연 보러 가실래요?
A **When does it start?**　　　　　　　　　　　　언제 시작하는데요?

우회적 응답　Yes / No에 해당하는 내용을 직접적으로 말하는 대신 참고할 수 있는 상황 등을 우회적으로 제시하는 답변도 나와요.

Q **Could I borrow** your book on finance?　　　　갖고 계신 금융 관련 책을 빌릴 수 있을까요?
A **I gave it to Amanda.**　　　　　　　　　　　그 책은 아만다에게 줬는데요.

ETS 유형 연습

650_P2_21 🎧

다음 질문을 먼저 읽고 음원을 들은 후 적절한 응답을 고르세요.

정답과 해설 p.046

1	Could I borrow your scissors for a minute?	(A)	(B)	(C)
2	Would you mind taking notes for me at the seminar?	(A)	(B)	(C)
3	Can I borrow a hammer?	(A)	(B)	(C)
4	Why don't we have pizza for dinner?	(A)	(B)	(C)
5	Why don't you join us for dinner tonight?	(A)	(B)	(C)

② 평서문

평서문은 정보 전달, 의견이나 감정의 제시, 문제점 제기, 제안 및 요청 사항 등을 언급하는 문장으로 매회 2~3문제가 나와요. 다양한 답변이 나올 수 있어 난이도가 가장 높은 문제 유형으로, 오답을 걸러내면서 들으면 정답을 고르는 데 도움이 될 수 있어요.

■ 빈출 질문 & 응답 패턴

정보 전달 응답 제시된 정보에 따른 후속 조치를 제안하거나 정보를 준 것에 대한 감사, 정보에 대해 호응하는 내용 등이 정답으로 자주 나와요.

Q **I need to look over** the report **before two**.　　　2시 전에 보고서를 검토해야 해요.
A **I'll get it to you right away.**　　　지금 바로 가져다 드릴게요.

의견 및 감정 제시 제시된 문장 내용에 대해 맞장구를 치는 등 호응하거나 반대 의사를 밝히는 응답이 나와요.

Q The security system **needs to be repaired**.　　　보안 시스템을 수리해야 해요.
A **Yes, it's urgent**.　　　맞아요, 시급합니다.

문제점 제기 문제점에 대한 해결책을 제시하는 답변이 가장 흔한 정답이에요.

Q **Mr. Miller hasn't arrived yet.**　　　밀러 씨가 아직 안 왔어요.
A **Let's start without him.**　　　우리끼리 시작합시다.

수락 / 거절 응답 제안 혹은 요청하는 내용에는 수락하거나 거절하는 응답이 정답이에요.

Q **Let's take a break** for fifteen minutes.　　　15분 동안 쉬도록 하죠.
A **That sounds like a good idea.**　　　좋은 생각이에요.

되묻는 응답 제시된 정보에 관련된 추가 정보나 상대의 의견을 되묻는 응답이 정답이 될 수 있어요.

Q **My doctor just opened a new office** in town.　　　제 주치의가 얼마 전 시내에 개원했어요.
A **Where's it located exactly?**　　　위치가 정확히 어디죠?

ETS 유형 연습 ....

650_P2_22 🎧

다음 질문을 먼저 읽고 음원을 들은 후 적절한 응답을 고르세요.　　　정답과 해설 p. 047

		(A)	(B)	(C)
1	I just bought a new telephone.	(A)	(B)	(C)
2	I really enjoyed the jazz festival last weekend.	(A)	(B)	(C)
3	Let's take a break for a few minutes.	(A)	(B)	(C)
4	You can store your luggage behind the hotel's front desk.	(A)	(B)	(C)
5	I didn't get a response to the job application I submitted.	(A)	(B)	(C)

T 실전 도움닫기 | 다음 말을 듣고 적절한 응답을 고르세요. 650_P2_23
다시 듣고 빈칸을 채우세요.

정답과 해설 p.048

1. Mark your answer.

(A)　(B)　(C)

> My computer _____.
>
> (A) We began at _____.
>
> (B) Yes, I _____ early.
>
> (C) Maybe it's not _____.

2. Mark your answer.

(A)　(B)　(C)

> _____ to the station?
>
> (A) That's a _____.
>
> (B) During my _____.
>
> (C) Because _____.

3. Mark your answer.

(A)　(B)　(C)

> There's _____.
>
> (A) _____, please?
>
> (B) _____ from?
>
> (C) They're _____.

4. Mark your answer.

(A)　(B)　(C)

> Would you _____ these boxes?
>
> (A) It was _____.
>
> (B) I'd _____.
>
> (C) _____.

5. Mark your answer.

(A)　(B)　(C)

> Could you _____ to the airport?
>
> (A) No, I _____ any.
>
> (B) Sure, _____ your flight?
>
> (C) About _____.

1. Mark your answer on your answer sheet.

2. Mark your answer on your answer sheet.

3. Mark your answer on your answer sheet.

4. Mark your answer on your answer sheet.

5. Mark your answer on your answer sheet.

6. Mark your answer on your answer sheet.

7. Mark your answer on your answer sheet.

8. Mark your answer on your answer sheet.

9. Mark your answer on your answer sheet.

10. Mark your answer on your answer sheet.

11. Mark your answer on your answer sheet.

12. Mark your answer on your answer sheet.

13. Mark your answer on your answer sheet.

14. Mark your answer on your answer sheet.

15. Mark your answer on your answer sheet.

16. Mark your answer on your answer sheet.

17. Mark your answer on your answer sheet.

18. Mark your answer on your answer sheet.

19. Mark your answer on your answer sheet.

20. Mark your answer on your answer sheet.

21. Mark your answer on your answer sheet.

22. Mark your answer on your answer sheet.

23. Mark your answer on your answer sheet.

24. Mark your answer on your answer sheet.

25. Mark your answer on your answer sheet.

■ 직업 / 직책

receptionist 접수직원

plumber 배관공

accountant 회계사

consultant 컨설턴트

mechanic 정비사

technician 기술자

architect 건축가

assistant 비서, 부하 직원

supervisor 관리자, 감독관

project manager 프로젝트 매니저(=PM)

department manager 부서장

director 이사

the board of directors 이사진

(vice) president (부)회장

CEO 최고경영자(=Chief Executive Officer)

■ 부서명

human resources (department) 인사부

accounting department 회계부

sales department 영업부

marketing department 마케팅부

customer service department 고객서비스부

shipping department 배송부

maintenance department 관리부

finance department 재무부

payroll department 경리부

quality control department 품질 관리부

public relations department 홍보부

■ 과거 표현

yesterday 어제

last year 작년에

three weeks ago 3주 전에

a couple of days ago 이틀쯤 전에

since last spring 지난 봄 이후로

in the past 과거에

the day before yesterday 그저께

■ 현재 표현

these days 요즘

right now 당장

currently 현재

almost every day 거의 매일

on a weekly basis 매주

sometimes 때때로(=occasionally)

quite recently 꽤 최근에

■ 미래 표현

this afternoon 오늘 오후에

in ten minutes 10분 후에

not until next Monday 다음 주 월요일이 되어야

by the end of the week 금요일까지

later today 오늘 늦게

within a week 한 주 내로

sometime next month 다음 달쯤에

soon 곧

at the latest 늦어도

■ 장소 / 행사 명사

warehouse 창고

auditorium 강당

headquarters 본사

main office 본사, 본점

branch (office) 지사, 지점

art exhibition 미술 전시회

conference 회의, 학회

press conference 기자 회견

■ 위치 / 방향 표현

in the conference room 회의실에서

on the third floor 3층에

in the auditorium 강당에서

down the street 길 따라 아래로

at the west terminal 서쪽 터미널에서

on the next corner 다음 모퉁이에

downstairs 아래층에

upstairs 위층에

right across the hall 복도 바로 맞은편에

behind the building 건물 뒤에

in front of the store 상점 앞에

right over there 바로 저쪽에

to the right[left] 오른쪽[왼쪽]으로

in the filing cabinet 파일 캐비닛 안에

somewhere in the north 북부쪽 어딘가에

in the mail box 우편함 안에

in the front[back] row 앞[뒷]줄에

on the bottom[top] shelf 맨 아래[위] 선반에

■ 이유

due to heavy traffic 교통 체증 때문에

due to severe weather 악천후 때문에

due to road construction 도로 공사 때문에

due to circumstance 상황 때문에

because of a schedule change 일정 변경 때문에

because of wrong size 사이즈가 맞지 않아

because of the power failure 정전 때문에

because it's too narrow 너무 좁기 때문에

because there wasn't enough space
충분한 공간이 없었기 때문에

because they postponed the launch
그들이 출시를 연기했기 때문에

because I'll be out of town
출장을 갈 예정이기 때문에

because he retired 그가 퇴직했기 때문에

■ 목적

to meet with the customer 고객을 만나기 위해

to thank us for our hard work
우리의 노고에 감사하기 위해

in order to get a refund 환불을 받기 위해

in order to finish early 빨리 끝내기 위해서

for a business trip 출장을 위해

for a dentist appointment 치과 예약 때문에

to welcome 환영하기 위해

to reserve 예약하기 위해

to discuss 토론하기 위해

to advertise 광고하기 위해

to increase efficiency 효율성을 높이기 위해

■ 방법 / 수단

in writing 서면으로

in person 직접, 손수(=personally)

by bus[plane] 버스[비행기]로

by cash 현금으로

by credit card 신용카드로

by overnight delivery 익일 배송으로

by accident 우연히

through an Internet search 인터넷 검색으로

through fund-raising events 모금 행사를 통해서

■ 기간 / 빈도

biweekly 격주로(=every two weeks)

for two days 이틀간

once in a while 가끔

once / twice 한 번/두 번

three times a week 일주일에 세 번

for years 수년간

during lunch 점심시간 동안에

during a break 쉬는 시간에

more than 10 years 10년 이상

at least once a month 최소 한 달에 한 번

within the next month 다음 달 내로

usually just on Saturdays 보통 토요일에만

until noon 정오까지

throughout the next three weeks
앞으로 3주 동안

as soon as we arrive 우리가 도착하자마자

no later than Friday 늦어도 금요일까지

■ 모른다

Nobody knows. 아무도 모르죠.

I don't really know. 잘 모르겠어요.

I have no idea. 몰라요.

I'm not sure. 잘 모르겠어요.

We're not sure yet. 아직 잘 모르겠어요.

Not that I know of. 제가 알기로는 아니에요

I don't know anything about it.
그것에 대해선 전혀 몰라요.

I wish I knew. 저도 알았으면 좋겠어요

She didn't mention it. 그녀가 말하지 않았어요.

I'll find out for you. 제가 알아볼게요.

Let's ask ~. ~에게 물어보죠.

■ 정해지지 않았다

I'm still considering it. 아직 고려 중이에요

I'm still waiting. 여전히 기다리고 있어요.

I'm still thinking about it.
아직 그것에 대해 생각 중이에요.

The manager is reviewing it.
매니저가 검토 중입니다.

I haven't decided yet.
아직 결정하지 않았어요.

It hasn't been decided yet.
아직 결정되지 않았어요.

It depends on the design.
그건 디자인에 따라 달라요.

It's not certain yet.
아직 확실하지 않아요.

It hasn't been announced.
발표가 안 났어요.

■ 둘 중 한 가지 선택

I prefer a window seat.
창가 쪽 좌석이 더 좋아요.

I feel like eating out. 외식을 하고 싶어요.

I'll take a bigger one. 큰 걸로 할게요.

It's nicer outside. 바깥이 좋겠네요.

Let's stay indoors. 실내에 있어요.

I'd better go soon. 바로 가는 게 좋겠어요.

Yes, I'll be with you shortly. 네, 곧 갈게요.

Sorry, I can't right now. 미안하지만, 지금은 안 돼요.

I chose July this year. 올해는 7월로 결정했어요.

Whichever costs less.
어느 것이든 더 저렴한 거요.

■ 둘 다 선택 / 상관 없음

Both would be good. 둘 다 좋겠어요.

I like both of them. 둘 다 좋아요.

It doesn't matter. 상관없어요.

It's up to you. 당신에게 달렸습니다.

Whichever you like. 원하시는 대로요.

Either is fine with me. 둘 중 어느 것이든 좋아요.

It doesn't matter. 상관없어요.

■ 둘 다 선택 안 함

I don't like either of them. 둘 다 아니에요.

I prefer neither. 둘 다 좋아하지 않습니다.

Neither, thanks. 고맙지만, 둘 다 됐습니다.

None of us can stay late.
우리 중 누구도 늦게까지 있을 수 없어요.

■ Yes 대체 표현(수락 / 동의)

Certainly. / Absolutely. / Definitely. / Why not?
물론이죠.

No problem. 문제 없어요.

Not at all. 전혀요.

I'd love to. / I'd be happy to. / I'm glad to. / I'd be delighted to. 그러고 싶어요.

That's what we expected.
그게 우리가 기대했던 바예요.

I think so too. 나도 그렇게 생각해요.

Go ahead. / Be my guest. 그렇게 하세요.

I'd be glad[happy] to. 그렇게 할게요.

I'd appreciate it. 그렇게 해주시면 고맙겠습니다.

That sounds good to me. 좋은 거 같네요.

Yes, I think we'd better. 네, 그게 낫겠어요

OK, I'll do it right away. 네, 바로 할게요.

■ No 대체 표현(거절 / 부정)

I'm sorry, (but) ~ 미안하지만 ~

Unfortunately, ~ 유감스럽게도[아쉽게도] ~

Sorry, I have an appointment then.
미안하지만 그때 약속이 있어요.

Actually, I already have. 실은 벌써 했습니다.

I'm almost done, thanks. 고맙지만, 거의 다 했어요.

I have other plans. 다른 약속이 있어요.

I'm afraid I can't. 그럴 수 없어서 유감이에요.

I wish I could. 그럴 수 있다면 좋겠지만요.

I'll consider it. 고려해 볼게요.

Just wait a minute, please. 잠시만 기다려 주세요.

I'll let you know later. 나중에 알려 드릴게요.

Part

짧은 대화

3

Part 3 | 짧은 대화 총 13지문, 39문항

Part 3은 남녀가 번갈아 가며 이야기하는 대화문을 듣고 그에 따른 문제를 푸는 유형이에요. 문제 수가 39개나 되니 LC에서 가장 비중이 큰 파트예요.

■ Part 1, 2와 이런 점이 다르다

1 대화문 하나를 듣고 문제를 세 개씩 풀어야 해요. 1세트가 [대화문1개+문제3개]로 총 13세트(39문제)예요.
2 시험지에 문제와 보기가 제시되어 있어, 대화문을 듣는 동시에 읽으면서 문제를 풀어야 해요.

Questions 32 through 34 refer to the following conversation.

◀») 음원

W Hello, I'm calling from the customer service department of Le Star Shoes. You recently purchased a pair of boots from us, and I wanted to know if you're satisfied with your purchase.

↓

M Oh. Yes, I'm very pleased with your service. I was especially impressed that I could order a pair of shoes and receive them the very next day!

↓

W That's great. We appreciate the positive feedback. Would you mind if we shared your comments on our Web site?

↓

32. Why is the woman calling? ⁸ᵉ
33. What does the man say about the service? ⁸ᵉ
34. What does the woman ask permission to do? ⁸ᵉ

📖 문제지

32. Why is the woman calling?
(A) To offer a refund
(B) To promote a new product
(C) To extend an invitation
(D) To collect feedback

↓

33. What does the man say about the service?
(A) Delivery is fast.
(B) Returning merchandise is easy.
(C) Representatives are helpful.
(D) Fees are reasonable.

↓

34. What does the woman ask permission to do?
(A) Postpone a shipping date
(B) Substitute an item
(C) Post some comments
(D) Charge an account

↓

다음 세트 준비!
[35~37]

■ Part 3 이렇게 풀자

① 음원을 듣기 전

1 문제 파악

문제를 미리 읽으면서 대화문을 듣는 동안 어떤 부분에 초점을 두어야 할지 파악해요. 성우가 파트 3의 Directions를 읽어주는 동안 첫 세트인 32번~34번 문제를 읽어 두어요.

---

2 키워드 표시

문제의 핵심이 되는 키워드를 표시해 두면, 정답 단서가 들렸을 때 더 쉽게 포착할 수 있어요. 키워드에는 의문사, 명사, 동사, 시간 표현 등이 해당돼요.

32. (Why) is the (woman) (calling)?   → **여자**가 **전화**를 건 **이유**?

33. (What) does the (man) say about the (service)?   → **남자**가 **서비스**에 대해 **무엇**을 말하나?

34. (What) does the (woman) (ask) (permission) to do?   → **여자**는 **무슨 허락**을 **구하는가**?

---

3 문제에 나온 화자 파악

문제에 나온 화자가 주로 정답의 단서를 말해요.

Why is the **woman** calling?   → 여자가 말하는 부분에서 정답이 나와요.

What does the **man** say about the service?   → 남자가 말하는 부분에서 정답이 나와요.

⚠ What **is the man asked** to do?   → 여자가 말하는 부분에서 정답이 나와요.

② 음원을 들으면서

4 정답 선택하기

정답의 단서는 대부분 문제 순서대로 나와요. 따라서 대화 전반부가 나올 때 첫 번째 문제를 보고 있다가 단서가 들리면 바로 정답을 고르고 다음 문제로 넘어가서 다음 단서를 기다리면 돼요.

③ 음원을 듣고난 후

5 문제를 읽어주는 동안 다음 세트 문제 파악

대화문이 끝나면 성우가 문제를 읽어줘요. 각 문제를 읽을 때마다 8초간의 문제 풀이 시간이 함께 주어지는데, 이 시간 동안 다음 세트의 문제들을 미리 파악해 두어요.

주제·목적 문제/화자·장소 문제

① 주제·목적 문제

주제·목적을 묻는 문제는 매회 4문제 정도 출제됩니다. 첫 화자가 화두를 꺼내면서 그와 관련된 내용의 대화가
이어지므로 인사말 이후 처음 2~3문장에서 대부분 답이 나와요.

주제	• What are the speakers discussing?	화자들은 무엇에 관해 이야기하고 있는가?
	• What are the speakers talking about?	화자들은 무엇에 관해 이야기하고 있는가?
	• What is the topic of the conversation?	대화의 주제는 무엇인가?
목적	• Why is the man/woman calling?	남자/여자는 왜 전화하고 있는가?

■ **핵심 포인트** | 주제와 목적은 첫 두 문장에서 단서를 포착하자.   650_P3_01 🎧

M Is that today's newspaper, Isabella? **There's an
   advertisement in there about a photography contest.**
   → 화두를 꺼낸 후 대화 주제가 바로 등장한다.

W I haven't seen it yet. What page is it on?

M I don't know, but it's in the Features section. I was thinking
   you should enter that great picture you took of the
   buildings in New York last summer.

남 그거 오늘 신문인가요? **거기에 사진
   공모전 광고가 실려 있던데요.**

여 아직 못 봤는데요. 몇 면에 있나요?

남 모르겠어요, 특집 기사면인데요. 당신이
   지난 여름 뉴욕에서 찍었던 멋진 건물
   사진을 출품하면 어떨까 생각했어요.

(What) are the (speakers) (discussing)?
(A) A book review
(B) A magazine article
(C) A newspaper advertisement
(D) A travel brochure

화자들은 무엇에 대해 **이야기하고 있는가?**
(A) 서평
(B) 잡지 기사
(C) 신문 광고
(D) 여행 책자

┌─ 정답이 들리는 단서 표현 ─

주제·목적 문제는 다음과 같은 표현이 들릴 때 정답을 포착해야 한다.

전화를 건 용건	**I'm calling to** get some assistance with my laptop.	노트북 컴퓨터에 대해 도움을 받고자 전화했어요.
상황/사실 언급	**I have an appointment** with Dr. Ramirez tomorrow, but I'm afraid I have to reschedule.	내일 라미레즈 박사님과 진료 예약이 잡혀 있는데 일정을 변경해야 할 것 같아요.
소식 전달	**Did you hear the news** about our company merger with Geller Solutions?	우리 회사가 겔러 솔루션즈와 합병할 거라는 소식 들으셨어요?
요청/제안문	**We need to plan** our strategy for next month's business exposition.	다음 달 비즈니스 박람회를 위한 전략을 세워야겠어요.

1. Why is the man calling?
   (A) To open an account
   (B) To report an error
   (C) To place an order
   (D) To return an item

M Hello, I'm _____ for a set of
   headphones I saw in your catalog.
W All right, I can _____. Can you give me
   the _____ for those?
M I have the catalog right here—if you can give me a
   moment, I'll check it and see.

2. What are the speakers discussing?
   (A) A telephone bill
   (B) An electricity bill
   (C) A weather report
   (D) A broken air conditioner

M I got a _____
   in the mail today. It's so expensive!
W Mine is too. I guess that's because I've been
   _____ so much in this hot weather.
M So have I, but I still don't think I should have been
   billed this much. Maybe I should _____
   and find out if the rates have gone up.

3. Why is the woman calling?
   (A) To open a bank account
   (B) To dispute a credit card charge
   (C) To change a billing address
   (D) To enroll in online banking

M Good afternoon, Jacobson Bank. How can I help you?
W Hi. Yes, there's a _____
   this month. I spent $5, but I was charged $50.
M I'm sorry. For _____ you will need
   to speak to someone from credit card transactions.
   Please hold while _____.

4. What are the speakers mainly
   discussing?
   (A) Holding a workshop
   (B) Creating a menu
   (C) Organizing a trip
   (D) Reviewing some applications

M Ms. Johnson, I'm planning the company's
   cafeteria menu for next month, and I'd like to add
   _____ to what I'll be cooking. Would
   that be OK with you?
W That'd be fine. I'm sure _____ for
   vegetarian dishes.
M I have _____ for vegetarian meals.
   I can make a few for _____.

② 화자 · 장소 문제

화자 · 장소 문제는 매회 6문제 정도 출제됩니다. 단서가 대화 초반에 대부분 제시되지만 그렇지 않은 경우에는 다른 문제들을 먼저 풀고 나서 마지막에 정답을 선택해도 좋아요.

직업 · 신분	• Who is the woman?	여자는 누구인가?
	• What is the man's job?	남자의 직업은 무엇인가?
근무처	• Where do the speakers most likely work?	화자들은 어디에서 일할 것 같은가?
대화 장소	• Where most likely are the speakers?	화자들은 어디에 있겠는가?

■ **핵심 포인트** | 업무 관련 어휘로 화자와 장소를 파악하자.   650_P3_03 🎧

W Excuse me, do you work here? **I'm interested in one of the cameras on display behind the counter.** → 카메라 가게에서 일어난 대화임을 알 수 있다.	여 실례합니다만 여기 직원이신가요? **제가 카운터 뒤에 진열된 카메라들 중 하나에 관심이 있어서요.**
M Oh, you mean this one—the Balani X13? → 남자의 직업은 카메라 가게 점원이다.	남 아, 이거 말씀하시는 거죠, 발라니 X13?
W Yes, that's it.	여 네, 맞아요.
M Just so you know, the battery that's included doesn't last very long—you might want to buy an extra one if you're planning to use the camera a lot.	남 참고로 말씀드리면, 카메라에 들어 있는 배터리는 오래 가지 않아요. 카메라를 자주 사용하실 거라면 여분으로 하나 더 사시는 게 좋을 겁니다.

(Who) most likely is the (man)?
(A) A store clerk
(B) A magazine journalist
(C) A museum director
(D) A professional photographer

남자는 누구이겠는가?
(A) 가게 점원
(B) 잡지사 기자
(C) 박물관 관장
(D) 전문 사진작가

정답이 들리는 단서 표현

화자 · 장소 문제는 다음과 같은 표현이 들릴 때 정답을 포착해야 한다.

자기 소개	Mr. Colson, **I'm a journalist** for *Health and Wellness Magazine.* 직업 A journalist	콜슨 씨, 저는 <헬쓰 앤 웰니스 매거진>의 기자입니다. 기자
업무 관련 단어	Take a look at the layout for the **next issue** of our **cooking magazine**. 근무처 At a magazine publisher	우리 요리 잡지 다음 호 레이아웃을 좀 보세요. 잡지 출판사
제품	A customer is looking for **this winter boot** in a size ten. 대화 장소 At a shoe store	손님이 이 겨울 부츠를 10사이즈로 찾고 있어요. 신발 매장

1. Where most likely are the speakers?
(A) At a restaurant
(B) At a theater
(C) At a sports stadium
(D) At a shopping center

M I was here for _____, and I think I left my jacket _____. I was sitting in the _____.
W I'll have to check. Can you _____ like?
M It's dark blue and _____ on the left side.

2. Who most likely is the woman?
(A) A travel agent
(B) A librarian
(C) A museum employee
(D) A university administrator

M Hi. I noticed that the Ancient Egypt exhibit _____ today. Can you recommend _____ on ancient civilizations?
W Yes, we do have _____ here that feature artifacts from different cultures.
M Well, I'd like to see exhibits of as _____ as possible.
W Well, then _____ starting with our Ancient World tour.

3. Where does the man work?
(A) At a car rental agency
(B) At an automotive repair shop
(C) At an express delivery service
(D) At a driver's license office

M Hi, this is Larry from Millwood Automotive Repairs. I'm _____ on a truck. I'm calling to see whether your _____. The model number on the tires is RCL forty-four.
W I'm afraid we don't have it _____ right now. I could order it for you, and it would be _____ in three working days. _____?
M Not really.

4. Where is the conversation taking place?
(A) At a train station
(B) At an airport
(C) At a bus terminal
(D) At a car rental agency

M Hello, I'd like to _____ for the 3 o'clock train to Chicago.
W Unfortunately, sir, that train's _____. Here's a copy of the _____.
M Hmmm... if I wait for the 3:40 train, I'll have time to _____ before leaving.

1. What are the speakers discussing?

   (A) A staff workshop
   (B) A promotion decision
   (C) A relocation plan
   (D) A vacation schedule

2. What does the man say he is happy about?

   (A) A budget has been increased.
   (B) A consultant is available.
   (C) A deadline has been changed.
   (D) A larger space will be reserved.

3. What does the woman offer to do?

   (A) Bring more chairs to the room
   (B) Choose a different date
   (C) Conduct an interview
   (D) Contact department managers

4. Why is the woman calling the restaurant?

   (A) To ask if her client is there
   (B) To reserve a table by the window
   (C) To ask about a missing item
   (D) To request a special menu

5. What does the man ask the woman to do?

   (A) Provide a description
   (B) Confirm a credit card number
   (C) Supply a guest list
   (D) Choose an event date

6. According to the man, what will happen in one hour?

   (A) A manager will call back.
   (B) An announcement will be made.
   (C) A transaction will be approved.
   (D) A business will close.

7. Who most likely is the man?

   (A) A computer repair person
   (B) A customer service representative
   (C) A photojournalist
   (D) A graphic designer

8. What does the woman inquire about?

   (A) Taking a photography lesson
   (B) Applying an online discount
   (C) Replacing a camera battery
   (D) Extending a warranty

9. According to the man, what should the woman do?

   (A) Visit a store
   (B) Call a manufacturer
   (C) Print some photographs
   (D) Download an instruction manual

10. Where does the woman work?

    (A) At a university
    (B) At a television station
    (C) At a public library
    (D) At a newspaper office

11. How does the woman know Alex Stanford?

    (A) They are writing a book together.
    (B) They used to work at the same company.
    (C) He recently submitted a résumé.
    (D) He is a local celebrity.

12. What does the woman suggest that the man do?

    (A) Visit a career fair
    (B) Travel after graduation
    (C) Participate in an internship
    (D) Submit a writing sample

13. What is the conversation mainly about?

    (A) Making travel arrangements
    (B) Submitting receipts for expenses
    (C) Applying for a business loan
    (D) Having a computer repaired

14. According to the man, why is the new system better?

    (A) Payments are processed faster.
    (B) It is less expensive to operate.
    (C) Scheduling is done online.
    (D) A warranty is included.

15. What will the woman most likely do next?

    (A) Change an appointment time
    (B) Consult with another colleague
    (C) Create electronic documents
    (D) Correct a bank statement

16. Where is the conversation taking place?

    (A) At a training session
    (B) At a theater performance
    (C) At a product demonstration
    (D) At a staff meeting

17. What problem does the woman mention?

    (A) She cannot find a building.
    (B) She did not receive an e-mail.
    (C) She was unable to attend an event.
    (D) She is having technical problems.

18. What does the man ask the woman to do?

    (A) Turn off her mobile phone
    (B) Take notes
    (C) Sit in the back row
    (D) Read an overview

19. Why is the man calling?

    (A) To invite the woman to a company picnic
    (B) To reserve space for an event
    (C) To volunteer to teach a course
    (D) To inquire about parking rules

20. What does the woman ask about?

    (A) The size of an area
    (B) The weather forecast
    (C) The date and time of an event
    (D) The number of people attending

21. What does the woman suggest?

    (A) Calling a rental company
    (B) Bringing more food
    (C) Going to another venue
    (D) Using public transportation

22. What are the speakers mainly discussing?

    (A) Improved train service
    (B) New bicycle pathways
    (C) A community festival
    (D) A renovation to city hall

23. What problem does the woman mention?

    (A) A lack of funding
    (B) A shortage of volunteers
    (C) Some travel delays
    (D) Some broken equipment

24. What do the men plan to do?

    (A) E-mail some friends
    (B) Call some city officials
    (C) Post an online announcement
    (D) Attend a meeting

LC

PART 3

세부 사항 문제 / 문제점 · 걱정거리 문제

① 세부 사항 문제

'누가 / 언제 / 어디서 / 무엇을 / 어떻게 / 왜'의 의문사로 다양한 세부정보를 묻는 문제로, 매회 12문제 정도 출제됩니다.
특히, 화자가 언급한 내용을 묻는 질문에서는 say나 mention 뒤에 제시된 단어나 구문이 핵심어예요.

언급 내용	• What does the woman say about an item?	여자가 제품에 대해 언급하는 것은 무엇인가?
세부 정보	• What is the man unable to do?	남자가 할 수 없는 것은 무엇인가?
	• Why is Mr. Dubois unavailable?	두보아 씨가 시간이 안 되는 이유는 무엇인가?

■ 핵심 포인트 | 질문 속의 키워드가 그대로 나오거나 패러프레이징된다.　　　　650_P3_06 🎧

M　You know, there's a new Indian restaurant that opened on Samson Street yesterday. It's just five minutes away. Why don't you try it?

W　Oh, that sounds good. It's so nice to be able just to walk to a restaurant from home and not have to worry about parking my car.

M　**If you go there this week, you'll get a ten percent discount** because it's their opening week.
→ 질문의 키워드인 this week가 그대로 등장했다.

남　어제 샘슨 가에 인도 식당이 새로 개업했어요. 5분 거리밖에 안 돼요. 한번 가 보세요.

여　오, 좋아요. 집에서 식당까지 그냥 걸어서 갈 수 있고 주차 걱정도 안 해도 되니까 너무 좋아요.

남　이번 주에 거기 가면 개업 첫 주라서 **10퍼센트 할인 받을 거예요.**

What does the man say is available (this week)?
(A) Reserved parking
(B) Product samples
(C) Cooking classes
(D) Discounted prices

남자가 **이번 주에** 가능하다고 말한 것은 무엇인가?
(A) 예약 주차
(B) 제품 샘플
(C) 요리 교실
(D) 할인가

┌─ 정답이 들리는 단서 표현 ─

세부 사항 문제는 다음과 같은 표현이 들릴 때 정답을 포착해야 한다.

질문	지문 속 단서
What **recently happened** in the company? 최근에 회사에 무슨 일이 있었는가?	We **recently/just** hired several new people. 우리는 최근에 신입사원을 몇 명 고용했어요.
What does the man say he will do **in March**? 남자는 3월에 무엇을 하겠다고 말하는가?	I'll be on vacation **in March**. 저는 3월에 휴가를 갈 거예요.
Why does the man **apologize**? 남자는 왜 사과하는가?	(I'm) **sorry, but** I'm running late. 죄송하지만, 늦을 것 같아요.
What does the woman want to buy? 여자는 무엇을 사길 원하는가?	**I'd like to** purchase some furniture for my restaurant. 제 식당에 들어갈 가구를 구입하고 싶어요.

1. When will the man probably start seeing clients tomorrow?
(A) At 9 A.M.
(B) At 10 A.M.
(C) At 11 A.M.
(D) At 1 P.M.

M Susan, could you _____ tomorrow?
W Sure, Mr. Miller. When is the _____ him?
M The mechanic told me that my car should be ready by ten. So, _____.
W OK, I'll _____ in at eleven.

2. What event do the women want to have at the restaurant?
(A) A client meeting
(B) A department luncheon
(C) A birthday party
(D) A retirement celebration

W1 I'm glad we _____ for lunch. The food is absolutely delicious.
W2 I agree. My whole meal was excellent.
W1 You know, this might _____ to have George's _____.
W2 Why don't we ask the server if we can _____ for a large group?

3. Why is the woman unable to answer the man's question?
(A) She has not heard back from a hotel.
(B) She does not have Internet access.
(C) An event budget has not been provided.
(D) A director has been out of town.

M Divya, I have a question about the _____. Do you know _____ this year?
W I'm still waiting to _____ from the South York Hotel that we can use their ballroom. _____, we can host as many clients as we like.
M Oh, OK. Please let me know _____.

4. What does the man say about the Claremont property?
(A) It is close to his business.
(B) It has a historical building.
(C) He hopes to redevelop it.
(D) He has decided to sell it.

W Hello, Mr. Wilson? This is Susan Chung—a reporter for the local newspaper. I'm following up on a report that you _____ the vacant Claremont property site.
M I lead a community group that _____ the Claremont property into the biggest park in the city. _____ are really excited about this possibility.
W I imagine you'll need to _____ to the city.
M That's right.

LC

PART 3

② 문제점·걱정거리 문제

기기 고장, 교통편 및 일정 지연, 예약, 업무 등과 관련된 문제점이나 걱정거리를 묻는 문제로, 매회 2문제 정도 출제돼요.

언급 내용	• What problem does the woman mention?	여자는 어떤 문제를 언급하는가?
세부 정보	• What is the man concerned about?	남자는 무엇을 걱정하는가?
	• Why are the speakers concerned?	화자들은 왜 걱정하는가?

■ **핵심 포인트** | 반전·역접의 표현 뒤에 문제점·걱정거리가 언급된다.   650_P3_08 🎧

M We really enjoyed meeting you at the interview, and I'd like to offer you the position of Assistant Director.

W Thanks so much for the offer. I'm very interested in the job, **but my only concern is how I would get to work. I don't own a car, and I know there aren't any public transportation options in the area.**
→ 반전·역접의 표현인 but 뒤에 바로 이어 문제점을 말하고 있다.

M Actually, I have some good news for you. Our company has just launched an employee shuttle service from the nearby train station.

남 면접에서 만나 봬서 정말 즐거웠어요. 조감독 자리를 제안하고 싶어요.

여 제안해 주셔서 정말 감사합니다. 그 일에 관심이 많지만, **단 하나 걱정스러운 건 어떻게 출근할까 하는 거예요. 전 차가 없는데 제가 알기로 이 지역에는 대중교통 수단이 없거든요.**

남 실은 좋은 소식이 있어요. 회사에서 얼마 전 가까운 기차역에서 직원 셔틀 서비스를 시작했어요.

(What) is the (woman) (concerned about)?
(A) The availability of staff
(B) The cost of a move
(C) A delay in production
(D) A lack of transportation options

여자가 걱정하는 것은 무엇인가?
(A) 직원 활용 가능성
(B) 이사 비용
(C) 생산 지연
(D) 교통편 부족

┌─ 정답이 들리는 단서 표현 ─

문제점·걱정거리 문제는 다음과 같은 표현이 들릴 때 정답을 포착해야 한다.

반전·역접 표현	But/However	그러나
	Unfortunately	유감스럽게도
	Actually	실은
고장이 난	out of order/down/broken down/not working/ not functioning/malfunctioning	고장이 난
부족한·떨어진	out of power	전원이 나간
	out of fuel	연료가 떨어진
	out of stock	품절된
일정 지연	delayed	지연된
	behind schedule	일정보다 늦게

1. What is the man's problem?
   (A) He lost his room keys.
   (B) He was late coming to work.
   (C) He cannot access his computer.
   (D) He forgot his computer password.

> **M** Have you had any problems using your computer this morning? I _____.
> **W** Our _____ last night. You have to go to the technical services office to _____.
> **M** OK... that's down on the first floor by the machine room, right?
> **W** It's on the first floor, but you need to _____ _____. It's right _____.

2. What problem does the woman mention?
   (A) She cannot locate a store.
   (B) She cannot install a program.
   (C) She cannot print some documents.
   (D) She cannot replace an ink cartridge.

> **W** Hi, I'm _____. The problem is, um, every time I try to _____ on both sides of the paper, the _____ in the machine.
> **M** I'm sorry to hear that. Unfortunately we can't _____ over the phone.
> **W** I guess I'll _____ to the store this afternoon.

3. What is the woman concerned about?
   (A) The rate of production
   (B) The availability of staff
   (C) The temperature of a room
   (D) The cost of shipping

> **W** I'm _____ on assembly line number three. The machine that seals the mobile phone boxes isn't _____ it should.
> **M1** Oh, we've had trouble with that machine in the past. _____ again, I think we'd better just replace it.
> **M2** I agree. But we should try to get a new one put in as soon as possible, or we might have to _____ _____.

4. What problem does Ms. Reed mention?
   (A) An invoice is incomplete.
   (B) An office has closed.
   (C) A document is missing.
   (D) A measurement is incorrect.

> **M** Hello? Ms. Reed?
> **W** Hello, Mr. Park. Could you possibly _____ _____? I _____ for the front entrance.
> **M** Certainly. It'll _____ to print the plan, though. If you come by my office around three o'clock, I'll _____ by then.

LC

PART 3

1. What do the speakers like about the restaurant?

   (A) The variety of menu items
   (B) The price of the dishes
   (C) The live music
   (D) The promptness of the service

2. What are the speakers considering?

   (A) Ordering a dessert
   (B) Changing a meeting time
   (C) Having an event catered
   (D) Writing a recommendation

3. What does the man say he will do?

   (A) Ask for driving directions
   (B) Make a reservation
   (C) Leave a business card
   (D) Talk to a manager

4. What event are the speakers discussing?

   (A) A film festival
   (B) A groundbreaking ceremony
   (C) A lecture series
   (D) A picnic

5. What problem does the man mention?

   (A) A weather forecast is bad.
   (B) A building permit has not been issued.
   (C) A structure is being repaired.
   (D) A guest speaker is unavailable.

6. What does the woman decide to do?

   (A) Request a refund
   (B) Reschedule an event
   (C) Reserve a different venue
   (D) Speak with a supervisor

7. Why is the man going to the restaurant?

   (A) To host a business dinner
   (B) To attend a job interview
   (C) To celebrate a birthday
   (D) To conduct an inspection

8. What would the man like to do?

   (A) Reserve a larger table
   (B) Change a meeting time
   (C) Order dishes before guests arrive
   (D) Speak with the owner

9. What does the woman say about the private dining area?

   (A) It is unavailable.
   (B) It is less noisy.
   (C) It has recently been remodeled.
   (D) It costs extra money.

10. Where does the woman work?

    (A) At a post office
    (B) At a restaurant
    (C) At a computer repair shop
    (D) At a pharmacy

11. What is the man concerned about?

    (A) Hours of operation
    (B) Fees for a service
    (C) A lost item
    (D) A mistake on an invoice

12. What will the woman most likely do next?

    (A) Check on an order
    (B) Speak to a colleague
    (C) Verify an address
    (D) Take a break

13. Who is the woman?

(A) An interior designer
(B) A furniture store owner
(C) A factory inspector
(D) A hotel manager

14. What is special about the products?

(A) They were featured in a magazine article.
(B) They were locally made.
(C) They are affordably priced.
(D) They are environmentally friendly.

15. What does the man offer to do for the woman?

(A) Take some measurements
(B) Send her some samples
(C) Change a warranty period
(D) Reduce a product's cost

---

16. Where does the man most likely work?

(A) At a post office
(B) At a motor vehicles department
(C) At a public library
(D) At a utility company

17. Why will the woman return tomorrow?

(A) To make a payment
(B) To complete a job application
(C) To provide an additional document
(D) To purchase some equipment

18. What additional benefit does the man mention?

(A) Express shipping
(B) An extended warranty
(C) Price reductions
(D) Internet access

19. What problem does the woman mention?

(A) Ticket sales have been slow.
(B) Bad weather has been predicted.
(C) Some volunteers are not feeling well.
(D) Some posters are in the wrong location.

20. What most likely is the focus of the festival?

(A) Crafts
(B) Dance
(C) Music
(D) Food

21. What does the woman remind the men to pick up?

(A) Instruction manuals
(B) Paychecks
(C) ID badges
(D) T-shirts

---

22. Where do the speakers work?

(A) At a furniture manufacturer
(B) At an art supply store
(C) At a restaurant supplier
(D) At an automobile repair shop

23. Why have customers complained about a product?

(A) It is too heavy.
(B) It is too expensive.
(C) It is not sturdy.
(D) It is unattractive.

24. What does the woman say she will do in the afternoon?

(A) Take some photographs
(B) Create a cost estimate
(C) Contact some customers
(D) Review a manual

① 요청·제안 문제

주로 세 번째 문제로 출제되며, 매회 5문제 정도 나와요. 대화의 후반부에 단서가 언급돼요. 요청이나 제안을 할 때 사용하는 빈출 패턴을 알아두면 쉽게 답이 들려요.

요청	• What does the man ask the woman to do?	남자가 여자에게 해 달라고 요청하는 것은 무엇인가?
	• What does the woman ask the man for?	여자가 남자에게 요청하는 것은 무엇인가?
	• What is the woman asked to do?	여자가 하라고 요청 받은 것은 무엇인가?
제안	• What does the woman offer to do?	여자가 하겠다고 제안하는 것은 무엇인가?
	• What does the man suggest/recommend?	남자가 제안/추천하는 것은 무엇인가?

■ 핵심 포인트 | 요청·제안의 표현을 놓치지 말고 포착하자.

650_P3_11

W I was looking for the cookware that was used in your cooking demonstration last week, but I don't see any on the shelf. Do you have any more in stock?

M No, sorry. We sold out of those quickly.

W Do you know if one of your other stores might have them in stock?

M Let me check. Here, it looks like we have them at our Silver Creek store. **I'll call and ask them to hold a set for you.**
→ 제안의 표현인 I'll이 등장했어요.

여 지난주 요리 시연에 사용된 조리 기구를 찾고 있었는데, 진열대에 안 보이네요. 재고가 더 있나요?

남 없어요, 죄송합니다. 빨리 매진되었어요.

여 다른 매장들 중 한 곳에 재고가 없을까요?

남 확인해 볼게요. 여기 있네요, 실버 크릭 매장에 있는 것 같아요. **제가 전화해서 고객님을 위해 한 세트 챙겨 놓으라고 요청할게요.**

(What) does the (man) (offer) to do?
(A) Check a catalog
(B) Wrap a gift
(C) Issue a refund
(D) **Call another store**

남자가 하겠다고 **제안**한 일은 **무엇인가?**
(A) 카탈로그 확인
(B) 선물 포장
(C) 환불
(D) **다른 매장에 전화하기**

정답이 들리는 단서 표현

요청·제안 문제는 다음과 같은 표현이 들릴 때 정답을 포착해야 한다.

요청	**I'll need** your photo ID.	사진이 있는 신분증을 주세요.
	Could you place an order for some more bottles today?	오늘 병 몇 개를 추가로 주문해 주시겠어요?
	(Please) switch off the power of the machine.	기계의 전원을 꺼 주세요.
제안	**(I think) you should** consider leading a discussion.	토론을 진행하는 걸 고려해 보셨으면 해요.
	I'll check with him and see if he can start to work earlier.	내가 그가 일을 더 일찍 시작할 수 있는지 확인해 볼게요.
제공	**(If you'd like,) I could[can]** mail you some samples.	원하시면, 제가 샘플을 몇 개 보내 드릴게요.
	I can take care of that. I'll send an e-mail to them.	제가 처리할게요. 그들에게 이메일을 보낼게요.

1. What does the woman ask for?
(A) An address
(B) A password
(C) A phone number
(D) An account number

M Hello, my name is Fred Kane, and I'm calling from the Clearsea Electronics Company. I'd like to _____ from our short-term savings account to our long-term account.
W No problem, sir. What's the _____ that you're _____?
M The account number is 67843.

2. Where does the woman suggest going?
(A) To a restaurant
(B) To a coffee shop
(C) To an ice cream shop
(D) To a company cafeteria

W Do you want to _____ near the ice cream shop?
M Oh, I went there last week and I _____. There were too many people and there wasn't _____ between the tables.
W Really? That's too bad.

3. What does the man ask the woman to do?
(A) Wait in the lobby
(B) Update an application
(C) Wear a badge
(D) Provide photo identification

W Hi, I'm Petra Barlow. I have an _____ in the accounting department here at Houseman Incorporated.
M Hello, Ms. Barlow. Let me _____. While I do that, would you _____ so it's easy to see?
W Yes, of course.

4. What suggestion does the man make about the logo?
(A) Fixing the position
(B) Adding a picture
(C) Changing the color
(D) Increasing the size

W Did you have a chance to _____ of the new book cover?
M Yes, I _____, and I think it's really good. I do have one suggestion though. I think our publishing company's logo is very small compared to the other information. How about _____ so people can see it better?
W That's a good idea.

② 다음에 할 일 문제

화자가 다음에 할 일을 묻는 문제로 매회 2~5문제 정도 나와요. 주로 세 번째 문제로 출제되며, 대화의 마지막 부분에
단서가 언급돼요.

다음에 할 일	• What will the man do next?	남자가 다음에 할 일은 무엇인가?
	• What is the man going to do next?	남자는 다음에 무엇을 할 것인가?
	• What does the woman say she will do?	여자는 무엇을 하겠다고 말하는가?
	• What will the speakers most likely do next?	화자들은 다음에 무엇을 할 것 같은가?

■ **핵심 포인트** | 미래 시점이나 제안을 나타내는 표현에서 단서를 포착하자.   650_P3_13 🎧

M I'd like to discuss a marketing strategy with you.

W OK, What did you have in mind?

M I was thinking of using social media to connect with customers directly.

W That's a wonderful plan! **Why don't I set up a meeting with the rest of the marketing team**?

→ 제안의 표현이 곧 정답으로 연결된다.

남 당신과 마케팅 전략을 논의하고 싶어요.

여 좋아요, 생각해 둔 게 있나요?

남 소셜 미디어를 이용해서 고객과 직접 연결할까 생각하고 있었어요.

여 멋진 계획이에요! **나머지 마케팅 팀원들과 회의를 잡아 볼게요.**

(What) does the (woman) say she (will do)?
(A) Revise a project timeline
(B) Obtain a construction estimate
(C) Provide a sales forecast
(D) Arrange a team meeting

여자는 무엇을 하겠다고 말하는가?
(A) 프로젝트 일정표 수정
(B) 공사 견적서 입수
(C) 예상 매출 제공
(D) 팀 회의 주선

┌─ 정답이 들리는 단서 표현 ─────────────────────────

다음에 할 일을 묻는 문제는 다음과 같은 표현이 들릴 때 정답을 포착해야 한다.

미래 시점	**I'll have** a technician **look** at the equipment.	기술자를 불러 장비를 점검하도록 할게요.
	I'll call Khan **and ask** him if he'd be able to switch shifts with me.	칸에게 전화해서 저와 근무시간을 바꿀 수 있는지 물어볼게요.
	I'll stop by your office right now.	지금 바로 사무실로 들를게요.
제안	**I can call** some landscaping firms to get some prices.	조경 회사 몇 군데에 전화해서 가격을 알아볼게요.
	I can e-mail you our latest brochure for your reference.	참고해 보실 수 있게 이메일로 당사의 최신 안내책자를 보내 드리겠습니다.
	Let me ask my manager if I can leave early tomorrow.	내일 일찍 퇴근할 수 있는지 제 상관에게 물어볼게요.

1. What will the man most likely do next?
- (A) Make an appointment
- (B) Provide a reference
- (C) Purchase some merchandise
- (D) Leave a message

M I'm _____ and your company for the great job you did catering for our business luncheon last week.

W Oh, don't thank me. Your event was _____, Nadia.

M If Nadia's in the office, I'd like to _____.

W Actually, she's out today. But I can _____ _____ so that you can leave her a message.

2. What will the speakers do next?
- (A) Look at fuel prices
- (B) Review customer complaints
- (C) Update staffing schedules
- (D) Organize training programs

W I hear that we've had _____ recently.

M In fact, I've just been _____. Our driver _____, but there was heavy traffic on the way to the airport, and she nearly missed her flight.

W We should probably _____ scheduled in the area.

M And we have some other issues to consider as well. _____—we'll need to decide what to do.

3. What does the woman say she will do next?
- (A) Update a file
- (B) Sign a contract
- (C) Discuss a price
- (D) Transfer a call

W I have a _____ on the phone. Since I'm really busy today, I was going to ask Steven to show the apartment, but he isn't _____.

M I noticed he forgot his mobile phone on his desk there. I might have _____ to show the client the third-floor apartment.

W That would be great. OK, I'll _____ now.

4. What will the man probably do next?
- (A) Schedule a meeting
- (B) Give a presentation
- (C) Take a lunch break
- (D) Work on a report

W _____ in London?

M I was worried about _____. But in fact, the room was full.

W Terrific. How was the _____ for you there?

M I _____. We should book it for next year's conference too! Oh, which reminds me— I have to _____ on the other speakers' presentations. I've got to start on that right now.

1. Where are the speakers?

   (A) At a conference
   (B) At an airport
   (C) At an office
   (D) At a bookstore

2. Why did the woman decide not to attend the final presentation?

   (A) She wanted to avoid rush hour traffic.
   (B) She had to prepare for a meeting.
   (C) She wanted to contact a publisher.
   (D) She had heard the speaker before.

3. What does the woman suggest the man do?

   (A) Check a calendar
   (B) Guide a discussion
   (C) Work extra hours
   (D) Book a flight

4. Where do the speakers work?

   (A) At a national park
   (B) At a travel agency
   (C) On a farm
   (D) In a market

5. What does the woman ask the man to do?

   (A) Arrange a display
   (B) Unload some boxes
   (C) Update a contact list
   (D) Order supplies

6. Why does the man say he cannot complete the task today?

   (A) He has to make a delivery.
   (B) He needs additional information.
   (C) No one is available to help.
   (D) The weather is bad.

7. What does the man say he has tickets for?

   (A) A city tour
   (B) An art show
   (C) A baseball game
   (D) A music concert

8. Why does the woman say she does not want the tickets?

   (A) She plans to work late that night.
   (B) She will be at a different event.
   (C) She will be away on vacation.
   (D) She prefers other types of events.

9. What will the man most likely do next?

   (A) Place information on a bulletin board
   (B) Attend a lunch meeting with clients
   (C) Prepare for a sports game
   (D) Call to ask for a refund

10. What is the report about?

    (A) Loan applications
    (B) Software updates
    (C) Revised hiring plans
    (D) Possible business locations

11. What does the woman say she is pleased about?

    (A) The changes in market prices
    (B) The availability of skilled workers
    (C) The presentation of some information
    (D) The reduction of some expenses

12. What does the man suggest?

    (A) Hiring a consultant
    (B) Including more photographs
    (C) Rescheduling a presentation
    (D) Requesting a product demonstration

13. What does the woman want to do?

(A) Make an airline reservation
(B) Renew a driver's license
(C) Apply for a research grant
(D) Obtain a passport

14. What will the woman most likely do next?

(A) Fill out some forms
(B) Show some identification
(C) Use a computer
(D) Speak to a travel agent

15. What can the woman pay extra for?

(A) A window seat
(B) A faster processing time
(C) Additional printouts
(D) Technical assistance

16. Where are the speakers?

(A) At a movie theater
(B) At a fitness center
(C) At an art museum
(D) At a research laboratory

17. What problem does the woman mention?

(A) She cannot find a supervisor.
(B) She has lost a card.
(C) A license has expired.
(D) A facility will close early.

18. What does the supervisor ask the woman to do?

(A) Check a directory
(B) Pay a service fee
(C) Come back later
(D) Fill out a form

19. Where most likely are the speakers?

(A) At an electronics store
(B) At a garden center
(C) At a car dealership
(D) At a utility company office

20. What does the woman want to talk to a manager about?

(A) Long waiting times
(B) A misleading advertisement
(C) A helpful employee
(D) High-quality merchandise

21. What does the man suggest the woman do?

(A) Return at another time
(B) Try out a product
(C) Provide written feedback
(D) Read a manual

22. Where does the woman most likely work?

(A) At a hotel
(B) At an architectural firm
(C) At a movie theater
(D) At a restaurant

23. What is causing a problem?

(A) A delayed opening
(B) An incorrect bill
(C) Noise from construction work
(D) A shortage of trained staff

24. What will the woman probably do next?

(A) Speak to her manager
(B) Send a confirmation e-mail
(C) Offer a reduced rate
(D) Check for an available room

LC

PART 3

① 의도 파악 문제

대화 중에 나올 짧은 문장 하나를 질문에서 미리 보여 주고, 그 말을 하는 화자의 숨은 의도를 묻는 문제로 매회 2문제씩 출제돼요. 주어진 문장의 앞뒤 대화의 전체적인 흐름을 파악해 문맥상 의미를 이해해야 문제를 풀 수 있어요.

문제유형
- Why does the man say, "~"?   남자가 "~"라고 말한 이유는 무엇인가?
- What does the man mean when he says, "~"?   남자가 "~"라고 말한 의도는 무엇인가?
- What does the woman imply when she says, "~"?   여자가 "~"라고 말한 의도는 무엇인가?

■ **핵심 포인트** | 제시문 앞뒤 문맥으로 의도를 파악하자.   650_P3_16 🎧

W   Hey, Samir. How's it going?

M   **I'm so tired of this financial report! I've been working on it for the last five hours.**
→ 남자가 재무 보고서를 5시간째 작성 중이라고 푸념하고 있다.

W   Well, the work day's almost over.

M   That's true – I'm off in half an hour.

여   안녕, 사미르. 잘 돼가요?

남   이 재무보고서 정말 지긋지긋해요! 5시간째 작성하고 있어요.

여   음, 근무시간이 거의 끝나가요.

남   그러네요. 30분 후면 퇴근이네요.

(Why) does the (woman) say, "the work day's almost over"?
(A) To end a meeting
(B) To express surprise
(C) **To comfort the man**
(D) To correct the man

여자가 "근무시간이 거의 끝나가요"라고 말한 이유는 무엇인가?
(A) 회의를 끝내려고
(B) 놀라움을 표현하려고
(C) **남자를 위로하려고**
(D) 남자의 실수를 바로잡으려고

┌─ 정답이 들리는 단서 표현 ─────────────────────

의도 파악 문제는 다음과 같은 표현이 들릴 때 정답을 포착해야 한다.

거절	W Can you lead a tour of our factory tomorrow morning?	내일 오전에 공장 견학을 진행할 수 있어요?
	M **I'm supposed to train some new employees all morning.**	오전 내내 신입 사원들을 교육해야 해요.
	의도 He cannot take on the job.	남자는 일을 맡을 수 없다.
지연	M Why is the elevator still out of order?	왜 엘리베이터가 여전히 고장이죠?
	W **They are waiting for some new parts to arrive.**	새 부품이 도착하길 기다리고 있어요.
	의도 To explain a delay	지연 이유를 설명하기 위해

1. What does the man mean when he says, "It was time for something like that"?
(A) He is concerned about a work deadline.
(B) He wants to hold meetings more often.
(C) He thinks a project is a good idea.
(D) He hopes to hold a special event.

M I just noticed they _____ in the lobby.
W It's just _____—to improve the lobby's overall appearance.
M Oh, OK… It was time for something like that.
W I heard the crews will even put up antique photos showing the _____—more than a century ago.

2. Why does the man say, "The train leaves in one minute"?
(A) To urge a quick decision
(B) To announce an early departure
(C) To deny a ticket purchase
(D) To assure the woman that she has arrived in time

W Hello. Can I still _____ for the 9:05 train to Amsterdam? It's not too late, is it?
M I'm sorry. The train leaves in one minute. However, there are trains at 10:50 A.M. and 12:30 P.M. There are _____.
W I'll _____.

3. Why does the woman say, "If you wouldn't mind"?
(A) To suggest a solution
(B) To ask for permission
(C) To make a complaint
(D) To accept an offer

M This is Jacob from the landscaping company. I'm afraid we won't be able to _____ _____ tomorrow.
W I'm going to _____ for two weeks starting this Thursday. I wanted to give you a key to the gate, so you'd be able to _____ _____.
M OK. Then what if I come by tomorrow anyway, just to _____?
W If you wouldn't mind. I'll be at home _____.

4. What does the man mean when he says, "That's not a bad idea"?
(A) He would like to hear more suggestions.
(B) He prefers the original plan.
(C) He agrees with the proposed solution.
(D) He has a better idea.

W We'll have to _____ we've asked you to do.
M Do you know _____ you'd like to put off?
W Well, I know we talked about _____ —but that's very expensive. So, if we don't make that addition, that's all we may need to cut.
M You know, that's not a bad idea. Let's see _____ if I take the library out of the renovation proposal.

② 시각 정보 문제

'Look at the graphic.'으로 시작하는 문제로 매회 2~3문제씩 출제되며, 대화 내용을 시각 정보와 연계시켜야만 정답을 고를 수 있어요. 대화에서 언급되는 내용을 시각 정보에서 확인하고, 확인된 정보를 보기와 연계시키면 답이 나와요.

문제유형
- Look at the graphic. Which product did the woman buy?　시각 정보를 참고해, 여자는 어떤 제품을 샀는가?
- Look at the graphic. When will the man work at the event?　시각 정보를 참고해, 남자는 언제 행사에서 일할 것인가?
- Look at the graphic. Which road will the speakers take next?　시각 정보를 참고해, 화자들은 다음에 어떤 길로 갈 것인가?

■ 핵심 포인트 | 시각 정보에 제시된 키워드를 놓치지 말고 포착하자.

650_P3_18 🎧

W　How can I help you?

M　Hi, my mobile phone isn't working correctly.

W　**OK. First, can you tell me the phone's serial number?**
  → 시각 정보의 키워드인 serial number가 그대로 등장했다.

M　Sorry, I'm not exactly sure where to find that.

W　The serial number is under the settings menu.

M　OK, give me a second to find that.

여　무엇을 도와 드릴까요?

남　안녕하세요, 제 휴대폰이 제대로 작동하지 않아요.

여　그렇군요. **먼저, 휴대폰 일련 번호를 알려 주시겠어요?**

남　죄송해요, 어디에 있는지 잘 모르겠어요.

여　일련 번호는 설정 메뉴 밑에 있어요.

남　알겠어요, 잠깐만 기다려 주시면 찾을게요.

Software version	8.2	>
Model	250–73	>
Capacity in GB	124	>
(Serial Number)	36998	>

소프트웨어 버전	8.2
모델	250-73
용량(GB)	124
일련 번호	**36998**

(Look at the graphic). (Which number) will the (man) (give) the (woman)?

(A) 8.2　　　　　　　　　(B) 250-73
(C) 124　　　　　　　　　**(D) 36998**

시각정보를 참고해, 남자는 여자에게 어떤 번호를 주겠는가?
(A) 8.2　　　　　(B) 250-73
(C) 124　　　　　**(D) 36998**

정답이 들리는 단서 표현

막대 그래프와 선 그래프에서는 최고점이나 최저점을 나타내는 최상급 표현이 정답으로 자주 등장해요.

the largest number	가장 큰 수치
the second most popular	두 번째로 인기 있는
the least amount	가장 적은 양
what they like **the best**	가장 좋아하는 것
the lowest rate	최저 요금
It's clear which one our customers like **the best**.	우리 고객들이 어떤 맛을 가장 좋아하는지가 분명하네요.

1.

Guest Name:	Eric Peterson
Nightly Rate:	$95.00
Airport Transfer:	$15.00
Restaurant Charges:	$45.00 (two meals)
Miscellaneous:	$20.00

Look at the graphic. Which amount on the bill will be changed?

(A) $95   (B) $15

(C) $45   (D) $20

W May I have the key card to your room so I can begin
_____?

M I _____. Sorry about that. My name's
Eric Peterson. I was in room 615.

W So... I will have to _____
of seven dollars to your bill for the key card.

2.

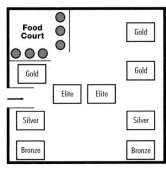

Look at the graphic. What type of booth does the man reserve?

(A) Elite   (B) Gold

(C) Bronze   (D) Silver

M Hello, I'd _____ for this year's garden
show.

W We have _____. I suggest one of the
"Elite" locations.

M I will take one of the spots _____.
I'm guessing there'll be _____ there.
Do I need to pay now?

W Just a deposit.

3.

Nutrition Information
Serving Size: 200 grams
Calories: **150**

	Amount Per Serving
Fat	5 grams
Protein	11 grams
Sugar	32 grams
Sodium	40 milligrams

Look at the graphic. Which of the ingredients does the man express concern about?

(A) Fat   (B) Protein

(C) Sugar   (D) Sodium

M Is there a yogurt that's _____ but also
has a lot of protein?

W Here's one of _____ of blueberry
yogurt. See, there's a lot of protein…

M Mmm—nice! But my doctor told me I shouldn't _____
_____—and it would put me over the daily
amount he recommended. That's more than 30 grams!

W In that case, I'd suggest _____ of this
yogurt.

1. What does the company sell?

   (A) Calculators
   (B) Cameras
   (C) Laptop computers
   (D) Kitchen appliances

2. Why does the woman say, "our customers want a compact design"?

   (A) To reject a suggestion
   (B) To express surprise
   (C) To offer reassurance
   (D) To ask for help

3. What will the woman do tomorrow?

   (A) Meet some clients
   (B) Select some images
   (C) E-mail a report
   (D) Make a presentation

---

4. What does the woman imply when she says, "Two hours wasn't enough"?

   (A) A deadline has been extended.
   (B) A project took longer than expected.
   (C) She was late arriving to an event.
   (D) She enjoyed a performance.

5. Why has the man been busy?

   (A) He was preparing for a presentation.
   (B) He was designing a brochure.
   (C) He was reporting on customer comments.
   (D) He was reviewing a performance.

6. What does the woman suggest the man do?

   (A) Arrive early
   (B) Invite a coworker
   (C) Test a new product
   (D) Recommend some medicine

MOUNTAIN VALLEY THEATER	
The World of Birds–Movie Times	
Theater 1	5:30
Theater 2	6:15
Theater 3	7:15
Theater 4	8:00

7. Why does the man apologize?

   (A) A price has increased.
   (B) A showtime is sold out.
   (C) A movie is no longer playing.
   (D) A coupon cannot be used.

8. Look at the graphic. Which theater will the woman go to?

   (A) Theater 1
   (B) Theater 2
   (C) Theater 3
   (D) Theater 4

9. Where does the man recommend going before the movie?

   (A) To a department store
   (B) To a local restaurant
   (C) To a library
   (D) To a park

---

10. Where do the speakers need to be at 2:00 P.M.?

(A) At an office
(B) At an airport
(C) At a train station
(D) At a convention center

11. What will the speakers do in Janville?

(A) Conduct some research
(B) Present at a seminar
(C) Inspect a facility
(D) Meet with investors

12. What does the man mean when he says, "we'll have Internet access at all times"?

(A) He has changed an Internet provider.
(B) He does not need to make any copies.
(C) The woman should not complain about poor service.
(D) The woman can complete an assignment online.

13. What are the speakers mainly discussing?

(A) Sales figures
(B) Dining options
(C) Team roles
(D) Inventory levels

14. Why does the woman say, "It's been a while"?

(A) To correct an error
(B) To complain about a delay
(C) To agree with a suggestion
(D) To praise a coworker

15. What does the man suggest doing next?

(A) Checking an account
(B) Updating a Web site
(C) Delivering a package
(D) Printing a document

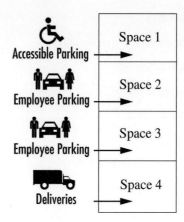

16. What did the woman order?

(A) A microwave oven
(B) A laptop computer
(C) Office furniture
(D) Printer paper

17. Why will the woman arrive late to the store?

(A) She has to give a coworker a ride.
(B) She cannot find a receipt.
(C) She is scheduled to work overtime.
(D) Her car is being repaired.

18. Look at the graphic. Which parking space should the woman use?

(A) Space 1
(B) Space 2
(C) Space 3
(D) Space 4

■ 업무 전반

headquarters 본사(=head office)

branch office 지점

paperwork 서류 업무

deadline 마감시한

paycheck 급여

extension 내선, 구내전화

return one's call 답신 전화하다

security badge 사원증(=ID badge)

bulletin board 게시판

transfer 인사이동 시키다

identification card 신분증

promote sales 판촉하다

sign a contract 계약서에 서명하다

submit a proposal 제안서를 제출하다

work overtime 초과 근무하다, 잔업하다

work late 야근하다

■ 출퇴근 / 휴가

medical leave 병가(=sick leave)

maternity leave 출산 휴가

access card 출입증

flexible working hours 탄력근무제

take a day off 하루 휴가를 내다

get out of work 퇴근하다

call in sick 아파서 결근하겠다고 전화하다

cover the shift 근무를 대신하다

■ 회의 / 일정

presentation 프레젠테이션, 발표

meeting room 회의실

conference call 전화회의

videoconferencing 화상회의

agenda 의제, 안건

handout 유인물, 인쇄물

chart 차트, 도표

(annual) budget report (연간) 예산 보고서

market survey 시장 조사

available (사람을 만날) 시간이 있는

scheduling conflict 일정 겹침

attend the meeting 회의에 참석하다

■ 사내 행사

banquet 연회

invitation 초대장

attendee 참석자

retirement 퇴직, 은퇴

venue 개최지, 행사장

register 등록하다

corporate event 기업 행사

company retreat 회사 야유회

trade show 무역 박람회

foundation ceremony 창립식

attend a training session 교육 과정에 참석하다

call off 취소하다(=cancel)

■ 인사 업무

coworker 동료

colleague 동료

employee 직원, 종업원

staff (전체) 직원

predecessor 전임자

replacement 후임자(=successor)

performance 업무 실적

raise 급여 인상

benefit (급여 외) 혜택, 수당

cover 맡다, 담당하다

time sheet 근무 시간 기록표

take over the position 직책을 맡다

■ 구인&구직

position 일자리, 직위

résumé 이력서

qualifications 자격요건

candidate 지원자, 후보자

complete (양식을) 작성하다

submit 제출하다

hire 고용하다

recruit 모집하다

portfolio 포트폴리오, (사진 · 그림 등의) 작품집

employment agency 직업 소개소

recommendation letter 추천서

job opening 일자리 공석(=job vacancy)

■ 사무기기

office supplies 사무용품

copier 복사기(=photocopier)

computer components 컴퓨터 부품

installation 설치

stockroom 비품 저장실

malfunction (기계가) 제대로 작동하지 않다

run out of ~이 떨어지다

place an order 주문하다

out of order 고장 난

find a new supplier[vendor]
새로운 납품업체를 구하다

■ 여가

leave 휴가; 떠나다

vacation 휴가; 휴가를 보내다

sightseeing 관광

destination 목적지

accommodations 숙박시설

single room 1인실

itinerary 여행 일정표

landmark 랜드마크, 주요 지형지물

jet lag 시차증

go on a trip 여행 가다

make a reservation 예약하다(=book)

travel agency 여행사

take a guided tour 가이드가 딸린 여행을 하다

■ 쇼핑

brand-new 새로 출시된

inventory 재고

damaged item 손상된 물품

refund 환불

shipment 배송

flyer 전단, 광고지

deliver 배송하다(=ship)

receipt 영수증

■ 은행

deposit 예금하다

withdraw 인출하다

transfer 송금하다(=remit)

balance 잔고, 잔액

due (돈을) 지불해야 하는

exchange rate 환율

savings account 보통 예금

interest rates 금리, 이자율

■ 식당

cuisine 요리법, 요리

beverage 음료

chef 주방장

food stand 매점

assorted 여러 가지의, 갖은

vegetarian 채식주의자(의)

spicy 양념 맛이 강한, 매운

■ 부동산

rent 임대료

lease 임대[임차]하다

deposit 보증금

landscaping 조경

tenant 세입자

property 부동산, 건물

renovation 개보수(=improvement)

■ 병원

checkup (건강) 검진

examine 검진하다(=see a doctor)

symptom 증상

treatment 치료, 처치

prescription 처방전

medication 약

pharmacy 약국

act up (병이) 재발하다

■ 교통

departure 출발

timetable 시간표

flight 비행; 비행편

express train 급행 기차

one-way[round] trip 편도[왕복] 여행

aisle[window] seat 통로[창가] 쪽 좌석

tow 견인하다

be stuck in traffic 교통 체증으로 꼼짝달싹 못하다

■ 패러프레이징 빈출 표현(단어→단어)

rule 규칙	→ regulation 규정
deliver 배달하다	→ ship 배송하다
attach 첨부하다	→ include 포함하다
journal 학술지	→ publication 출판물
display 진열하다	→ exhibit 전시하다
event 행사	→ occasion 행사
holiday 휴가	→ vacation 휴가
footwear 신발(류)	→ shoes 신발
switch 전환하다	→ transfer 옮기다
upcoming 다가오는	→ future 미래의
relocate 이전하다	→ move 이사하다
aircraft 항공기	→ flight 비행기
produce 생산하다	→ develop 개발하다
show 보여 주다	→ present 제시하다
profitable 수익성 있는	→ lucrative 이익이 되는
donate 기부하다	→ contribute 기부하다
paperwork 서류	→ document 문서
feedback 피드백	→ comment 의견
sufficient 충분한	→ adequate 충분한
abroad 해외로	→ overseas 해외로
thoroughly 철저히	→ carefully 신중하게
inside 내부에	→ indoors 실내에
free 무료의	→ complimentary 무료의
walk 걷다	→ stroll 여유롭게 걷다
reasonable 가격이 적정한	→ affordable 가격이 알맞은

■ 패러프레이징 빈출 표현(단어→구)

submit 제출하다	→ turn in 제출하다
postpone 연기하다	→ put off 연기하다
cancel 취소하다	→ call off 취소하다
land 착륙하다	→ touch down 착륙하다
attend 참석하다	→ participate in 참석하다
review 검토하다	→ go over 검토하다
visit 방문하다	→ drop by 들르다
contact 연락하다	→ get in touch with 연락하다
collaborate 협력하다	→ work together 협력하다
exercise 운동하다	→ work out 운동하다
revise 수정하다	→ make a correction 수정하다
distribute 배부하다	→ hand out 나눠 주다
install 설치하다	→ set up 세우다
mayor 시장	→ government official 공무원
ship 배송하다	→ send out 발송하다
consult 참고하다	→ refer to 참고하다
register 등록하다	→ sign up 등록하다
detour 우회도로	→ alternate route 우회로
assistant 조수, 보좌	→ staff member 직원
quarterly 분기마다	→ every three months 3개월마다
telecommuting 재택근무	→ working from home 재택근무
unavailable 이용할 수 없는	→ out of stock 재고가 없는
join 가입하다	→ become a member 회원이 되다

Part

짧은 담화

4

Part 4는 한 사람이 말하는 담화문을 듣고 그에 따른 세 문제를 푸는 유형으로, 총 10세트[담화문10개＋문제30개]가 출제돼요.

■ 2인 이상이 말하는 대화문이 아닌 혼자서 말하는 담화문인 점만 제외하면
→ Part 3과 똑같다!

Questions 71 through 73 refer to the following announcement.

◁)) 음원

M Hi everyone. I hope you're enjoying the conference. Uhm... before we get started with the next presentation, I have a quick announcement.

↓

You should have received a prepaid ticket for the welcome dinner tonight, in your registration packet. But it looks like some of the packets were missing them.

↓

So... if you didn't get one, I'll be in the lobby distributing tickets during the break at three o'clock. You just need to present your conference badge in order to receive your ticket. So don't forget it, OK?

↓

71. Who most likely are the listeners?
72. What problem does the speaker mention?
73. According to the speaker, what will some listeners need to do?

📖 문제지

71. Who most likely are the listeners?
    (A) Concert performers
    (B) Technical support staff
    (C) Conference attendees
    (D) Restaurant servers

↓

72. What problem does the speaker mention?
    (A) A room has not been reserved.
    (B) Some tickets were not distributed.
    (C) A speaker is unavailable.
    (D) A microphone is not working.

↓

73. According to the speaker, what will some listeners need to do?
    (A) Keep their receipts
    (B) Follow some signs
    (C) Wait in line
    (D) Show some identification

↓

다음 세트 준비!
[74~76]

■ Part 4 이렇게 풀자

① 음원을 듣기 전

1 문제 파악

문제를 미리 읽으면서 담화문을 듣는 동안 어떤 부분에 초점을 두어야 할지 파악해요. 성우가 파트 4의 Directions를 읽어주는 동안 첫 세트인 71번~73번 문제를 읽어 두어요.

2 키워드 표시

문제의 핵심이 되는 키워드를 표시해 두면, 정답 단서가 들렸을 때 더 쉽게 포착할 수 있어요. 키워드에는 의문사, 명사, 동사, 시간 표현 등이 해당돼요.

71. (Who) most likely are the (listeners)?   → **청자들은 누구**일 것 같은가?
72. (What problem) does the (speaker) (mention)?   → **화자는 무슨 문제를 언급**하는가?
73. According to the speaker, (what) will some   → **청자들은 무엇을 해야 하는가?**
    (listeners) (need to do)?

3 화자와 청자 구분

문제에서 화자(speaker)에 대해 묻는지 청자(listener)에 대해 묻는지를 구분해야 해요.

Where does the **speaker** most likely work?   → 화자가 일하는 곳
Who most likely are the **listeners**?   → 청자의 직업

② 음원을 들으면서

4 정답 선택하기

정답의 단서는 대부분 문제 순서대로 나와요. 따라서 담화 전반부가 나올 때 첫 번째 문제를 보고 있다가 단서가 들리면 바로 정답을 고르고 다음 문제로 넘어가서 다음 단서를 기다리면 돼요.

③ 음원을 듣고난 후

5 문제를 읽어주는 동안 다음 세트 문제 파악

담화문이 끝나면 성우가 문제를 읽어줘요. 각 문제를 읽을 때마다 8초간의 문제 풀이 시간이 함께 주어지는데, 이 시간 동안 다음 세트의 문제들을 미리 파악해 두어요.

전화 메시지   예약 확인 및 변경, 업무 협조 요청, 프로젝트 진행 상황 공유 등과 같은 내용이 나와요.

녹음 메시지   업체 소개, 영업시간, 내선번호 등을 안내하는 ARS 녹음 메시지가 주로 나와요.

650_P4_01

정답과 해설 p.083

■ 담화의 흐름과 문제 구성

인사/소개	Hello, Mr. Clark. ❶ **This is Roger calling from the Lost Property office at the Wharton train station.**	❶ 저는 와튼 기차역 분실물 관리소의 로저입니다.
용건	❷ **A passenger found your wallet this morning and turned it in to us.**	❷ 한 승객이 오늘 아침 귀하의 지갑을 습득해서 저희에게 돌려주셨습니다.
요청/당부	When you come to retrieve your wallet, ❸ **you will need to give the attendant your item reference number.** It's 5492. Please remember to have this number when you come to the station. We cannot return your wallet unless you present this information.	❸ 안내원에게 조회 번호를 제시하셔야 합니다.

1. (Where) does the (speaker)(work)?

화자는 어디에서 근무하는가?

장소 문제 → 인사 직후 자기소개에 주목

정답   **At a train station**

기차역

2. (What) is the speaker (calling about)?

화자는 무엇에 대해 전화하는가?

주제 문제 → 초반부 듣고 주제 파악하기

정답   **A lost item**

분실물

3. (What) does the speaker (ask) the (listener) to do?

화자는 청자에게 무엇을 해달라고 요청하는가?

요청 사항 문제 → 요청문에 주목

정답   **Present a reference number**

조회 번호 제시하기

질문의 단서가 되는 주요 표현

"**Thank you for calling** Chester City Theater's business office."   화자는 어디에서 일하는가?

"**I'm calling to** confirm your reservation for a one-way shuttle bus."   전화의 목적은 무엇인가?

"**Please** call us again during regular office hours."   화자는 무엇을 요청하는가?

"**This is** Jim from Thompsonville Garage with a message for Gloria Blanton."   화자는 누구인가?

[1-2]

1. What type of facility does the message give information about?
   (A) A concert hall
   (B) A library

2. How can a caller reach John Olsen?
   (A) By dialing extension 25
   (B) By calling after 3:00 P.M.

> Thank you for calling the Gould Music Library. _____ are from nine A.M. to three P.M., Monday through Thursday. Access to our special archives can _____ John Olsen _____. If you would like to _____ for our administrative office, please _____ and then begin speaking. Thank you.

[3-4]

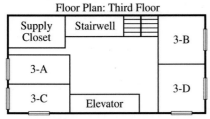

Floor Plan: Third Floor

Supply Closet	Stairwell	
3-A		3-B
3-C	Elevator	3-D

3. Who most likely is the message for?
   (A) A repair person
   (B) A real estate agent

4. Look at the graphic. Which apartment does the Garcia family live in?
   (A) 3-A   (B) 3-B

> I'm calling because one of the apartment units has _____. Could you _____ later this afternoon or tomorrow morning? It's the one the Garcia family lives in… you know… the corner apartment on the third floor, _____ _____? Their phone number is 555-0148. Please _____ to arrange a time to make the repair.

[5-6]

5. What is the purpose of the message?
   (A) To confirm an appointment
   (B) To request contact information

6. What is Mr. Lee asked to do?
   (A) Call a company
   (B) Register a product

> Hi, this is Lisa Sherman calling from Speed Mobile service. Mr. Lee, I'm calling because _____ to us in the mail, due to an incorrect address. We need your _____ so that we can resend a copy of your statement. _____ at 555-3421 between 9 A.M. and 5 P.M. Monday through Friday. Thank you for your time and have a nice day.

1. What is the purpose of the trip to Chicago?
   (A) To recruit new staff
   (B) To inspect a factory
   (C) To sign a contract
   (D) To give a sales presentation

2. Why is Tanya Levin unable to go to Chicago?
   (A) She is feeling sick.
   (B) Her flight has been canceled.
   (C) She has to work on another assignment.
   (D) Her previous trip has been extended.

3. What does the speaker say he will send to the listener?
   (A) A payment form
   (B) A list of clients
   (C) Some sales figures
   (D) Some slides

4. Why is the woman calling?
   (A) To reschedule a flight reservation
   (B) To notify a customer of a delay
   (C) To confirm transportation details
   (D) To provide driving directions

5. What time will the shuttle bus arrive at Jackson Telecommunications?
   (A) 3:15 P.M.
   (B) 4:15 P.M.
   (C) 5:15 P.M.
   (D) 6:15 P.M.

6. What is the listener asked to do?
   (A) Give payment to the driver
   (B) Be prepared to provide identification
   (C) Allow extra time for check-in
   (D) Confirm the number of passengers

7. What business most likely created the message?
   (A) An art gallery
   (B) A movie theater
   (C) A photography studio
   (D) A job recruitment agency

8. When is the business office closed?
   (A) On Sundays
   (B) On Mondays
   (C) On Tuesdays
   (D) On Wednesdays

9. What are job seekers advised to do?
   (A) Visit a Web site
   (B) Mail in a résumé
   (C) Come to the office
   (D) Call during office hours

10. Who most likely is the speaker?
    (A) An electrician
    (B) A car mechanic
    (C) A carpenter
    (D) A telephone repair person

11. What does the speaker say he will have to do?
    (A) Contact another store
    (B) Collect a deposit
    (C) Replace a broken part
    (D) Consult a colleague

12. Why should the listener call back?
    (A) To set up an appointment
    (B) To confirm a delivery time
    (C) To speak to a department manager
    (D) To authorize a charge

13. What type of business is Fresh Goods?

(A) A food manufacturer
(B) A grocery store
(C) A restaurant
(D) A vegetable grower

14. Why should listeners contact Barbara Hughes?

(A) To place an order
(B) To schedule an event
(C) To arrange transportation
(D) To report a problem

15. According to the message, what is available on the Web site?

(A) Driving directions
(B) Menu options
(C) A promotional offer
(D) Photos of the business

---

16. Who is the speaker most likely calling?

(A) A family member
(B) A friend
(C) A client
(D) A coworker

17. What does the speaker imply when he says, "It's rush hour"?

(A) A business' schedule has changed.
(B) A project was poorly timed.
(C) A suggestion will not work.
(D) A bus is crowded.

18. What does the speaker ask the listener to do?

(A) Give a presentation
(B) Make an appointment
(C) Mail some packages
(D) Purchase a gift

Turner's Furniture Store				
Employee	Tuesday, April 5	Wednesday, April 6	Thursday, April 7	Friday, April 8
Li	X	X	X	
Isamu		X	X	X
Karima	X	X		X
Hans	X		X	X

19. Look at the graphic. What day of the week is the speaker discussing?

(A) Tuesday
(B) Wednesday
(C) Thursday
(D) Friday

20. What event does the speaker mention?

(A) A discount sale
(B) A product launch
(C) A training workshop
(D) A job fair

21. What does the speaker offer the listener?

(A) A free meal
(B) A salary bonus
(C) A new uniform
(D) An extra vacation day

공지 / 안내	공공장소(상점, 공연장 등)에서 운영시간/행사/주의 사항 안내 등의 내용이 나와요.
회의	회사 관련 소식이나 업무에 대한 공지 사항을 직원들에게 전달하고 협조를 구하는 내용이 주로 나와요.

650_P4_04
정답과 해설 p.088

■ 담화의 흐름과 문제 구성

회의 주제/ 대상	① **Congratulations on completing your flight attendant training!** You're now ready for your first work assignments. ② **You have all submitted your lists of airports that you would like to be assigned to.** I'm reviewing your preferences and will give you your location assignments by the end of the week.	① 비행기 승무원 교육을 완수하신 것을 축하드립니다.
세부 사항		② 여러분 모두가 배정받고 싶은 공항 목록을 제출하셨습니다.
요청/당부	But before you leave, ③ **we're going to take a group photo, so please come to the front of the room.** We'll post the photo on our internal company Web site.	③ 단체 사진을 찍을 테니, 방 앞쪽으로 나와 주세요.

1. (Who) most likely are the (listeners)?
청자들은 누구일 것 같은가?

대상 문제 → 도입부에 청자의 직업 정보에 주목

정답 **Flight attendants**
비행기 승무원

2. According to the speaker, (what) did the (listeners) (submit)?
화자에 따르면, 청자들은 무엇을 제출했는가?

세부 사항 문제 → 초반부 키워드 'submitted'에 주목

정답 **Work location preferences**
선호하는 근무 장소

3. (What) are the (listeners) (asked) to (do) (next)?
청자들은 다음에 무엇을 하라고 요청 받는가?

요청 사항 문제 → 후반부의 요청문에 주목

정답 **Assemble for a photo**
사진을 찍기 위해 모이기

┌─ 질문의 단서가 되는 주요 표현 ─

"Welcome you all on your first day of work." 청자는 누구일 것 같은가?

"Sign up[Register] for the program today." 화자가 청자들에게 하라고 권장하는 것은 무엇인가?

"I'd like to show a video of our president's speech." 청자들이 다음에 할 일은 무엇인가?

"Come up with some ideas by the end of the week." 청자들이 하라고 요청 받은 일은 무엇인가?

[1-2]

1. What problem does the speaker mention?
   (A) A building will be without power.
   (B) Some computers must be replaced.

2. What does the speaker say he will do?
   (A) Send colleagues a message
   (B) Meet with team leaders

> Our office building will be _____
> Saturday morning and, uh, the _____
> for about three hours. For any of you planning to
> come in on Saturday, _____ by one
> o'clock. I'll _____ once the work's
> done.

[3-4]

3. What type of product does the business sell?
   (A) Clothing
   (B) Footwear

4. What did the business do after it relocated?
   (A) It placed some advertisements.
   (B) It organized an inauguration event.

> I have _____ at today's staff meeting.
> I just handed out a graph summarizing our _____
> _____. And, well... I think
> this information is particularly interesting since
> we _____ this year. During the
> quarter we moved, we experienced the lowest shoe
> sales of the entire year. However, thanks to the
> _____ we put out, business picked
> up quickly, and we ended the year by making a record
> number of sales.

[5-6]

5. What is the purpose of the announcement?
   (A) To report a schedule change
   (B) To give directions to an event

6. When will the event begin?
   (A) At 1:00 P.M.
   (B) At 6:00 P.M.

> Ladies and gentlemen, I'm sorry to announce that
> tonight's football game _____ by
> _____, due to heavy rain conditions.
> We _____. In the meantime, we
> encourage you to _____, which are
> now open. Please note there are no refunds, but
> you can exchange your ticket for a future game by
> _____ next to the main gate.

1. Where most likely is the announcement being made?

   (A) At a paint store
   (B) At a post office
   (C) At a manufacturing plant
   (D) At a construction site

2. What has caused a problem?

   (A) Some paint has spilled.
   (B) Some machinery is jammed.
   (C) Some packages have not been delivered.
   (D) Some products have been damaged.

3. What are the listeners instructed to do?

   (A) Turn off their machines
   (B) Meet with a supervisor
   (C) Clean up the area
   (D) Go to the staff room

4. Who most likely are the listeners?

   (A) New employees
   (B) Department heads
   (C) Potential clients
   (D) Outside consultants

5. What does the speaker say the listeners will do?

   (A) Conduct interviews
   (B) Review submissions
   (C) Answer inquiries
   (D) Draft contracts

6. What will most likely happen next?

   (A) Some materials will be presented.
   (B) Attendees will introduce themselves.
   (C) Work spaces will be assigned.
   (D) A building tour will take place.

7. What is the main topic of the announcement?

   (A) A recycling policy
   (B) An inventory procedure
   (C) Employee payroll
   (D) Computer maintenance

8. Why is the company making a change?

   (A) To increase revenue
   (B) To attract new employees
   (C) To comply with the local laws
   (D) To take advantage of a new technology

9. According to the speaker, what will happen on Thursdays?

   (A) Discarded materials will be picked up.
   (B) Machinery will be serviced.
   (C) Employees will be paid.
   (D) Supply orders will be processed.

10. Where most likely is the announcement being made?

    (A) At a library
    (B) At a bookshop
    (C) At a gift shop
    (D) At a department store

11. Why does the speaker say, "It's 9:30 P.M."?

    (A) To announce an event will begin
    (B) To decline an invitation
    (C) To suggest changing locations
    (D) To remind listeners of a closing time

12. What does the speaker encourage the listeners to do?

    (A) Purchase a promotional item
    (B) Enroll in a program
    (C) Attend a book reading
    (D) Apply for a job

13. What are listeners being asked to decide?

(A) What kind of printers to buy
(B) How to improve a procedure
(C) Where to locate some equipment
(D) When to have a celebration

14. What does the speaker say about the budget?

(A) It has not been finalized.
(B) There is extra money in it.
(C) There will be a new category.
(D) It will be lower next year.

15. What are listeners requested to do after the meeting?

(A) Request travel vouchers
(B) Meet with a committee member
(C) Register for a class
(D) Indicate a preferred product

16. Who most likely is the audience for this talk?

(A) Catering staff
(B) A maintenance crew
(C) A group of musicians
(D) Concert attendees

17. Why are listeners invited to visit the green tents?

(A) To get water
(B) To purchase food
(C) To check a schedule
(D) To pick up a T-shirt

18. According to the woman, what will happen at 6:00 P.M.?

(A) A contest winner will be announced.
(B) Performers will sign autographs.
(C) Equipment will be checked.
(D) Cleanup will begin.

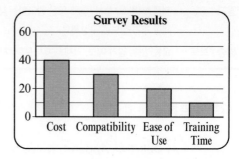

19. Where do the listeners most likely work?

(A) At a financial advising firm
(B) At an electronics store
(C) At a telephone company
(D) At a software company

20. Look at the graphic. What concern does the speaker say can be addressed?

(A) Cost
(B) Compatibility
(C) Ease of Use
(D) Training Time

21. What will the listeners do next?

(A) Talk in small groups
(B) Contact important customers
(C) Watch a tutorial
(D) Collect additional data

광고	제품/서비스/행사/업체 등을 광고하는 내용으로 주로 광고 대상 소개, 특징 및 장점 설명, 연락처/할인 등에 대한 추가 정보로 구성돼요.
방송/보도	교통 방송, 일기 예보, 경제/건강/문화/지역 소식을 다루는 라디오 방송이 나와요.

650_P4_07 🎧
정답과 해설 p.093

■ 담화의 흐름과 문제 구성

광고 대상 소개	① **At Oak Tree Apparel, we've built a reputation for making men look their very best in the latest formal wear fashions.**	① 오크 트리 어패럴은 최신 정장 패션으로 남성분들을 최고의 모습으로 꾸며 드린다는 명성을 쌓아 왔습니다.
세부 사항	② **It's the individualized attention from our helpful staff that keeps our customers coming back.**	② 고객분들이 계속 재방문하시는 것은 저희 직원들의 개별 맞춤 서비스 때문입니다.
다음에 일어날 일	And now, to serve you better, ③ **we're keeping our doors open longer. Beginning next week, we'll be open for business from nine A.M. until nine P.M. every day.** Come in and see why we're ranked number one in the city for customer satisfaction.	③ 다음 주부터, 매일 아침 9시부터 저녁 9시까지 영업 시간을 연장할 것입니다.

1. (What) is the (speaker) (advertising)?

화자는 무엇을 광고하는가?

광고 대상 문제 → 광고 도입부의 업체 소개에 주목

정답 **A clothing store**
옷 가게

2. According to the speaker, (what) do (customers) (like) about the business?

화자에 따르면, 고객들이 업체에 대해 좋아하는 점은 무엇인가?

세부 사항 문제 → 키워드 'customers like'에 주목 → keeps our customers coming back

정답 **Its personalized service**
맞춤형 서비스

3. (What) will (happen) at the business (next week)?

다음 주에 업체에 일어날 일은 무엇인가?

다음에 일어날 일 문제 → 'next week'에 주목

정답 **Operating hours will be extended.**
영업 시간이 연장될 것이다.

┌─ 질문의 단서가 되는 주요 표현 ─

"**Are you looking for** healthy lunch options? Come to VG Bistro."   광고되고 있는 업체는 무엇인가?

"**This is** Jin Lim for TEK News, reporting live from the Trade Show."   화자는 누구이겠는가?

"**Visit our Web site to** watch our video tutorials."   청자들은 왜 웹사이트를 방문해야 하는가?

"**I'm now going to** speak with some local citizens."   화자는 다음에 무엇을 할 것인가?

"**Our new shoes will** last much longer **than ordinary shoes.**"   신제품은 어떤 점이 특별한가?

"**I'll be right back after** a commercial break."   청자들이 다음에 듣게 될 것은 무엇인가?

[1-2]

1. What is the main topic of the radio show?
   (A) Financial planning
   (B) Web site design

2. What has recently become available online?
   (A) Audio recordings
   (B) Product reviews

> This is Scott Durlin, and you're listening to Scott's
> _____ on WYBR Radio Ninety-One,
> where we discuss how to _____
> and home-budget topics. I want to let listeners know,
> that as of today, you can _____ of
> past broadcasts of our show from my newly updated
> Web site, www.scottsadvice.com. This is in addition to
> the _____ on topics from the show.

[3-4]

Mishu E-readers	
Model	**Display Size**
PT-250	15 centimeters
DX-16	16 centimeters
DX-32	17 centimeters
DX-64	18 centimeters

3. Look at the graphic. Which e-reader has an app for video chatting?
   (A) PT-250
   (B) DX-64

4. What does the speaker say visitors to the Mishu Web site can do?
   (A) Read customer reviews
   (B) Purchase a product

> Buy a Mishu E-reader today and _____.
> Mishu customers can carry _____ on
> one device! The model with _____
> even has an application installed for video chatting.
> Visit the Mishu Web site "Customer Feedback" section
> to read for yourself what _____ about
> their devices.

[5-6]

5. What benefit of the project did the governor mention?
   (A) Shorter commutes
   (B) More local jobs

6. Who will be interviewed after the break?
   (A) The governor
   (B) Community residents

> At a press conference today, the governor
> announced that _____ in Starks
> County. The governor emphasized that the hospital
> will _____—helping to boost the
> local employment rate. After the break, I'll talk with
> _____ of Starks County. They've
> raised concerns that the _____
> will have a negative impact on wildlife in the area.

LC

PART 4

1. What type of business is being advertised?

   (A) A graphic design agency
   (B) A garden supply center
   (C) A grocery store
   (D) A restaurant

2. What does the speaker say is special about Carla's?

   (A) It accepts all forms of payment.
   (B) It offers express delivery.
   (C) It uses fresh ingredients.
   (D) It has a convenient location.

3. What is the business offering with certain purchases?

   (A) A free dessert
   (B) A coupon
   (C) A recipe book
   (D) A digital download

4. What did the city council do yesterday?

   (A) Responded to questions
   (B) Announced a festival
   (C) Approved a budget
   (D) Worked on revising a law

5. According to the speaker, what will be different about the bridge after the renovation?

   (A) It will have a bicycle lane.
   (B) It will be stronger.
   (C) It will be covered.
   (D) It will require users to pay a toll.

6. What will the bridge reopen just in time for?

   (A) A local parade
   (B) A road race
   (C) A firework display
   (D) A music performance

7. Who most likely is the speaker?

   (A) A marine biologist
   (B) A news reporter
   (C) A local official
   (D) A boat captain

8. According to the speaker, what can business owners expect?

   (A) An increase in customers
   (B) A reduction in energy costs
   (C) Higher tax rates
   (D) Fewer parking restrictions

9. What will Marjorie Kelley most likely discuss?

   (A) Road conditions
   (B) Business opportunities
   (C) Wildlife conservation
   (D) Boating safety

10. What is the hotel advertising?

    (A) A restaurant addition
    (B) A special offer
    (C) A celebrity appearance
    (D) A second location

11. What is said about the hotel rooms?

    (A) They have ocean views.
    (B) They are near the mountains.
    (C) They are equipped with Wi-Fi.
    (D) They are large and modern.

12. According to the advertisement, what happens after dinner?

    (A) A film is shown on the beach.
    (B) Dessert is served on the patio.
    (C) Music is performed outside.
    (D) Boat rides are available.

13. What is the talk mainly about?

(A) Designing an office space
(B) Restoring old furniture
(C) Finding furniture bargains
(D) Touring a furniture factory

14. Why does the speaker say, "you only need to make a few changes"?

(A) To justify an expense
(B) To confirm that a task is easy
(C) To question the steps of a plan
(D) To indicate that no assistance is available

15. Why should the listeners visit a Web site?

(A) To watch videos
(B) To submit photographs
(C) To enter a contest
(D) To register for discounts

16. Where is the speaker?

(A) At a television studio
(B) At a car dealership
(C) At a parking garage
(D) At city hall

17. According to the speaker, what happened yesterday?

(A) A contract was signed.
(B) A new product went on sale.
(C) An article was published.
(D) A construction project began.

18. What will the speaker do next?

(A) Demonstrate a process
(B) Review a product
(C) Take a tour
(D) Conduct an interview

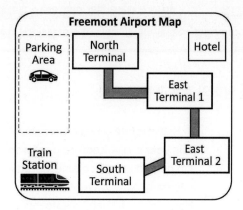

Freemont Airport Map

19. Why was a construction project approved?

(A) To provide investment opportunities
(B) To accommodate more travelers
(C) To make use of a budget surplus
(D) To meet stricter safety regulations

20. Look at the graphic. Which terminal is being built?

(A) North Terminal
(B) East Terminal 1
(C) East Terminal 2
(D) South Terminal

21. According to the speaker, what is special about the new terminal?

(A) It will have a variety of retail stores.
(B) It will be environmentally friendly.
(C) It will feature artwork from local artists.
(D) It will offer international flights.

Unit | **16** 인물 / 강연 / 설명

인물	회사에서 새로운 직원/임원, 워크숍 등의 행사에서 연설자, 시상식에서 수상자 등을 소개하는 내용이 나와요.
강연 / 설명	학회, 박람회, 직원 교육 등의 행사에서 각종 주제에 대한 강연, 행사 일정 등에 대해 설명하는 내용이 나와요.

650_P4_10 🎧
정답과 해설 p.099

■ 담화의 흐름과 문제 구성

인사	❶ **Hi everyone, I hope that you've been enjoying this year's architecture conference.**	┈┈ ❶	안녕하세요, 여러분. 올해의 건축 학술회의를 즐기고 계시길 바랍니다.
담화의 목적	I'm here to introduce a new product from my company, New Wave Printers.		
세부 사항	Now, you've all used a software program to create models to present a building idea to clients. Well, ❷ **with our new 3D printer, the Replicon 3000, you'll experience the most accurate tool on the market** for making professional-quality presentation models.	┈┈ ❷	저희 3D 프린터인 레플리콘 3000으로, 시중에서 가장 정확한 도구를 경험하게 되실 겁니다.
다음에 일어날 일	❸ **I'd like to show you models that I've made with the Replicon 3000** so you can see just how precise the outcome is.	┈┈ ❸	제가 레플리콘 3000으로 만든 모형 몇 개를 보여 드리고 싶습니다.

1. (Where) is the (talk) most likely (being given)?
담화의 장소는 어디일 것 같은가?

장소 문제 → 인사 중 언급되는 장소에 주목

정답 **At a professional conference** 전문 회의

2. (What) does the speaker (emphasize) about the (Replicon 3000)? 화자가 레플리콘 3000에 대해 강조하는 것은 무엇인가?

세부 사항 문제 → 키워드 '레플리콘 3000'에 주목

정답 **Its accuracy**
정확성

3. (What) will the (speaker) (do next)?
화자가 다음에 할 일은 무엇인가?

다음에 할 일 문제 → 앞으로 할 행동을 표현하는 'I'd like to'에 주목

정답 **Display some models**
몇몇 모형의 전시

┌─ 질문의 단서가 되는 주요 표현 ─

"**I'm honored by this award** for the employee of the year."

"**I'll be your instructor** for this beginning art class."

"**Thank you for attending** tonight's Business Seminar."

"Dr. Smith **is known for his work** as the director of the research lab."

"**Please** join me in giving them a warm round of applause."

연설의 목적은 무엇인가?

화자가 말하고 있는 대상은 누구인가?

청자들이 참석한 행사의 종류는 무엇인가?

스미스 박사는 무엇으로 유명한가?

청자들은 무엇을 하라고 요청 받는가?

실전 도움닫기 | 문제를 먼저 읽은 후 담화를 들으면서 답을 고르세요. 650_P4_11
다시 듣고 빈칸을 채우세요.

정답과 해설 p.099

[1-2]

1. Where is the announcement taking place?
   (A) At a retirement party
   (B) At a science seminar

2. What does Dr. Heller plan to do?
   (A) Write for a newspaper
   (B) Volunteer at a school

Good evening, everyone. Welcome to this _____ of Dr. Anthony Heller, who is retiring after 35 years with the Society for Environmental Sciences. Now, there's no doubt that Dr. Heller is best known for _____ as the director of the research center. But, as some of you will remember, Dr. Heller began _____ as a field biologist. Now that he's retiring, he plans to _____ for *The Hartland Daily Newspaper*.

[3-4]

3. What is the purpose of the speech?
   (A) To inaugurate a company
   (B) To accept an award

4. Why does the speaker say, "I couldn't have done it without my team"?
   (A) She does not have the skills for a task.
   (B) She wants to thank her colleagues.

I feel truly honored by _____ here at Flint and Gray Banking. At the beginning of the year, I was asked to _____ for our account holders. After ten months of _____, we are now able to release a fully functioning application to our users. But I _____ without my team of programming specialists. They all did a fabulous job. So for that, please join me in giving them a _____.

[5-6]

5. What type of event are the listeners attending?
   (A) An outdoor festival
   (B) A club meeting

6. Who is Charlotte Blake?
   (A) A writer
   (B) A film director

Welcome to the June meeting of the Maplewood _____. The film we're showing this month is the award-winning *Evening Rain*. The club is especially happy to have Ms. Charlotte Blake, _____, here with us today. After the movie, you'll be able to ask her about the _____. We hope you'll stay for the discussion.

LC

PART 4

1. Where most likely is the interview being held?

   (A) At a health clinic
   (B) At a radio station
   (C) At a publishing company
   (D) At a television studio

2. What is Dr. Meyer's specialty?

   (A) Allergy treatments
   (B) The science of exercise
   (C) Nutritional supplements
   (D) The study of sleep

3. What will Dr. Meyer talk about today?

   (A) A trip she has taken
   (B) An award she has received
   (C) A book she has written
   (D) A foundation she has started

4. What is the purpose of the speech?

   (A) To welcome new employees
   (B) To express appreciation for a company's
       success
   (C) To announce the launch of a new
       product
   (D) To describe the reorganization of a
       business

5. What did *Electronics Magazine* report about
   the company?

   (A) It has a high rate of customer satisfaction.
   (B) It is an excellent place to work.
   (C) It is environmentally responsible.
   (D) It has an effective mentorship program.

6. What does the speaker recognize Dan Gao's
   department for?

   (A) Meeting project deadlines
   (B) Organizing the anniversary celebration
   (C) Finding talented employees
   (D) Designing innovative products

7. Who is the speaker most likely addressing?

   (A) Equipment suppliers
   (B) Factory employees
   (C) A board of directors
   (D) Potential customers

8. According to the speaker, what will listeners
   do first?

   (A) Have their pictures taken
   (B) Fill out a survey
   (C) Meet with a nurse
   (D) Watch a video

9. What will the supervisors do?

   (A) Demonstrate machinery operation
   (B) Review an annual budget
   (C) Submit performance records
   (D) Distribute special clothing

10. What field does Dr. Hoffman work in?

    (A) Business
    (B) Education
    (C) Medicine
    (D) Engineering

11. What is said about young people aged
    thirteen to eighteen?

    (A) They buy more electronics than adults do.
    (B) They frequently participate in after-
        school programs.
    (C) They prefer online reading sources.
    (D) They are healthier than young people of
        previous generations.

12. What will Dr. Hoffman do at the end of the
    week?

    (A) Release a report
    (B) Host a conference
    (C) Accept an award
    (D) Start a new job

13. Where is the talk taking place?

(A) In a factory
(B) In a retail store
(C) At a car dealership
(D) At a conference center

14. What has Watson Research recently done?

(A) Upgraded equipment
(B) Opened a new location
(C) Improved a product
(D) Hired additional technicians

15. What will listeners probably do next?

(A) Read a brochure
(B) Watch a video
(C) Examine a mobile phone
(D) Speak with a representative

---

16. Who most likely are the listeners?

(A) Warehouse employees
(B) Delivery drivers
(C) Administrative assistants
(D) Store cashiers

17. According to the speaker, what is an advantage of the new devices?

(A) They are user-friendly.
(B) They shorten a process.
(C) They have a long battery life.
(D) They reduce training expenses.

18. What does the speaker imply when he says, "They're on that table"?

(A) The listeners should return later.
(B) The listeners should pick up some items.
(C) Some missing items have been found.
(D) A task has been finished.

Project	Cost
Bike Lanes	$1 million
Library Expansion	$2 million
Parking Garage	$2.5 million
Community Center	$3 million

19. Who most likely is the speaker?

(A) An accountant
(B) A business owner
(C) A city official
(D) An architect

20. Look at the graphic. How much will the selected project cost?

(A) $1 million
(B) $2 million
(C) $2.5 million
(D) $3 million

21. What will the speaker do next?

(A) Show a video
(B) Provide additional information
(C) Visit a library
(D) Present an award

여행	관광지나 관광 버스 안에서 가이드가 일정을 안내하거나 장소를 소개하는 내용, 교통 안내방송(공항, 비행기 내 등)에서 운행 시간/탑승구 변동을 알리는 내용이 나와요.
견학 / 관람	박물관, 공원, 공장 등의 견학 시 가이드가 장소 및 관람 순서 등에 대해 설명하고 권고하는 내용이 주로 나와요.

650_P4_13 🎧
정답과 해설 p.105

■ 담화의 흐름과 문제 구성

인사/소개	① **Welcome to the Museum of Ancient History.** I'm your guide.	┈┈┈	① 고대사 박물관에 오신 것을 환영합니다.
안내 및 세부 사항 설명	Right now we're in the Egyptian Gallery. We have a lot of unusual artifacts on display. ② **Some of you have already asked if you'll get to see some of the famous painted masks you've heard about in books and movies.** As our art conservation experts have told us, those objects are easily damaged by light.	┈┈┈	② 몇 분께서 책과 영화에서 몇몇 유명한 채색 가면을 볼 수 있는지 벌써 물으셨는데요.
관련 정보	However, ③ **if you'd like to learn more about the masks, we have a fantastic book available in the gift shop.**	┈┈┈	③ 가면에 대해 더 알고 싶으시면, 기념품점에서 구입하실 수 있는 책이 있습니다.

1. (Where) is the tour (taking place)?
관람이 이루어지고 있는 장소는 어디인가?

장소 문제 → 인사 중 언급되는 장소에 주목

정답 **At a history museum**
역사 박물관

2. (Why) does the speaker say, "those objects are easily damaged by light"?
화자는 왜 "그 물건들은 빛에 쉽게 손상됩니다"라고 하는가?

의도 파악 문제 → 인용문 앞에 언급되는 내용에 주목

정답 **To explain why some items are not on display**
일부 품목이 전시되지 않은 이유를 설명하려고

3. (How) can the (listeners) (find) more (information)?
청자들이 추가 정보를 찾을 수 있는 방법은 무엇인가?

세부 사항 문제 → 키워드 'find more information'에 주목 → learn more

정답 **By purchasing a book**
책의 구입

┌─ 질문의 단서가 되는 주요 표현 ─

"**Welcome to** the Museum of Contemporary Art."
화자는 어디에서 일하는가?

"**On this tour, we'll** visit some buildings with different architectural styles."
관광의 주된 초점은 무엇인가?

"**Let me show you** how those machines work. **Follow me.**"
사람들이 다음에 갈 장소는 어디인가?

"a reminder that our show will begin **in 10 minutes**"
10분 뒤에 일어날 일은 무엇인가?

"**We apologize for the delay because of** poor weather conditions."
지연의 원인은 무엇인가?

T **실전 도움닫기** | 문제를 먼저 읽은 후 담화를 들으면서 답을 고르세요. 다시 듣고 빈칸을 채우세요.

650_P4_14

정답과 해설 **p. 105**

[1-2]

1. Where does the speaker most likely work?
   (A) At a photography studio
   (B) At an art museum

2. What is *Blanchard's Gaze*?
   (A) A book
   (B) A painting

> We will now be _____ named Gold Hall. For this next part of our tour, I ask that you please _____. The first painting, here on our right, is *The Look*, arguably _____ by Esmeralda Blanchard. What exactly is the woman in the painting looking at? Well, if _____ by the pond, you are correct. Historians have recently confirmed this through a letter Blanchard wrote to her sister. You can read more about the correspondence in *Blanchard's Gaze*, _____ which is available in the gift shop.

[3-4]

3. What most likely will listeners do first?
   (A) Watch how tea is produced
   (B) Touch the texture of tea leaves

4. What does the speaker imply when he says, "you won't be able to go through all of them"?
   (A) A product comes in many varieties.
   (B) Some items are very expensive.

> Welcome to Danmere Tea Company's factory tour. The first thing we'll do on our tour is to visit interactive Introduction Hall, where you'll have the chance to _____ of various textures. Then we'll see the _____ on the factory floor, and finally—in our new Danmere Tasting Room— you'll get to _____ a wide range of _____. Trust me… you won't be able to go through all of them. I encourage you to walk around and _____ before making your choices. Now, if everyone is ready, let's begin the tour.

[5-6]

5. Who is this announcement for?
   (A) Train passengers
   (B) Airline travelers

6. When will this work take place?
   (A) In April
   (B) In June

> Attention all passengers: _____ scheduled for the month of June, trains on the R-2 line will not be running between the hours of one and four P.M. beginning tomorrow, _____, and continuing through _____. There will be _____ to transport passengers by bus between stations during this time. Passengers may board the bus across the street in front of the National Transportation Building. We apologize for this inconvenience and look forward to serving you for all of _____.

1. According to the speaker, what will be the main focus of the tour?

   (A) Architectural styles
   (B) Local cuisine
   (C) Literary figures
   (D) Traditional farming

2. What does the speaker say about Morales Avenue?

   (A) A famous author used to live there.
   (B) It is the location of a yearly festival.
   (C) It is closed to vehicles.
   (D) A city wall used to stand there.

3. According to the speaker, what can listeners do at the museum?

   (A) View a short film
   (B) Purchase some souvenirs
   (C) See a reproduction of the city
   (D) Attend a lecture

4. What is the speaker introducing?

   (A) A lecture about art
   (B) An inspection of a building
   (C) A tour of a factory
   (D) An office meeting

5. What does the speaker say about Tundra Mountain?

   (A) It is a source of water.
   (B) It is often photographed.
   (C) A conference is being held there.
   (D) Many people ski there.

6. Where will the people probably go next?

   (A) To the top of a mountain
   (B) To a conference room
   (C) To a gift store
   (D) To a room with machines

7. Where is the announcement most likely being heard?

   (A) At a banquet hall
   (B) At a shopping center
   (C) At an aquarium
   (D) At an art museum

8. According to the speaker, what can visitors do at the customer service desk?

   (A) Enter a raffle
   (B) Get a map of the building
   (C) Sign up for a membership
   (D) Rent a locker

9. What does the speaker say will happen in fifteen minutes?

   (A) A show will start.
   (B) The café will begin serving lunch.
   (C) Advance tickets will go on sale.
   (D) A tour group will meet.

10. What is the subject of the talk?

    (A) The score from a sporting event
    (B) The contents of an art exhibit
    (C) The route for a boat ride
    (D) The view from a tower

11. According to the speaker, what is unusual about today?

    (A) Tickets are half price.
    (B) The sky is clear.
    (C) A bridge is closed.
    (D) An island is crowded.

12. What will listeners do in 30 minutes?

    (A) Get on a bus
    (B) Exit a room
    (C) Meet at a bench
    (D) Return a headset

13. Where is the announcement being made?

(A) In an art museum
(B) At a concert hall
(C) At a photography studio
(D) In a conference room

14. Why is the audience asked to be quiet?

(A) The event is being recorded.
(B) The event is being broadcast live.
(C) The event is being photographed.
(D) The event is being filmed.

15. According to the announcement, what is not permitted at this event?

(A) Food and beverages
(B) Standing in the aisles
(C) Flash photography
(D) Recording equipment

16. What type of volunteer work are the listeners going to do?

(A) Arts education
(B) Health services
(C) Community development
(D) Environmental conservation

17. Why does the speaker say, "each of you will be assigned a mentor"?

(A) To reject a proposal
(B) To request feedback
(C) To correct some information
(D) To encourage participation

18. What does the speaker remind the listeners about?

(A) Taking some notes
(B) Wearing safety glasses
(C) Signing a waiver
(D) Reading a manual

Exhibit	On loan from ...
Painting Achievements	The Portuguese Fund
Modern Printing	The Acker Family
Swiss Photography	Bern University
Dutch Sculpture	The Amsterdam Collection

19. What did the Megahurst Art Gallery recently do?

(A) It opened a new location.
(B) It began offering art classes.
(C) It joined an art organization.
(D) It stopped permitting photography.

20. What is included with the brochure?

(A) A discount coupon
(B) A restaurant menu
(C) A schedule of events
(D) A membership application

21. Look at the graphic. What exhibit will the tour group visit first?

(A) Painting Achievements
(B) Modern Printing
(C) Swiss Photography
(D) Dutch Sculpture

■ 제품 / 서비스 문의 메시지

contact 연락하다

extension 내선번호

respond to ~에 대해 회신하다

inquiry about ~에 대한 문의

receipt 영수증

policy 정책, 방침

manufacturer 제조업체, 생산자

discount 할인(하다)

bill 청구서, 계산서

statement 내역서

purchase 구매

shipment 운송품, 선적

merchandise 상품, 물품(=goods)

retailer 소매업자

place an order 주문하다

customer service representative
고객 서비스 담당자

■ 고장 / 수리 메시지

recall 회수하다

replace 교체하다

fix 수리하다, 고치다(=repair)

manufacturing flaw 제조 결함

inconvenience 불편

compensate 보상하다

purchase price 구매가

mailing address (우편물을 받는) 주소

■ 일정 문의

appointment 약속, 예약

reschedule 예정을 다시 세우다, 일정을 변경하다

delay 늦추다, 지연되다

shop hours (가게의) 영업 시간

office[business] hours 업무 시간

hours of operation 운영 시간

confirm a reservation 예약을 확정하다

make a reservation 예약하다

■ 메시지

reach 연락이 닿다

beep 삐 하는 소리

hotline 핫라인, 직통 전화 (번호)

tone 발신음, 신호음

connect 연결하다

star key (전화기) 별표(*)

pound key (전화기) 우물 정자(#)

voice mail 음성 사서함

automated message 자동 응답 메시지

leave a message 메시지를 남기다

take a message 메시지를 받아 적다

return one's call ~에게 회신 전화를 하다

get back to 나중에 회신 전화를 하다

stay on the line 전화를 끊지 않고 기다리다

after the tone 신호음이 나온 후에

extension number 내선 번호

■ 사내 공지

bulletin board 게시판

board of directors 이사회

on short notice 충분한 예고 없이, 갑자기

security policy 보안 정책

ID badge 신분증, 사원증

go into effect 실시되다

check in 출입 절차를 밟다

work assignment 작업 할당

modify 변경하다, 바꾸다

maintenance 관리, 정비

installation 설치

expand 확장하다

service person 수리공, 정비공

replace 교체하다

energy-efficient 에너지 효율성이 좋은

safety measure 안전 조치

■ 교통 안내방송

attention 안내 말씀 드립니다

flight 항공편

destination 목적지

arrivals board 도착 안내 게시판

due to ~ 때문에

engine trouble 엔진 고장

proceed to ~으로 가다

shut down (기계가) 멈추다, 정지하다

■ 쇼핑센터

patron 고객; 후원자

register 금전등록기, 계산대

sales representative 영업사원

grocery 식료품, 잡화

retail outlet 소매점

raffle 추첨 행사, 경품 행사

shopping complex 쇼핑 단지

coatroom 휴대품 보관소

checkout 계산대

customer service counter 고객 서비스 창구

■ 행사장

performance 공연

exhibition 전시회

ticket counter 매표소

complimentary 무료의

audience 청중, 관람객

demonstration 시범 설명

sound equipment 음향 장비

auditorium 강당

hold 열다, 개최하다

arrange 미리 정하다, 준비하다

opening ceremony 개막식, 개회식

contribute 기여하다, 공헌하다

prepare for ~을 준비하다

can't wait to 빨리 ~하고 싶어 하다

■ 인물 소개

commitment 헌신, 전념

congratulate 축하하다

guest speaker 초청 연사

keynote speaker 기조 연설자

inspire 격려하다, 영감을 주다

positive attitude 긍정적인 태도

contribute 공헌하다, 기여하다

■ 시상식

honored 영예로운

fabulous 멋진

present an award to ~에게 시상하다

best-known for ~로 가장 유명한[잘 알려진]

do an outstanding job 뛰어난 업적을 이루다

the prestigious award 권위 있는 상

awards ceremony 시상식

recognize (공로를) 인정하다, 표창하다

devoted 헌신적인

thanks to ~ 덕분에

on behalf of ~을 대표해서

be pleased to ~하게 되어 기쁘다

announce that ~이라는 것을 알리다

make a speech 연설하다(=give a speech)

win an award 상을 받다

meet[achieve] a goal 목표를 달성하다

give a round of applause for
~에게 큰 박수를 보내다

■ 관광/견학

performance 공연

exhibition 전시회

kiosk 매점

refreshments 다과, 음식물

ticket counter 매표소

audience 청중, 관람객

landmark 경계표, 역사적 건조물

state-of-the-art 최첨단의, 최고급의

sound equipment 음향 장비

turn off mobile phones 휴대폰을 끄다

take pictures of 사진 찍다

■ 광고

a new line (상품의) 새로운 종류

beverage 음료

machine 기계

appliance 가전제품

office furniture 사무용 가구

art supplies 미술용품

event hall 이벤트 홀

catering orders 출장 음식 주문

cafeteria 구내 식당

snack bar 매점

establishment 시설, 업체

product 상품, 물품

■ 패러프레이징 빈출 표현(단어→단어)

see 보다	→ view 보다
staff 직원	→ employee 직원
e-mail 이메일을 보내다	→ send 보내다
submit 제출하다	→ send 보내다
gather 모이다	→ meet 만나다
type 타자를 치다	→ enter 입력하다
release 공개하다	→ introduce 소개하다
encourage 권장하다	→ advise 조언하다
supermarket 슈퍼마켓	→ store 상점
outing 야유회	→ trip (짧은) 여행
productivity 생산성	→ efficiency 효율성
movie 영화	→ film 영화
footwear 신발(류)	→ shoes 신발
policy 정책	→ procedure 절차
head 책임자, 장	→ supervisor 관리자
competition 경연대회	→ contest 시합
thoroughly 철저히	→ carefully 신중하게
recently 최근에	→ lately 최근에
space 공간	→ room 자리, 공간
author 저자	→ writer 작가
electronically 온라인으로	→ online 온라인으로
revitalize 부흥시키다	→ improve 향상시키다
singer 가수	→ performer 공연자
dessert 디저트	→ refreshments 다과
appointment 진료 예약	→ consultation (의사와의) 상담

■ 패러프레이징 빈출 표현(단어→구 / 구→단어)

film 촬영하다	→ direct a film 영화를 감독하다
expo 박람회	→ trade show 무역 박람회
collaborate 협력하다	→ work together 함께 일하다
in-flight 기내의	→ on an airplane 기내에서
order 주문하다	→ place an order 주문하다
mayor 시장	→ city's officer 시장
distribute 배부하다	→ hand out 나누어 주다
establish 설립하다	→ set up 세우다
economist 경제학자	→ economic expert 경제 전문가
guitar 기타	→ musical instrument 악기
detour 우회도로	→ alternate route 대체 도로
sign up 신청하다	→ register 등록하다
come up with ~을 생각해 내다	→ brainstorm 아이디어를 모으다
take a look at ~을 살펴보다	→ inspect 점검하다
schedule an appointment 약속을 잡다	→ contact 연락하다
receive your money back 돈을 돌려 받다	→ refund 환불
a lot less noisy 훨씬 덜 시끄러운	→ quiet 조용한
song writer and singer 작곡가 겸 가수	→ musician 음악가

Part

단문, 장문 빈칸 채우기

5&6

Part 5&6 | 단문, 장문 빈칸 채우기 Part 5 30문항, Part 6 16문항

Part 5는 하나의 완전한 문장을 만들기 위해 빈칸에 들어갈 단어나 어구를 선택지에서 고르는 유형으로, 총 30문제가 출제돼요. Part 6은 완전한 지문을 만들기 위해 4개의 빈칸에 들어갈 단어나 어구, 문장을 선택지에서 고르는 유형으로, 총 4개의 지문(16문제)이 출제돼요.

■ Part 5와 6은 이런 점이 다르다

1. Part 5는 완전한 한 문장을 완성하고, Part 6는 완전한 한 지문을 완성해요.
2. Part 6는 Part 5와는 달리 한 문장 안에서 정답의 근거를 찾지 못하는 경우가 많아요.

Questions 131-134 refer to the following e-mail.

To: Marty Leung <mleung@dwightdunham.com>
From: Megan Takkar <mtakkar@dwightdunham.com>
Subject: New Employee Forms
Date: March 1

Dear Mr. Leung,

Congratulations on your acceptance to our firm. ------. I have attached a few documents that will help
you begin your career with us. They provide a brief ------ to Dwight Dunham & Associates, as well as
131   132
explaining our company's various workplace policies and codes of conduct. You will need to agree with
these policies, and some pages will require your signature to this effect. After you ------ those pages,
133
please submit them to Lauren Matthiasen in the human resources department. She ------ them for you.
134
Again, congratulations, and I look forward to working with you. If you have any questions, don't hesitate to
contact me at extension 144.

Regards,
Megan Takkar

Enclosure

---

131. 문장 고르기 문제
(A) Ms. Matthiasen will assist you in preparing
your documents.
(B) Your application will be processed within
two weeks.
(C) We are excited to have you at Dwight
Dunham & Associates.
(D) Please offer any support you can to our
new coworker.

132. 어형 문제
(A) orient
(B) oriental
(C) oriented
(D) orientation

133. 어휘 문제
(A) edit
(B) sign
(C) type
(D) e-mail

134. 문법 문제
(A) will file
(B) had filed
(C) file
(D) filing

131 문장 고르기 문제

Part 6에서만 출제되는 유형입니다.

❶ 전반적인 지문 흐름을 파악하여, 빈칸 앞뒤 문장을 확인합니다.

❷ 선택지를 빈칸에 넣어 글의 흐름이 자연스러운지 확인합니다.

❸ 지문에서 언급하지 않은 아이디어를 사용한 오답을 소거합니다.

→ 빈칸 앞에서 회사에 채용된 것을 축하한다는 내용을 언급하고 있어요. 따라서 빈칸에는 회사의 일원으로 맞게 되어 기쁘다는 내용이 나오는 것이 글의 흐름상 자연스러우므로 (C)가 정답이에요.

132 어형 문제

Part 6의 어형 문제도 Part 5의 어형 문제와 마찬가지로 대개 개별적인 한 문장 안에서 정답을 찾을 수 있어요. 문장의 주어와 동사, 빈칸에 필요한 품사 등을 파악할 수 있으면 비교적 쉽게 해결할 수 있는 문제 유형입니다.

→ 빈칸은 동사 provide의 목적어 자리이자 a brief의 수식을 받는 명사 자리이므로 명사 (D) orientation이 정답이에요.

133 어휘 문제

Part 6의 어휘 문제는 Part 5의 어휘 문제와 달리 한 문장 안에서 정답을 찾을 수 없는 경우도 있어요. 따라서 크게는 전체 글의 흐름을 파악해야 하거나, 작게는 문장 앞뒤의 유기적 관계를 파악해야 한다는 점에 유의해야 합니다.

→ 바로 앞 문장 some pages will require your signature to this effect에서 서명이 필요하다고 언급하고 있어요. 따라서 서명한 후에 인사부의 로렌 마티아센 씨에게 제출하라는 의미가 되어야 하므로 (B) sign(서명하다)이 정답이에요.

134 문법 문제

Part 6의 문법 문제 중 특히 시제 문제는 Part 5의 시제 문제와 달리 시제의 단서가 한 문장 안에 제시되지 않을 수도 있습니다. 이럴 때는 앞뒤 문맥이나 글의 종류 및 주제 등을 통해 시제를 결정해야 해요.

→ 빈칸은 주어인 She 뒤의 동사 자리이자 흐름상 '그녀가 서류를 정식으로 제출할 것이다'라는 미래의 의미를 나타내고 있으므로 미래시제 (A) will file이 정답이에요.

Unit | 01 문장의 구성 요소

① 주어와 동사

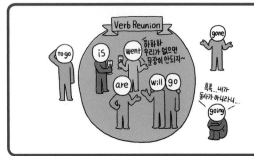

문장에는 반드시 동사가 있으며
be동사, 일반동사, <조동사＋동사>의 형태로 존재해요.

■ 주어: 동작을 행하는 주체

주어는 우리말로 '~은(는), ~이(가)'에 해당하는 말로, 주로 사람이나 사물, 개념을 나타내는 (대)명사가 주어 역할을 담당해요. 물론 주어인 명사를 꾸미는 말이 함께 와서 길어질 수도 있어요.

All **employees** must wear a uniform. 모든 직원은 유니폼을 입어야 한다.
　　　주어

The **flight to Tokyo** was delayed. 도쿄행 비행기가 지연되었다.
　　주어 └─────┘ 주어를 꾸미는 말(Unit 12 전치사 참고)

The **computers repaired by the technician** are now ready for use.
　　주어 　└─────┘ 주어를 꾸미는 말(Unit 11 분사 참고)

그 기술자에 의해 수리된 컴퓨터들은 이제 사용할 수 있다.

> | 기본기 다지기 | **주어 없이 동사원형으로 시작하는 명령문**
>
> 명령문은 주어인 'you'가 생략된 형태, 즉 주어 없이 동사로 시작하는데, 이때 동사는 동사원형으로만 등장합니다.
>
> Please **send** me your final draft. 당신의 최종 원고를 제게 보내세요.
> 　~~sends, sending~~

■ 동사: 사람이나 사물의 움직임이나 상태를 나타내는 말

동사는 주어 뒤에서 주어의 동작이나 상태를 나타내는 말이에요. be동사는 물론이고 <조동사(will, can 등)＋동사원형>도 이에 해당합니다. 한 개의 절에는 한 개의 동사만 존재하고요, 동사 앞에 to가 붙거나 동사 뒤에 -ing가 붙은 형태(Unit 10~11 참고)는 진짜 동사가 아니랍니다.

Mobile phones are very useful. 휴대전화들은 매우 유용하다.

We replaced the fax machine. 우리는 팩스기를 교체했다.

Employees working late should lock the door. 늦게까지 일하는 직원들은 문을 잠가야 한다.

STEP 1

1. The main _____ of the new electronic notepad is Internet use.
   (A) function
   (B) functional

2. Mr. Lee recently _____ a tour of the company's main production facility.
   (A) to conduct
   (B) conducted

3. _____ of the shipment should be expected within ten days.
   (A) Receive
   (B) Receipt

4. Please _____ the enclosed survey and return it to our office.
   (A) complete
   (B) completed

STEP 2

5. Fred's superb _____ to detail is his best attribute as a graphic artist.
   (A) attends
   (B) attended
   (C) attendant
   (D) attention

6. The _____ of the carpet can be completed as soon as the office furniture is moved.
   (A) installed
   (B) installation
   (C) installers
   (D) install

7. The time needed to acquire all of the necessary materials _____ on several factors.
   (A) depend
   (B) depends
   (C) depending
   (D) to depend

8. The _____ of water in Orlova Valley has dropped over the last two years.
   (A) consume
   (B) consumer
   (C) consumption
   (D) consumed

② 목적어

타동사 뒤에는 목적어가 오는데
명사, 대명사, to부정사, 동명사, 명사절이
대표적인 목적어 형태예요.

■ **목적어**: 주어 + 동사 + 목적어

대부분의 동사 뒤에는 우리말의 '~을, ~를'에 해당하는 목적어가 등장해요. 이렇게 뒤에 목적어가 필요한 동사들을 '타동사'라고 부르며 (대)명사나 명사구, 명사절이 타동사 뒤에서 목적어 역할을 하게 됩니다.

명사   We **had** a discussion with the sales staff. 우리는 영업사원들과 논의했다.
                동사   목적어(명사)

             Mr. Baek **gives** new employees an orientation. 백 씨가 신입사원들에게 예비 교육을 해준다.
                      동사   목적어 1(~에게) 목적어 2(~을)

            → 동사에 따라 목적어가 두 개 나란히 오는 경우도 있어요. give(주다), offer(제공하다) 등의 동사가 이에 해당돼요.

명사구   This brochure **contains** detailed information. 이 안내서는 상세한 정보를 담고 있다.
                 동사   목적어(형용사 + 명사로 이루어진 명사구)

대명사   Corv Graphics **will help** us to create a new logo. 코브 그래픽 사는 우리가 새 로고를 만드는 데 도움을 줄 것이다.
                  동사   목적어(대명사)

to부정사   They **agreed** to revise the plan. 그들은 계획을 수정하는 것에 동의했다.
               동사   목적어(to부정사, Unit 10 참고)

동명사   Ms. Eaves **suggested** changing the current supplier. 이브 씨는 현 납품 업체를 바꿀 것을 제안했다.
               동사   목적어(동명사, Unit 10 참고)

명사절   Apollo, Inc. **announced** that it is acquiring Luzon Manufacturing.
                  동사   목적어(주어 + 동사로 이루어진 명사절)

            아폴로 사는 루존 제조사를 인수할 것이라고 발표했다.

| 기본기 다지기 | **목적어가 필요 없는 자동사**

동사 뒤에 목적어가 없는 경우도 있어요. 예를 들어 '오르다, 상승하다'라는 뜻의 rise 같은 동사가 '~을 상승하다'라고 해석되면 어색하죠? 이렇게 목적어가 필요 없는 동사들을 '자동사'라고 부르는데 이런 자동사 뒤에는 주로 부사나 전치사구가 등장한다는 점을 기억해 두세요.

Prices **are rising** sharply. 물가가 급격히 오르고 있다.
               부사

The CEO **spoke** to the shareholders. CEO는 주주들에게 호소했다.
          전치사(to) + 명사(the shareholders)로 이루어진 전치사구

STEP 1

1. The city's library will accept _____ of used books until June 30.
   (A) donates
   (B) donations

2. Local artists sell their handmade _____ every Saturday morning.
   (A) creative
   (B) creations

3. Mr. Martin has decided _____ the planning meeting because of a scheduling conflict.
   (A) postpones
   (B) to postpone

4. After remaining high for several days, temperatures finally fell _____ yesterday.
   (A) slight
   (B) slightly

STEP 2

5. CEO Donald Farajo issued a brief _____ on the merger proposal to the international financial press.
   (A) stated
   (B) stating
   (C) statement
   (D) state

6. Our service department has received numerous _____ about the new TZ-2000 processor overheating.
   (A) complain
   (B) complaining
   (C) complainer
   (D) complaints

7. Epulo, Inc., offers _____ for events ranging from formal banquets to casual buffets.
   (A) cater
   (B) catering
   (C) caters
   (D) catered

8. Mr. Oliver gave the customers some samples to show _____ what the fabric looked like.
   (A) they
   (B) them
   (C) their
   (D) themselves

어휘 | **1.** accept 받다 used 사용된, 중고의 **2.** handmade 수제의, 수공의 creative 창조의, 창의적인 creation 창조, 창작, 창작품 **3.** decide 결정하다 planning 기획 scheduling conflict 일정상의 충돌 **4.** slightly 조금 **5.** issue 발표하다 brief 간략한 merger proposal 합병 제안 financial 재정의 press 언론 **6.** numerous 다수의, 수많은 processor (컴퓨터의) 프로세서 overheating 과열 complain 불평하다, 항의하다 complainer 불평가, 투덜대는 사람 complaint 불평, 불만 **7.** range from A to B 범위가 A에서 B에 이르다 banquet 연회 cater (행사 등에) 음식을 공급하다 catering 음식 공급(업) **8.** fabric 옷감

③ 보어

동사 뒤에는 주어나 목적어를
보충하는 보어가 오는데
명사나 형용사가 그 역할을 해요.

He is
an actor.
(명사 보어)

He is
famous.
(형용사 보어)

■ 주격 보어: 주어 + 동사 + 주격 보어

보어는 주어나 목적어의 성질, 상태, 신분 등을 보충 설명하는 말로, 명사나 형용사가 보어 역할을 합니다. 주격 보어란 주어의 의미를 보충하는 말이에요.

| 주어 | + | be동사 ~이다 / appear ~인 듯하다 / become ~이 되다 / seem ~처럼 보이다 / remain ~인 채로 남다 / stay ~인 채로 머무르다 | + | 주격 보어 |

The number of technicians available **is** insufficient. 작업 가능한 기술자 인원이 불충분하다.
→ 보어가 주어의 상태를 표현할 때, 즉 '~(하)다'라고 해석이 되는 주격 보어 자리에는 형용사가 옵니다.

Mr. Kraus **was** a major **asset** to the sales team. 크라우스 씨는 판매팀의 핵심 인재였다.
→ 보어가 주어와 동격(크라우스 씨 = 핵심 인재)일 때, 즉 '~이다'라고 해석이 되는 주격 보어 자리에는 명사가 옵니다.

■ 목적격 보어: 주어 + 동사 + 목적어 + 목적격 보어

목적격 보어란 목적어를 보충 설명하는 말로, 명사나 형용사가 사용되며 부사는 보어가 될 수 없답니다. 구조가 어렵게 느껴질 수 있지만 '목적어와 목적격 보어'를 '주어와 주격 보어'의 관계처럼 이해하세요.

| 주어 | + | make ~를 …하게 만들다 / find ~가 …임을 알다/깨닫다 / keep ~를 …로 유지하다 / consider ~를 …라고 여기다 | + | 목적어 | + | 목적격 보어 |

The music made the performance (**impressive** / ~~impression~~ / ~~impressively~~). 음악은 공연을 감명 깊게 만들었다.
→ 목적격 보어가 목적어인 the performance의 상태를 설명하므로 형용사 impressive가 옵니다.

I **found** the book **easy**. 나는 그 책이 쉽다고 생각했다.
I **found** the book **easily**. 나는 그 책을 쉽게 찾아냈다.
→ easy는 목적어인 the book의 상태를 설명하는 목적격 보어로 쓰였어요. 하지만 easily는 목적격 보어가 아니라 동사 found를 수식하는 부사고요, 그래서 보어와는 달리 생략할 수도 있어요.

STEP 1

1. Sun Foods, Inc., has become a
   _____ in selling processed foods in
   China.
   (A) leader
   (B) leading

2. Ms. Chu was extremely _____ to
   receive the award for outstanding sales
   performance.
   (A) happy
   (B) happily

3. With its light weight, the latest
   Apurage vacuum cleaner is _____
   to carry.
   (A) ease
   (B) easy

4. Experts remain _____ about the
   stability of Eastside Technology's
   stock.
   (A) optimistically
   (B) optimistic

STEP 2

5. Participation in the Louisville Business
   Workshops is _____ to all business
   owners.
   (A) open
   (B) opener
   (C) opens
   (D) openly

6. Due to her strong background,
   Ms. Sakai was a natural _____ to
   lead Celina Legal Associates.
   (A) choose
   (B) chosen
   (C) to choose
   (D) choice

7. One of Mr. Oh's primary duties is
   the _____ of the corporate food
   service.
   (A) manage
   (B) manages
   (C) manageable
   (D) management

8. Many of our employees have reported
   that they have found the new
   computer program quite _____.
   (A) benefit
   (B) benefits
   (C) benefitting
   (D) beneficial

어휘 | **1.** processed food 가공식품 **2.** extremely 극도로, 매우　outstanding 뛰어난　performance 실적 **3.** weight 무게　vacuum
cleaner 진공 청소기 **4.** expert 전문가　stability 안정성　stock 주식 **5.** participation 참가, 참여　owner 소유주　openly
공공연하게 **6.** due to ~ 때문에　background 배경, 경력　choice 선택된 사람[것] **7.** primary 주요한　duty 임무, 의무　corporate
기업의 **8.** benefit 혜택; 이익을 얻다, ~에게 이롭다　beneficial 유익한, 이로운

1 The ------- of five franchise businesses helped to boost Letman Company's revenue last year.
   (A) acquire
   (B) acquired
   (C) acquisition
   (D) acquisitional

2 Amplono Industries' latest product is a ------ of a mobile phone and a lightweight tablet computer.
   (A) combine
   (B) combination
   (C) combines
   (D) combined

3 The minutes from last week's board of directors meeting showed that all of the board members were in -------.
   (A) attended
   (B) attends
   (C) attendance
   (D) attending

4 The Felton Engineering Conference ------ are pleased to have Dr. Gerard Wylie as this year's keynote speaker.
   (A) organizers
   (B) organizing
   (C) organizational
   (D) organizationally

5 The consensus among the members of the focus group is that the salad dressing is ------- enough.
   (A) sweeten
   (B) sweet
   (C) sweetly
   (D) sweetest

6 Please ------- the owner's manual before using your Kivi Craft oven for the first time.
   (A) consulting
   (B) consulted
   (C) consults
   (D) consult

7 It is Namgung Consulting's policy to make a job ------- without delay when the right applicant is found.
   (A) offerings
   (B) is offered
   (C) offer
   (D) offers

8 The finance department has submitted an initial budget ------- for upgrading our billing system.
   (A) estimate
   (B) estimates
   (C) estimating
   (D) estimations

9 Marta Capek, president of Leafster Holding Ltd., has no ------- of retiring this year.
   (A) intended
   (B) intending
   (C) intents
   (D) intention

10 Caliber Paper, Inc., has hired MacRae Advertising to increase the company's ------- in foreign markets.
   (A) recognize
   (B) recognizing
   (C) recognition
   (D) recognized

Questions 11-14 refer to the following article.

More Health Providers Are Going Paperless

According to the Bureau of Health Services, hospitals and medical providers are adopting technology at an increasing rate. Digitization of health records has become especially -------.
11.
Digital records can be accessed more easily by medical professionals. ------- can refer to them at
12.
any place and at any time. -------. In addition, when laboratory reports are digitized and centrally
13.
stored, patients ------- about carefully maintaining their own records.
14.

---

11. (A) popular
    (B) complex
    (C) tiresome
    (D) unsustainable

12. (A) Doctors
    (B) Suppliers
    (C) Executives
    (D) Economists

13. (A) Health records are subject to confidentiality rules.
    (B) Patients are encouraged to make an appointment.
    (C) Such information allows them to provide better care.
    (D) The bureau conducts such studies on an annual basis.

14. (A) not worrying
    (B) having no worries
    (C) not having to worry
    (D) do not have to worry

① 명사의 역할과 자리

명사는 문장에서
주어, 목적어, 보어 역할을 해요.

■ **명사의 형태:** -tion / -sion / -ance / -ment / -ty 등으로 끝나는 단어

participation 참가   discussion 토론   assistance 도움   movement 이동   ability 능력

■ **명사의 역할**

❶ 주어	동사 앞	The **seminar** **was canceled** because of rain. 비 때문에 세미나가 취소되었다.
❷ 목적어	타동사 뒤	The inspectors **checked** the **equipment** yesterday. 조사관들이 어제 장비를 점검했다.
	전치사 뒤	Dr. Aoki is an expert **in** **education**. 아오키 박사는 교육 분야의 전문가이다. → 전치사 뒤에는 항상 명사가 따라오는데 그 명사를 전치사의 목적어라고 해요.
❸ 보어		Mr. Bacon **was** a **consultant** at a hospital. 베이컨 씨는 한 병원의 상담가였다.

→ 동사나 전치사 바로 뒤에 항상 명사부터 나오는 것은 아니에요. 명사를 수식하는 형용사가 먼저 오는 경우도 많아요.

The company provides **educational** programs. 그 회사는 교육 프로그램을 제공한다.
　　　　　　동사　　　　형용사 └──────┘ 명사

■ **명사의 자리**

❶ a(n) / the 뒤

The receptionist called **an** ambulance. 접수원이 구급차를 불렀다.

❷ 소유격 뒤

The price of **Ashland Food's** stock increased. 애쉴랜드 푸드 사의 주가가 올랐다.

❸ 형용사 뒤

We hired **additional** employees. 우리는 추가 인력들을 고용했다.

STEP 1

1. A _____ of souvenirs can be found in the gift shop.
   (A) various
   (B) variety

2. Please remember to include your _____ at the bottom of the order form.
   (A) signed
   (B) signature

3. The _____ of cameras is prohibited during the performance.
   (A) operate
   (B) operation

4. For reasons of _____, anyone entering the construction area must wear a hard hat.
   (A) safety
   (B) safely

STEP 2

5. The article about the planned refinery _____ appeared in the *Jackson City Sentinel*.
   (A) expand
   (B) expands
   (C) expansive
   (D) expansion

6. A thorough _____ of paragraph 6 should be made before the letter is signed.
   (A) revision
   (B) revised
   (C) revising
   (D) revise

7. Any changes to your reservation should be made at least three days prior to your _____ at the hotel.
   (A) arrive
   (B) arrival
   (C) arrives
   (D) arrived

8. Kumiko Sekine will give a _____ on watercolor techniques on May 3.
   (A) demonstration
   (B) demonstrating
   (C) demonstrated
   (D) demonstrators

어휘 | **1.** souvenir 기념품 **2.** at the bottom of ~의 하단에, 밑바닥에 **3.** be prohibited 금지되다 performance 공연
4. construction area 건설 현장 hard hat 안전모 **5.** refinery 정유공장, 제련소 appear 발행되다, 나타나다 expand 확장하다,
확대하다 expansion 확장, 확대 **6.** thorough 철저한 revision 검토, 수정 **7.** prior to ~에 앞서 **8.** give a demonstration
시연해 보이다 watercolor 수채화 technique 기법 demonstrator 시연하는 사람

Unit 02 명사 **139**

② 셀 수 있는 명사와 셀 수 없는 명사

명사에는 셀 수 있는 명사와 셀 수 없는 명사가 있는데
셀 수 없는 명사는 앞에 a(n)을 쓰지 않고,
뒤에 -(e)s를 붙일 수 없어요.

■ 셀 수 있는 명사: 가산명사

셀 수 있는 명사를 쓸 때는 하나(단수)인지, 여러 개(복수)인지를 반드시 표시해야 해요. 단수명사 앞에는 하나를 의미하는 a/an을 붙이고 복수명사는 마지막에 -(e)s를 붙여요.

We plan to hire +

an assistant.   우리는 보조 한 명을 고용할 계획이다.
assistants.   보조들을
~~assistant.~~   → 가산명사는 관사나 -(e)s 없이 단독으로 쓸 수 없어요.

> **빈출 가산명사**
>
> | | | | |
> |---|---|---|---|
> | price 가격 | estimate 견적(서) | opening 공석 | product 제품 |
> | permit 허가증 | refund 환불 | location 위치 | order 주문 |
> | discount 할인 | result 결과 | increase 증가 | plan 계획 |

■ 셀 수 없는 명사: 불가산명사

셀 수 없는 명사들은 단수, 복수의 개념이 없어서 앞에 a/an이 올 수 없으며 뒤에 -(e)s도 붙지 않아요. 하지만 형태는 단수와 동일하므로 뒤에 오는 동사도 단수 형태가 됩니다.

Access
~~An access~~ + to this building is restricted.   이 건물에 대한 접근이 제한된다.
~~Accesses~~

> **빈출 불가산명사**
>
> | | | | |
> |---|---|---|---|
> | advice 조언 | research 연구 | information 정보 | furniture 가구 |
> | access 접근 | employment 고용 | luggage/baggage 짐 | machinery 기계류 |
> | consent 동의 | stationery 문구류 | equipment 장비 | merchandise 상품 |

| 기본기 다지기 | 사람 명사는 대표적인 가산명사

동사 뒤에 -er[or], -ee, -ant, -ist 등이 붙으면 '~하는 사람'을 의미하는 명사가 돼요.

employer 고용주	employee 직원	consumer 소비자	supervisor 상사
applicant 지원자	accountant 회계사	assistant 조수	client 고객
candidate 후보자	representative 직원	receptionist 접수원	guide 안내인
architect 건축가	critic 비평가	professional 전문가	official 공무원

STEP 1

1. The best salespeople first establish a _____ of trust with their potential buyers.
   (A) sense
   (B) senses

2. A processing fee of $3.00 will be added to _____ received by telephone.
   (A) order
   (B) orders

3. Mr. Rivera has just been appointed to a senior management _____.
   (A) position
   (B) positions

4. Star Transportation ordered new office _____ last month.
   (A) furniture
   (B) desk

STEP 2

5. The supervisors decided to delay _____ until they could fill the entire order.
   (A) ship
   (B) shipped
   (C) shipper
   (D) shipment

6. So far this quarter, regional sales of compact cars have surpassed industry analysts' _____.
   (A) predicts
   (B) predicted
   (C) predictions
   (D) predictable

7. D & Y Beauty Corporation plans to add at least one _____ overseas in the next year.
   (A) locations
   (B) location
   (C) locates
   (D) locating

8. A shipment of plastic _____ will be delivered to the Soto Soda factory tomorrow.
   (A) contain
   (B) containing
   (C) contained
   (D) containers

어휘 | **1.** establish 확립하다 trust 신뢰 potential 잠재적인 **2.** processing fee 수수료 order 주문, 주문품 **3.** be appointed 임명되다 management 경영, 관리 **4.** transportation 교통 order 주문하다 last month 지난달 **5.** supervisor 감독자 decide 결정하다 delay 미루다, 지연시키다 entire 전체의 **6.** so far 지금까지 quarter 사분기 sales 매출 compact car 소형차 surpass 초과하다 analyst 분석가 predict 예상하다, 예측하다 prediction 예상, 예측 **7.** at least 최소, 적어도 overseas 해외에 **8.** shipment 우송물, 선적품 deliver 배달하다, 전달하다 contain 포함하다, 함유하다 container 용기, 통

③ 한정사의 개념과 종류

한정사는 명사의 의미를
한정하는 말로, 명사에 따라
어울리는 한정사가 각기 달라요.

some/all/
little
advice (O)

little all some every

every
advice (X)

advice

■ 한정사의 개념

명사의 의미를 한정시키는 말을 한정사라고 하는데 셀 수 있는 명사(가산명사)의 단수형 앞에는 반드시 한정사가 와야 해요.

■ 한정사의 종류

❶ **관사:** a/an 뒤에는 셀 수 있는 명사(가산명사)의 단수형을 쓰고, the 뒤에는 어떤 명사든지 쓸 수 있어요.

관사	셀 수 있는 명사	셀 수 없는 명사
a(n)	a computer, a~~computers~~	an~~equipment~~
the	the computer, the computers	the equipment

❷ **소유격:** my(나의), Mr. Glenn's(글렌 씨의) 등의 소유격 뒤에는 모든 종류의 명사가 올 수 있어요.

❸ **수량 표현:** 수나 양을 나타내는 수량 표현의 경우 각각 어울리는 명사의 종류가 정해져 있어요.

수량 표현	가산명사				불가산명사	
	단수		복수			
each 각각의 every 모든	each every	computer				
both 둘 다 few 거의 없는 a few 몇몇의 several 몇몇의 many 많은 a number of 많은 a variety of 다양한			both few a few several many a number of a variety of	computers		
little 거의 없는 a little 조금 있는 much 많은					little a little much	equipment
some 약간의 most 대부분의 all 모든			some most all	computers	some most all	equipment

Please answer **each** question in the form. 양식에 있는 각각의 질문에 답하세요.
~~many~~

→ every는 <every+기수+복수명사> 형태로 쓰여 '~마다'라는 의미를 나타낼 수도 있어요.

They reorder products **every two months**. 그들은 두 달마다 제품을 재주문한다.

STEP 1

1. Mr. Montoya's biography of former president John Kendall is the subject of _____ debate.
   (A) much
   (B) many

2. The new Boulin sports car has several _____ that distinguish it from last year's model.
   (A) feature
   (B) features

3. Due to an unavoidable _____, Mr. Khan will postpone the teleconference until Thursday.
   (A) conflict
   (B) conflicts

4. Maucir Travel Agency offers _____ flights at reduced prices.
   (A) much
   (B) some

STEP 2

5. _____ sample from Ando Biology Labs must be kept at the correct temperature.
   (A) All
   (B) Most
   (C) Few
   (D) Every

6. All _____ to the auto production plant must register at the security checkpoint.
   (A) visit
   (B) visitation
   (C) visitors
   (D) visiting

7. The president of Paterson Industrial Solutions has signed a number of important _____ this month.
   (A) contract
   (B) contracts
   (C) contracted
   (D) contracting

8. Most _____ have completed a paid internship at the company headquarters.
   (A) apply
   (B) applicants
   (C) applied
   (D) applicant

어휘 | **1.** biography 전기 former 이전의 subject 주제, 대상 debate 논쟁, 논란 **2.** distinguish A from B A와 B를 구별하다 **3.** due to ~ 때문에 unavoidable 피할 수 없는 postpone 미루다, 연기하다 teleconference 화상회의 **4.** at reduced prices 할인된 가격에 **5.** correct 올바른 temperature 온도 **6.** register 등록하다 security checkpoint 보안 검문소 visitation 방문, 시찰 **7.** contract 계약, 계약서 **8.** complete 완료하다, 끝내다 paid 유급의 headquarters 본사, 본부 applicant 지원자, 신청자

1 After collecting more information about its customer base, Kolby Corp. will present a business plan to potential ------- .
(A) investing
(B) investors
(C) invests
(D) invested

2 Through the Advance to Success program, Alliryx Ltd. hopes to develop ------- junior executive into a confident leader.
(A) other
(B) each
(C) these
(D) which

3 Kasis Art Gallery encourages every ------ to read the guidelines carefully before submitting exhibition proposals.
(A) apply
(B) applied
(C) applicant
(D) application

4 Cool Reads' Web site specializes in the ------- of electronic books to public libraries.
(A) distributed
(B) distributor
(C) distribution
(D) distributes

5 Combining humor and musical talent, ------ by the Arieli Sisters have attracted large audiences to Café Baron.
(A) performances
(B) performed
(C) performance
(D) to perform

6 Participants in Rodel's culinary-internship program should report to Mr. Gerard in the dining area to receive their initial ------- .
(A) assignment
(B) assigns
(C) assigned
(D) assigning

7 The entrance on Somers Street will be closed ------- day so that a new automatic door can be installed.
(A) like
(B) full
(C) all
(D) same

8 Last month the Dorchester restaurant chain launched a campaign to provide healthier options for its many ------- .
(A) patron
(B) patrons
(C) patronize
(D) patronizes

9 The marketing manager at Cortez International Foods is seeking ------- from her team for unique ways to boost sales.
(A) suggest
(B) suggested
(C) suggestions
(D) suggesting

10 Employee performance evaluations are conducted ------- six months.
(A) even
(B) less
(C) soon
(D) every

Questions 11-14 refer to the following notice.

Dear Valued Customer,

Please be advised that the Dellmere Bank branch on Vine Street will be ------- on April 5 and 6.
11.

During this period, the building will undergo much-needed -------. These include improvements to
12.

the teller line and transaction counters. -------.
13.

If you use any of our other branches, you will experience no ------- in processing your transactions.
14.

In addition, our online banking service will continue to be available 24 hours a day.

Thank you for your patience.

Jane Hegy
General Manager

11. (A) reserved
(B) cleaned
(C) closed
(D) funded

12. (A) renovated
(B) renovations
(C) renovates
(D) renovator

13. (A) Please complete all transactions early.
(B) The original flooring was kept.
(C) Forms are available in the lobby.
(D) We apologize for the inconvenience.

14. (A) delays
(B) decreases
(C) sales
(D) estimates

① 인칭대명사

■ 인칭대명사의 형태

명사를 대신해서 쓰는 말을 대명사라고 해요. 그 중 인칭대명사는 '나', '너', '그것들'처럼 사람이나 사물을 가리키는 말로, 문장에서 담당하는 역할(격)과 지칭하는 대상이 무엇인지 등에 따라 형태가 달라집니다.

		주격 ~은(는), ~이(가)	소유격 ~의	목적격 ~을, ~에게	소유대명사 ~의 것	재귀대명사 ~ 자신
1인칭	나	I	my	me	mine	myself
	우리	we	our	us	ours	ourselves
2인칭	너	you	your	you	yours	yourself
	너희	you	your	you	yours	yourselves
3인칭	그	he	his	him	his	himself
	그녀	she	her	her	hers	herself
	그것	it	its	it	—	itself
	그들 / 그것들	they	their	them	theirs	themselves

■ 주격, 소유격, 목적격

❶ **주격 인칭대명사**: 동사 앞 주어 자리에는 주격 인칭대명사를 씁니다.

She will quit her job next month. 그녀는 다음 달에 일을 그만둘 것이다.
주격

❷ **소유격 인칭대명사**: 명사 앞에서 명사를 수식하는 한정사로 쓰입니다.

Mr. Watts talked about **his report** briefly. 왓츠 씨는 자신의 보고서에 대해 간단히 말했다.
소유격

❸ **목적격 인칭대명사**: 동사나 전치사 뒤에는 목적격 인칭대명사를 씁니다.

Ms. Diaz is busy, but I could **ask her for you**. 디아즈 씨는 바쁘지만 내가 너를 위해 그녀에게 물어볼게.
목적격   목적격

STEP 1

1. The mechanics became more efficient as _____ began using the new technology.
   (A) themselves
   (B) they

2. Mr. Kensington has already filed the expense report for _____ recent trip to Hong Kong.
   (A) his
   (B) him

3. Ms. Williams has given _____ a detailed schedule for constructing the new workstations.
   (A) we
   (B) us

4. Although the staff has grown, Mr. Lee continues to conduct all client meetings _____.
   (A) him
   (B) himself

STEP 2

5. Ms. Nakasone will give you a copy of the report _____ always prepares after our meetings.
   (A) it
   (B) she
   (C) they
   (D) we

6. We hope to send _____ tax documents to you by the end of the week.
   (A) you
   (B) your
   (C) yours
   (D) yourself

7. We were informed by the property owner that the rent should be paid directly to _____.
   (A) her
   (B) hers
   (C) she
   (D) herself

8. With _____ new building and expanded hours, First Bank of Stubenville is ahead of the competition.
   (A) them
   (B) they
   (C) its
   (D) itself

어휘 | 1. mechanic 정비공 efficient 효율적인 **2.** file 제출하다; 보관하다 expense report 지출 결의서 **3.** detailed 상세한 construct 짓다, 건설하다 workstation 근무하는 자리 **4.** conduct 진행하다, 수행하다 **5.** prepare 준비하다 **6.** tax 세금 by the end of the week 금요일까지 **7.** inform 알리다 property owner 건물주 rent 임대료 directly 직접 **8.** expanded 확대된, 확장된 be ahead of ~에서 앞서다 competition 경쟁

② 소유대명사와 재귀대명사

소유격 + 명사 = 소유대명사

my + man = mine

■ 소유대명사

<소유격 + 명사>의 역할을 하는 소유대명사는 '~의 것'이라고 해석하며, 명사처럼 주어, 목적어, 보어 자리에 모두 쓸 수 있어요.

❶ 주어: 동사 앞에 와요.

My backpack is too heavy, but **yours** / ~~you~~ is lightweight. 내 배낭은 너무 무거운데, 네 것은 가볍다.
= your backpack (소유격 your + 명사 backpack)

❷ 목적어: 타동사나 전치사 뒤에 와요.

Of the three ideas, the judge chose **mine** / ~~me~~. 세 가지 아이디어 중에서 심사위원은 내 것을 선택했다.
= my idea

❸ 보어: 주어나 목적어의 보충어로 쓰여요.

The mobile phone on Ms. Ryo's desk is **hers** / ~~her~~. 료 씨의 책상에 있는 휴대폰은 그녀의 것이다.
= her mobile phone

■ 재귀대명사

myself(나 자신)처럼 인칭대명사의 소유격이나 목적격에 -self[selves]를 붙인 형태로 '~ 자신', '직접'이라고 해석해요.

조건	위치	예문
주어와 목적어가 같을 때	목적어 자리	**Carlos** can introduce himself/~~him~~ in English. 주어 ／ 목적어 = Carlos 카를로스는 영어로 자기 자신을 소개할 수 있다.
주어나 목적어를 강조할 때 (생략해도 문장이 성립해요)	문장 끝이나 명사 뒤	**The investors** visited the factory (themselves). 주어 ／ 주어 강조 = **The investors** (themselves) visited the factory. 투자자들은 공장을 (직접) 방문했다.
관용적 표현	전치사 뒤	Jill has written the article **by** herself. 질은 혼자서 그 기사를 썼다. → by oneself 혼자 힘으로, 혼자서 = on one's own

RC

PART 5&6

STEP 1

1. Drivers are asked to park _____ cars within the white lines.
   (A) their
   (B) theirs

2. To prepare _____ for a job interview, Mr. Paik read about the company's history.
   (A) yourselves
   (B) himself

3. Mr. Wong will travel to the management seminar in Singapore on _____.
   (A) his own
   (B) him

4. Barton Maintenance employees determined next month's work schedule _____.
   (A) them
   (B) themselves

STEP 2

5. We will position _____ as the premier refrigerator among quality kitchen appliances.
   (A) we
   (B) us
   (C) our
   (D) ours

6. Dr. Schmidt is not sure that her assistant can complete the investigation by _____.
   (A) his
   (B) him
   (C) his own
   (D) himself

7. Customer inquiries can be difficult to answer on _____.
   (A) yours
   (B) yourself
   (C) your own
   (D) you

8. The branch has already submitted its sales totals, but we have not finished calculating _____ yet.
   (A) us
   (B) ours
   (C) our
   (D) ourselves

어휘 | **1.** be asked to do ~하도록 요청 받다 **2.** prepare 준비하다 **3.** travel 여행하다 management 경영 **4.** maintenance 유지, 보수 determine 결정하다 **5.** position 배치하다, 자리를 잡다 premier 최고의 quality 우수한, 양질의 appliance 가전제품 **6.** be sure that ~을 확신하다 assistant 조수, 보조 complete 완수하다, 완성하다 investigation 조사 **7.** inquiry 문의 **8.** branch 지점 submit 제출하다 calculate 계산하다

③ 지시대명사와 부정대명사

those + 수식어구 = ~한 사람들

those interested in animation 애니메이션에 관심 있는 사람들

■ 지시대명사 this / these와 that / those

지시대명사는 이전에 언급된 사물이나 사람을 가리키는 말이에요. 거리나 시간상 가까운 것은 this(이것), 먼 것은 that(저것)으로 표현하며 복수형은 각각 these(이것들), those(저것들)예요. this와 that은 단수명사 앞, these와 those는 복수명사 앞에서 그 명사를 한정하는 지시형용사로 쓰일 수도 있어요.

This is a quick update on the program. 이것은 프로그램에 관한 간단한 수정 사항입니다.

These / Those programs are no longer available. 이/저 프로그램들은 더 이상 운영되지 않습니다.

| 기본기 다지기 | those who: ~하는 사람들

뒤에 수식어가 붙은 those는 '~하는 사람들'을 의미해요.

Those who use the parking area must obtain a permit. 주차장을 사용하는 사람들은 허가증을 받아야 한다.

Those (who are) **interested** in the seminar should register in advance. 그 세미나에 관심 있는 사람들은 미리 등록해야 한다.

■ 부정대명사

정해지지 않은 사람이나 사물 따위를 가리키는 말이에요.

수량	부정대명사	of the + 복수 / 불가산 명사: ~중에서	동사의 수
단수	one 하나 each 각각 either 둘 중 하나 neither 둘 중 어느 쪽도 아닌	of the restaurants (복수명사)	is great.
복수	few 거의 없음 both 둘 다 several 몇몇 many 많음 some 일부 any 누구든/무엇이든 most 대부분 all 전부	of the restaurants (복수명사)	are great.
단수	some 일부 any 누구든/무엇이든 most 대부분 all 전부 much 다량	of the information (불가산명사)	is great.

■ one, another, the other, (the) others의 차이

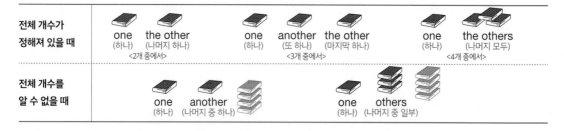

| 전체 개수가
정해져 있을 때 | one
(하나) | the other
(나머지 하나)
<2개 중에서> | one
(하나) | another
(또 하나) | the other
(마지막 하나)
<3개 중에서> | one
(하나) | the others
(나머지 모두)
<4개 중에서> |

전체 개수를 알 수 없을 때
one (하나) another (나머지 중 하나)   one (하나) others (나머지 중 일부)

Among five balls, **one** is red, **another** is yellow, and **the others** are blue.
5개의 공 중 하나는 빨강, 다른 하나는 노랑, 나머지 전부(3개)는 파랑이다.

→ each other(2명), one another(3명 이상)는 '서로'라는 의미의 대명사로, 목적어로 쓰여요.

STEP 1

1. _____ mechanic has worked at Mr. Kim's Auto Shop for years.
(A) This
(B) These

2. _____ of the employees are searching the archives for the missing folder.
(A) Much
(B) Many

3. Mr. Hahn and Ms. Smalls have similar job duties, and _____ hope for promotions.
(A) one
(B) both

4. Dr. Hemana and Dr. Wareham have known _____ since they were university students.
(A) another one
(B) each other

STEP 2

5. _____ who work in the shipping office must receive training in the new mailing procedures label.
(A) One
(B) Each
(C) Those
(D) Themselves

6. Of the two mobile phones, one has an 8 megapixel camera, and _____ features a 12 megapixel camera.
(A) another
(B) others
(C) the other
(D) the others

7. In order to finish the candidate interviews, _____ of the recruiters will need to stay another day.
(A) all
(B) much
(C) other
(D) others

8. _____ interested in the position should submit a completed form before February 21.
(A) These
(B) Those
(C) Every
(D) They

어휘 | **1.** mechanic 정비공 auto shop 자동차 정비소 **2.** archive 기록 보관소 missing 없어진 **3.** similar 비슷한 duty 의무 promotion 승진 **4.** since ~한 이래로 **5.** shipping office 배송 사무실 procedure 절차 **6.** megapixel 100만 화소 feature 특징을 이루다 **7.** candidate 지원자, 후보자 recruiter 채용 담당자 **8.** interested 관심이 있는 submit 제출하다 completed 완성된, 작성된

1 Mr. Pierce has confirmed that ------- will present the advertising campaign to the clients.
(A) his
(B) him
(C) he
(D) himself

2 Although Daminger Beauty Products and Sasso Cosmetics have not been profitable this year, ------- expect revenues to increase next quarter.
(A) another
(B) both
(C) either
(D) least

3 Apply to Joneston Stores today so as not to miss ------- chance to join a great sales team.
(A) you
(B) your
(C) yours
(D) yourself

4 Ms. Newman said she will complete the quarterly report ------- since most of the accounting staff is on vacation.
(A) she
(B) her
(C) hers
(D) herself

5 Maybear Bakery promises that ------- bread products are dairy free.
(A) themselves
(B) its
(C) itself
(D) they

6 Under the new regulations, development proposals in historic Dorcliff will be subject to a longer review process than ------- in neighboring towns.
(A) anyone
(B) whichever
(C) them
(D) those

7 The president of Macropa, Inc., took it upon ------- to investigate the reasons for the company's narrowing profit margin.
(A) his
(B) him
(C) himself
(D) he

8 Recent customer feedback shows that ------- Galpran line of footwear is lightweight and affordable.
(A) our
(B) us
(C) we
(D) ourselves

9 Personnel must submit estimated travel expense forms to ------- managers at least three days before departure.
(A) their
(B) they
(C) them
(D) theirs

10 Putting ------- preference aside, Ms. Shang approved the design favored by the majority.
(A) hers
(B) her own
(C) she
(D) herself

Questions 11-14 refer to the following letter.

Sparta Fitness Center

July 1
Luce Charpentier
317 North Street
Dundee 3000

Dear Ms. Charpentier:

We are writing to inform you that your Sparta Fitness Center membership has -------. We hope
                                                                          11.

that you are planning to renew your membership. If so, please fill out the ------- form and bring it
                                                                          12.

to any Sparta Fitness Center. -------. If you respond by August 1, we will waive the reinstatement
                               13.

fee.

------- fitness goals are important to us. We want to continue to help you maintain an active and
  14.

healthy lifestyle!

Sincerely,

Manabu Ishiyama
Membership Services
Sparta Fitness Center, Inc.
Enclosure

---

11. (A) begun
(B) expired
(C) doubled
(D) disappeared

12. (A) enclose
(B) enclosed
(C) encloses
(D) enclosing

13. (A) An associate will return your call within
one day.
(B) No action is required of you at this time.
(C) All forms must be printed on white paper.
(D) A complete list of our locations is
included on the form.

14. (A) Your
(B) Their
(C) Many
(D) These

Unit | 04 형용사

① 형용사의 개념과 역할

형용사는 명사를 수식하거나,
명사의 상태나 특성을 설명해요.

There is a delicious cake.

The cake is delicious.

■ 형용사의 개념과 형태

형용사는 good voice(좋은 목소리)에서 good처럼 명사의 성질이나 상태를 나타내는 말로, 일반적으로 -able, -ive, -ful 등으로 끝나는 형태가 많아요.

형용사 어미	형용사		형용사 어미	형용사	
-able[ible]	available 이용 가능한	possible 가능한	-al	personal 개인적인	additional 추가의
-ive	expensive 값비싼	creative 창조적인	-ous	famous 유명한	previous 이전의
-ful	careful 조심스러운	successful 성공적인	-ary	necessary 필요한	temporary 임시의
-ic	realistic 현실적인	specific 구체적인	-ate	private 사적인	fortunate 운 좋은

→ -able[ible]로 끝나면 '~할 수 있는, ~ 가능한'이라는 의미로 주로 해석돼요.

■ 형용사의 역할

❶ **명사 수식:** 주로 명사 앞에서 명사를 꾸미는 수식어 역할을 해요.

The staff is making **considerable changes**. 직원들은 상당한 변화를 이루어 내고 있다.
　　　　　　　　　　　　　└─────────┘명사

❷ **주어 보충:** be동사, become, seem, remain 등의 동사 뒤에서 주어를 보충하는 주격 보어로 쓰일 수 있어요.

The document **was informative**. 그 문서는 유익했다.
　　주어　　　　　　주격 보어

❸ **목적어 보충:** make, keep, find, consider 등의 동사가 있을 때 그 동사의 목적어 뒤에서 목적격 보어로 쓰일 수 있어요.

Most customers **found** the manual **helpful**. 대부분의 고객은 설명서가 유용하다고 생각했다.
　　　　　　　　　　목적어　　목적격 보어

STEP 1

1. If you have a _____ meal request, please tell the ticket agent when booking your flight.
   (A) special
   (B) specialize

2. The clothing shop is _____ because it sells quality uniforms at competitive prices.
   (A) success
   (B) successful

3. The coordinators are asking the focus groups to provide _____ criticism.
   (A) construction
   (B) constructive

4. The finance department will outline its _____ growth plans at the all-staff meeting.
   (A) strategic
   (B) strategically

STEP 2

5. Sarrelk Communications offers a _____ variety of social-media services.
   (A) wide
   (B) widen
   (C) widely
   (D) widest

6. The analyst's commentary in the progress report was sharply _____ of the leadership team.
   (A) critical
   (B) critic
   (C) critically
   (D) criticism

7. The sales goal set by the management team seems _____ to most of the staff.
   (A) realist
   (B) realism
   (C) realistic
   (D) realistically

8. The decision to hire _____ help was based largely on the concerns expressed by the employees.
   (A) addition
   (B) additions
   (C) additional
   (D) additionally

어휘 | **1.** ticket agent 탑승권 판매원 book one's flight 항공편을 예약하다 **2.** quality 품질이 좋은; 품질 competitive 경쟁력 있는 **3.** coordinator 진행자 criticism 비평, 비판 constructive 건설적인 **4.** finance department 재무부 outline 간략히 서술하다 strategic 전략적인 **5.** a wide variety of 매우 다양한 **6.** analyst 분석가 commentary 논평 progress report 경과 보고서 sharply 날카롭게 critical 비판적인 **7.** realistic 현실적인 **8.** help 인력, 고용인 be based on ~에 근거를 두다 concern 우려, 관심사 addition 추가된 것 additional 추가의 additionally 덧붙여

② 주의해야 할 형용사

The man is respected. (존경 받는)

respected

respectful

The others are respectful. (공손한)

■ 분사 형용사 (Unit 11 참고)

동사-ing로 끝나는 형용사		동사-ed로 끝나는 형용사	
leading 선두의	following 다음의	detailed 상세한	established 자리를 잡은
lasting 지속적인	promising 유망한	motivated 의욕적인	experienced 노련한
challenging 힘든	encouraging 고무적인	required 필수의	attached 첨부된

Mr. Kwon is a (**promising** / ~~promised~~) candidate. 권 씨는 유망한 후보자이다.

Advance registration is (**required** / ~~requiring~~) for the conference. 그 학회는 사전 등록이 필수적이다.

■ 헷갈리는 형용사

reliable / dependable 믿을 만한 reliant / dependent 의존적인	responsible 책임이 있는 responsive 민감한	considerable 상당한 considerate 사려 깊은	favorable 우호적인 favorite 좋아하는
comprehensible 이해할 수 있는 comprehensive 포괄적인	informative 유익한 informed 잘 아는	impressive 인상적인 impressed 감명 받은	confident 확신하는 confidential 기밀의
respectable 존경할 만한 respective 각각의	respected 존경 받는 respectful 공손한	successful 성공적인 successive 연속적인	industrial 산업의 industrious 근면한

All personal information is (**confidential** / ~~confident~~). 모든 개인 정보는 기밀이다.

■ be + 형용사 + 전치사

be responsible for	~에 대한 책임이 있다	be dedicated[committed] to	~에 헌신하다, 전념하다
be recognized for	~을 인정받다	be promoted to	~로 승진하다
be eligible for = be entitled to	~에 자격이 있다	be accessible by	~로 접근할[이용할] 수 있다
be dependent on	~에 의존하다	be aware of	~을 알다, 인지하다
be concerned[anxious] about	~에 대해 걱정하다	be capable of	~을 할 수 있다 (= be able to do)
be familiar with	~에 익숙하다	be exempt from	~가 면제되다

Team leaders **are responsible for** their teams. 팀장들은 팀을 책임진다.

Some Koreans **are capable of** speaking English. 일부 한국인은 영어로 말할 수 있다.
    = are able to speak English

실전 도움닫기

다음 문장의 빈칸에 들어갈 알맞은 말을 고르세요.   정답과 해설 p. 121

1. _____ assembly-line workers tend to be more attentive.
(A) Experienced
(B) Experiencing

2. Mr. Moore's speech made a _____ impression on the audience.
(A) lasted
(B) lasting

3. Everyone at the concert was _____ by Ms. Vincenzi's outstanding performance.
(A) impressive
(B) impressed

4. Wellbeing Aid, Inc., is _____ to meeting the specific needs of its customers.
(A) dedicated
(B) dedication

5. Farmers are predicting good crop harvests as a result of recent _____ weather conditions.
(A) favors
(B) favorable
(C) favor
(D) favoring

6. Winthrop Strategies is seeking to employ a _____ individual who consistently meets deadlines.
(A) motivate
(B) motivated
(C) motivation
(D) motivations

7. The division manager revised the report because the language in it was too _____.
(A) repetitive
(B) repeating
(C) repetition
(D) repeat

8. The malfunctioning printer will soon be replaced with a more _____ model.
(A) reliable
(B) reliably
(C) relying
(D) relied

어휘 | **1.** assembly-line 조립 라인 tend to ~하는 경향이 있다 attentive 세심한, 주의 깊은 experienced 숙련된 **2.** impression 인상 audience 청중 lasting 지속적인 **3.** outstanding 뛰어난 performance 공연 **5.** predict 예측하다, 예견하다 good crop 풍작 harvest 수확, 추수 as a result of ~의 결과로 weather conditions 기상 조건 favor 호의, 친절; 호의를 보이다, 찬성하다 favorable 순조로운, (기후가) 좋은, 양호한 favoring 형편에 맞는, 선호하는 **6.** individual 개인 consistently 일관되게 meet a deadline 마감일을 맞추다 **7.** division 부서 revise 수정하다 language 언어, 표현 repetitive 반복적인 repeating 반복하고 있는 repetition 반복 repeat 반복하다 **8.** malfunctioning 오작동하는 replace 교체하다 reliable 신뢰할 수 있는

1 Ms. Hidalgo was chosen as the new CEO of Parton Corporation based on her ------- knowledge of the textile industry.
(A) deep
(B) deepen
(C) deeply
(D) depth

2 The most ------- of Hillcrest-Linden's numerous overseas subsidiaries is Sri Lanka–based Colombo Tech.
(A) profit
(B) profits
(C) profitably
(D) profitable

3 Thanks to a highly ------- management team, Wu Logistics has experienced unprecedented growth this year.
(A) competency
(B) competently
(C) competence
(D) competent

4 Ms. Patel was ------- about her first day on the job at Haighton Industries, but everything went extremely well.
(A) anxious
(B) anxiously
(C) anxiety
(D) anxiousness

5 Warren Velasco's latest exhibit has been praised as his most ------- work to date.
(A) create
(B) creative
(C) creation
(D) creativity

6 The ------- issue of additional vacation time for first-year employees was settled at yesterday's managers' meeting.
(A) controversy
(B) controversially
(C) controversial
(D) controversies

7 An agreement was finally signed after a ------- negotiation between the legal advisers at the two corporations.
(A) lengthens
(B) lengthen
(C) lengthy
(D) length

8 After ------- effort, we have succeeded in redesigning the keyboard.
(A) consider
(B) considerable
(C) considerate
(D) considerably

9 Consumers have been very ------- of our efforts to reduce the amount of unsolicited mail that they receive.
(A) appreciating
(B) appreciate
(C) appreciative
(D) appreciation

10 There is no ------- evidence that the reformulated allergy medication is any more effective than the existing one.
(A) persuaded
(B) persuasion
(C) persuasive
(D) persuade

Questions 11-14 refer to the following information.

About Newspaper Advertising

Thank you for choosing to advertise in the *Belmore Times* weekly newspaper. -------. A clear,
11.

simply worded advertisement is often the most ------- way to catch your readers' attention while
12.

giving them the necessary information about your product or service. -------, an advertisement
13.

that is too wordy and dense may often be overlooked. Keep in mind that the average newspaper

reader spends fewer than five minutes on an individual page. Therefore, advertisements that can

be readily ------- in a matter of seconds will achieve the best results.
14.

---

11. (A) If our subscriber numbers change
significantly, we will alert you.
  (B) There are several ways to submit your
advertisement to us.
  (C) Please note that it can be very different
from online marketing.
  (D) To make the most of your investment,
consider the following tip.

12. (A) reliable
  (B) reliably
  (C) reliability
  (D) reliableness

13. (A) Later on
  (B) In contrast
  (C) As a result
  (D) Despite this

14. (A) printed
  (B) distributed
  (C) downloaded
  (D) comprehended

Unit | 05 부사

① 부사의 개념과 역할

the extremely hot weather

■ 부사의 개념과 형태

부사는 방법이나 정도 등을 설명하는 말로, (대)명사를 제외한 모든 품사뿐만 아니라 문장 전체도 수식할 수 있어요. 대체로 '~하게'라고 해석되며 '형용사+-ly'의 형태가 많아요.

형용사+-ly	strongly 강력하게	sharply 급격하게	carefully 신중하게	suddenly 갑자기
	highly 매우	closely 밀접하게	lately 최근에	hardly 거의 ~ 않다
	→ 명사+-ly는 형용사예요.	timely 시기 적절한 costly 비싼	orderly 질서 정연한	friendly 친절한
그 밖의 형태	well 잘, 훨씬	very 매우	then 그때	even 심지어
	also 또한	too 너무, 또한	quite 꽤	just 딱, 방금
	already 벌써(주로 긍정문)	still 여전히, 그런데도	yet 아직, 벌써	ever 언제나

■ 부사의 역할

❶ 동사 수식

주어+부사+동사	**The president personally greets** new employees. 회장은 직접 신입사원들을 환영한다.
동사(+목적어)+부사	Please **finish** the sales report **quickly**. 신속히 판매 보고서를 작성해 주세요.
조동사+부사+본동사	The client **must fully understand** all the paperwork. 고객은 모든 서류를 완전히 이해해야 한다.
be동사+부사+p.p.[-ing]	The meeting **was originally scheduled** for May 13. 회의는 원래 5월 13일로 예정되어 있었다.
have+부사+p.p.	Our office **has recently moved**. 우리 사무실이 최근에 이사했다.

❷ 형용사, 부사, 구, 문장 전체 수식

부사는 동사 외에도 형용사나 부사, 구, 문장 전체를 수식할 수 있어요.

The **extremely hot** weather lowered productivity. 극도로 더운 날씨가 생산성을 떨어뜨렸다.
　　　└──→ 형용사 수식

We would **very much** like to hire you as an advisor. 우리는 당신을 고문으로 모시길 간절히 바랍니다.
　　　└──→ 부사 수식

You should register for the seminar **well in advance.** 그 세미나는 한참 전에 등록해야 한다.
　　　　　　└──→ 전치사구 수식

Fortunately, no one was seriously injured. 다행히 아무도 심하게 다치지 않았다.
└──────────→ 문장 전체 수식

160

STEP 1

1. You can have a _____ different opinion from your colleagues on the matter.
   (A) complete
   (B) completely

2. All passengers' seat belts are _____ fastened prior to takeoff.
   (A) secure
   (B) securely

3. Please adjust the volume knob _____ so the sound is not too loud.
   (A) slight
   (B) slightly

4. The municipal road repaving project is _____ on schedule.
   (A) current
   (B) currently

STEP 2

5. Our sales figures increased last quarter, but this trend could _____ change.
   (A) easy
   (B) easier
   (C) easiest
   (D) easily

6. Kiva Business Center is _____ opening after three years of construction.
   (A) final
   (B) finality
   (C) finals
   (D) finally

7. Royalty payments will be divided _____ between the writers of a coauthored book.
   (A) equal
   (B) equally
   (C) equals
   (D) equality

8. Mi-Sun Park's artwork _____ combines classical elements with modern materials.
   (A) skill
   (B) skilled
   (C) skillful
   (D) skillfully

어휘 | **1.** opinion 의견 colleague 동료 matter 문제 **2.** seat belt 안전벨트 fasten 매다, 고정시키다 prior to ~전에 takeoff 이륙 securely 안전하게, 단단히 **3.** adjust 조절하다 knob 손잡이 loud 소리가 큰 **4.** municipal 시의 repave (도로를) 재포장하다 on schedule 예정대로인 **5.** sales figures 매출액 quarter 분기 trend 경향 **6.** finality 최종적임 **7.** royalty payment 인세 대금 divide 분배하다 coauthor 공동 집필하다 equally 균등하게 **8.** artwork 예술품 combine 결합하다 element 요소 material 재료

② 빈출 부사 정리

His scores have sharply increased.

■ 빈출 부사

증가/감소 강조 부사	증가 / 감소 / 변화를 나타내는 동사(increase, decrease, rise, fall, replace, change 등)와 잘 어울려요.
	sharply 급격하게 slightly 약간 gradually 점진적으로 steadily 꾸준히 considerably/substantially 상당히
	Customer satisfaction **increased steadily** after the store opened. 그 매장을 연 뒤로 고객 만족도가 꾸준히 높아졌다.
숫자 수식 부사	빈칸 뒤에 숫자 표현이 있으면 숫자 수식 부사와 어울려요.
	nearly/almost/approximately/about 대략, 거의 at least 최소한 just/only 오직
	The factory produces **approximately 300** vehicles per year. 그 공장은 1년에 대략 300대의 차량을 생산한다.
시간 강조 부사	before(~ 전에)나 after(~ 후에)의 앞에 위치하여 '직전에', '직후에'를 의미해요.
	shortly/immediately/soon/right 곧, 즉시
	There will be a snack break **immediately after** the lecture. 강연 직후에 간식 시간이 있을 것이다.
접속부사	앞뒤 문장의 의미를 연결하는 부사(접속사 아님)로, 주로 콤마(,)와 함께 사용돼요.
	however 하지만 nevertheless 그럼에도 불구하고 moreover 게다가 therefore 그러므로 otherwise 그렇지 않으면
	The new antivirus program is easy, cheap, and, **moreover**, it's effective. 새로운 바이러스 퇴치 프로그램은 쉽고 싸며, 게다가 효과적이다.
부정부사	부정(否定)의 의미를 나타내요.
	never 결코 ~ 않다 hardly/scarcely/seldom/rarely 거의 ~ 않다
	The tenants **hardly** use the back gate. 세입자들은 뒷문을 거의 이용하지 않는다.

■ 자주 어울려 쓰이는 부사 표현

reasonably[affordably] priced	가격이 적당한	conveniently located	위치가 편리한
originally scheduled	원래 예정된	temporarily closed	일시적으로 폐쇄된
review thoroughly[carefully]	철저히[꼼꼼히] 검토하다	widely known	널리 알려진
regularly check[inspect]	정기적으로 점검하다	clearly indicate	명확하게 나타내다

The clinic is **conveniently located** near the campus. 그 병원은 캠퍼스 인근 편리한 곳에 위치하고 있다.

STEP 1

1. The contractors say they will begin the renovation work _____ before 8 A.M. tomorrow.
   (A) shortly
   (B) short

2. The elevators in the north wing will be _____ closed for maintenance next week.
   (A) temporarily
   (B) cautiously

3. Sales of new cars are down _____ five percent this quarter.
   (A) nearly
   (B) quite

4. _____ opened as a modest tourist hotel, Agafya Inn is now a full-service resort.
   (A) Originally
   (B) Original

STEP 2

5. There is a coffee machine _____ located on the second floor of the Tabor Building.
   (A) conveniently
   (B) slightly
   (C) considerably
   (D) eventually

6. Please leave _____ six chairs in the conference room and remove any extras.
   (A) more
   (B) rather
   (C) just
   (D) quite

7. Kristi Driver is a well-known therapist, and her services are very _____ priced.
   (A) strongly
   (B) internally
   (C) reasonably
   (D) repeatedly

8. Mr. Grappin will be returning to New York _____ to finalize the project details.
   (A) soon
   (B) quite
   (C) closely
   (D) lately

어휘 | **1.** contractor 하청업체 renovation 보수 **2.** wing 부속 건물 temporarily 임시로 **3.** quarter 분기 **4.** modest 크지 않은 originally 원래 **5.** located ~에 위치한 floor 층 **6.** remove 치우다 **7.** well-known 잘 알려진 therapist 치료사 **8.** finalize 마무리하다

1 Ms. Simmons ------- conducted writing seminars while employed at the *Norris Weekly Circular*.
(A) frequent
(B) frequents
(C) frequently
(D) frequenting

2 The sofa sale at Seaview Furniture is ------ over, with just one day left to shop for discounted items.
(A) almost
(B) slightly
(C) only
(D) already

3 Rather than replace all machinery at once, engineers at the Hartford plant decided to replace it ------- over the next five years.
(A) slightly
(B) gradually
(C) familiarly
(D) previously

4 Although the job took ------- six hours to complete, the workers will be paid for a full eight-hour shift.
(A) during
(B) until
(C) right
(D) only

5 Monstad Construction, the company that will renovate our hotel lobby, comes ------ recommended.
(A) high
(B) higher
(C) highest
(D) highly

6 Ledgercore software products are designed ------- to meet the needs of large-scale accounting firms.
(A) specifically
(B) specifics
(C) specifies
(D) specific

7 Yesterday's speech was disrupted by problems with the sound system, but the president's message was ------ communicated to the audience.
(A) likewise
(B) whatever
(C) furthermore
(D) nevertheless

8 Recent reports show that the value of the nation's currency fell ------ during the recession.
(A) sharp
(B) sharply
(C) sharpen
(D) sharpness

9 Once the factory is ------- operational, it will require a workforce of 400.
(A) fully
(B) fuller
(C) fullest
(D) full

10 While apartment prices have changed ------ in the downtown section of River City, prices in other areas have stayed the same.
(A) drama
(B) dramas
(C) dramatic
(D) dramatically

Questions 11-14 refer to the following article.

Since the launch of the Hershland Commuter Rail Service in March, ridership has been growing

-------. Now, the City of Hershland has realized that some changes need to be made if the rail
  11.

service is to accommodate all passengers. "At this time, we just don't have enough room for

-------," says train conductor Herman Wagner. "The trains are very ------- during peak hours. Often
  12.   **13.**

there is standing room only, and sometimes there is no room at all for new passengers to board."

The City of Hershland has developed a plan to increase the rail service's capacity. With the aid of

a federal grant, it will acquire additional railcars. -------.
                                                        14.

11. (A) steady
    (B) steadily
    (C) steadied
    (D) steadying

12. (A) him
    (B) either one
    (C) both
    (D) everybody

13. (A) reliable
    (B) crowded
    (C) accessible
    (D) urgent

14. (A) So far, commuters have praised their
       comfortable seating.
    (B) No further railway track improvements
       have been announced.
    (C) The purchases are to be negotiated in
       the coming year.
    (D) Assistance is also available at
       www.hershland.gov/hcrs.

Unit | 06 동사의 형태와 종류

① 동사의 형태

동사에는 기본형(~하다),
완료형(~해 오다), 수동형(~되다),
진행형(~ 중이다) 등
다양한 형태가 있어요.

Something has changed. (완료형)

■ 동사의 형태 변화

종류	동사		동사 아님	
	현재형	과거형	과거분사형	현재분사형
의미	~이다 / ~하다	~했다	~된	~하는
be동사	is, are	was, were	been	being
규칙 변화 동사	return	return**ed**	return**ed**	return**ing**
불규칙 변화 동사	begin	began	begun	beginning

➜ 과거분사, 현재분사는 be동사나 have동사와 결합하면 동사로 쓰일 수 있어요.

■ 동사원형이 오는 경우

❶ 주어가 없는 명령문

Please change the layout of this chart. 이 도표의 구성을 바꾸세요.

❷ 조동사 뒤

The assistant **will change** the coffee filters. 비서가 커피 필터를 교체할 것이다. (will = 미래를 나타내는 조동사)

➜ 조동사는 동사에 가능, 의무 등 보조적 의미를 첨가하는 말로, can, must, will 등이 있어요.

❸ 주어가 3인칭 단수(he, she, it 등)가 아닌 경우 현재 시제를 나타낼 때

The rules change frequently. 규정이 자주 바뀐다.

Mr. Roberts often **changes** his mind. 로버츠 씨는 자주 마음을 바꾼다. (Mr. Roberts = 3인칭 단수)

➜ 주어가 3인칭 단수이면 동사원형에 -(e)s를 붙여요.

■ 과거분사형(p.p.)이 오는 경우

❶ 수동태 be+p.p.: ~되다

The plan **was changed** abruptly. 계획이 갑자기 바뀌었다. (Unit 9 능동태와 수동태 참고)

❷ 완료 시제 have+p.p.: ~했다

The Internet **has changed** our lives. 인터넷은 우리의 삶을 바꾸었다. (Unit 8 시제 참고)

■ 현재분사형(-ing)이 오는 경우

진행 시제 be+-ing: ~하고 있다

The paintings **are changing** the atmosphere of the room. 그림들이 방의 분위기를 바꾸고 있다. (Unit 8 시제 참고)

STEP 1

1. Please _____ your hotel key at the front desk when you go out.
(A) to leave
(B) leave

2. You should _____ hotel reservations several weeks ahead of time.
(A) make
(B) made

3. The Darlingstone Hotel _____ a complimentary breakfast to all of its guests.
(A) offering
(B) is offering

4. Mr. Hu's innovative ideas were _____ enthusiastically by the Bercier Group's marketing staff.
(A) received
(B) receive

STEP 2

5. The law offices of Peck and Sever have already _____ for the public holiday.
(A) close
(B) closed
(C) closing
(D) closure

6. To ensure prompt return of your laundry, _____ your hotel room number on the tag provided.
(A) wrote
(B) written
(C) write
(D) writing

7. All employees are _____ their best to meet the deadline for the construction project.
(A) does
(B) do
(C) doing
(D) did

8. All orders for office supplies must be _____ to Ms. Reaton by Thursday at noon.
(A) submitting
(B) submit
(C) submitted
(D) submission

어휘 | **1.** front desk 프런트 데스크 **2.** reservation 예약 ahead of time 사전에 **3.** complimentary 무료의 **4.** innovative 획기적인, 혁신적인 enthusiastically 열렬하게, 열광하여 **5.** law office 법률 사무소 public holiday 공휴일 **6.** ensure 보장하다 prompt 즉각적인 laundry 세탁물 tag 꼬리표, 번호표 **7.** do one's best 최선을 다하다 meet the deadline 마감일을 맞추다 construction 공사 **8.** order 주문, 주문품, 주문서 office supplies 사무용품 submit (서류 등을) 제출하다 submission 제출

② 자동사와 타동사

목적어가 필요 없는 자동사
VS.
목적어가 따라붙는 타동사

■ 자동사의 개념

목적어가 필요 없는 동사로, 자동사 뒤에는 명사가 오지 않고 주로 전치사구나 부사가 와요.

Some of the passengers **talked** loudly. 몇몇 승객들은 큰 소리로 이야기했다. (부사)
　　　　　　　　자동사 　in the station.　　역에서 (전치사구)
　　　　　　　　~~loudness.~~　　큰 소리를

■ 토익에 자주 출제되는 자동사 + 전치사

rely[depend] on ~에 의존하다	agree with[on] ~에 동의하다	collaborate with[on] ~와[~에] 협력하다
consist of ~로 구성되다	specialize in ~을 전문으로 하다	deal with ~을 다루다
comply with ~을 준수하다	adhere to ~에 들러붙다	refer to ~을 참고하다, 언급하다
participate in ~에 참가하다	respond[react] to ~에 응답[반응]하다	appeal to ~에 호소하다

The staff members usually **agree with** the manager's decisions. 직원들은 대체로 부장의 결정에 동의한다.

■ 타동사의 개념

타동사 뒤에는 목적어(명사)가 반드시 있어야 하고, 부사나 전치사구는 목적어 역할을 대신할 수 없어요.

Mr. Crown finally **finished the budget report**. 크라운 씨는 마침내 예산 보고서를 완성했다.
　　　　　　　　타동사　　　　목적어

■ 자동사로 헷갈리기 쉬운 타동사

discuss ~에 대해 논의하다	attend ~에 참석하다	accompany ~와 동반하다	oppose ~에 반대하다
explain ~에 대해 설명하다	contact ~와 연락하다	notify ~에게 통지하다	await ~을 기다리다

We will soon **discuss** ~~about~~ **technical matters**. 우리는 곧 기술적인 문제에 대해 논의할 것이다.

| 기본기 다지기 | 뒤에 전치사가 따라오는 자동사

동사 어휘를 선택할 때 자동사와 타동사 구별에 유의해야 해요. 문장을 해석하면서 빈칸 뒤에 전치사가 있는지 살펴보고 전치사가 있다면 그 전치사와 어울리는 자동사를 선택합니다.
Mr. Femi **(participated / ~~attended~~) in** the symposium. 페미 씨는 그 심포지엄에 참석했다.

STEP 1

1. Every member of the team should
   _____ with the new regulations.
   (A) comply
   (B) keep

2. The new line of products will surely
   _____ a lot of customers.
   (A) appeal
   (B) attract

3. All employees are required to
   _____ annual evaluations every
   December.
   (A) agree
   (B) complete

4. Ms. Ishimura generously offered to
   _____ the invitation in person.
   (A) respond
   (B) deliver

STEP 2

5. Please _____ our Web site to find
   unique recipes made with Hahm food
   products.
   (A) come
   (B) go
   (C) visit
   (D) take

6. Most residents of Vilica rely _____
   agriculture for their livelihood.
   (A) on
   (B) from
   (C) into
   (D) of

7. Medateli Foods _____ in crafting
   products that are rich in health-giving
   vitamins and minerals.
   (A) authorizes
   (B) modernizes
   (C) realizes
   (D) specializes

8. The construction workers _____
   with their colleagues to make sure
   that they meet the deadline.
   (A) collaborate
   (B) collaborating
   (C) collaborates
   (D) collaboration

어휘 | **1.** regulation 규정 comply 준수하다 **2.** surely 반드시 **4.** generously 관대하게, 친절하게 in person 직접 **5.** recipe 조리법
6. resident 주민, 거주자 livelihood 살림살이, 생계 **7.** craft 제조하다 authorize 재가하다 modernize 현대화하다 realize
깨닫다 specialize 전문으로 하다 **8.** collaborate 협력하다 collaboration 협력

1 The financial review board has stated that no budget proposal may ------- ten pages.
   (A) excessive
   (B) excess
   (C) exceeding
   (D) exceed

2 All new employees are required to ------- in the three-day orientation.
   (A) attend
   (B) take
   (C) inquire
   (D) participate

3 For the last fifteen years, Tatella, Inc. has ------- consistently among the nation's ten leading toy manufacturers.
   (A) rank
   (B) ranked
   (C) ranking
   (D) ranks

4 You must ------- the catering coordinator if you have more than twenty people in your group so that he can arrange a larger table.
   (A) display
   (B) notify
   (C) publish
   (D) reveal

5 Landscape architects are invited to ------- designs for a new garden at Anston Apartments.
   (A) submit
   (B) agree
   (C) call
   (D) base

6 Glideline Technologies ------- in archiving records and retrieving lost data.
   (A) consists
   (B) interests
   (C) inspects
   (D) specializes

7 The Tyneside Recreation Department ------- suggestions for new programs until the end of this month.
   (A) has accepted
   (B) will be accepting
   (C) accepting
   (D) to accept

8 Keyomon restaurants can be ------- in a wide variety of locations, from urban centers to coastal towns.
   (A) finding
   (B) found
   (C) having found
   (D) find

9 For the best results, allow the glue to dry for twenty minutes to ensure that it ------- to the surface of the wood.
   (A) utilizes
   (B) polishes
   (C) complies
   (D) adheres

10 The Director of Finance and the Director of Personnel responded quite ------- to the question about budget increases.
   (A) differently
   (B) difference
   (C) differed
   (D) differing

Questions 11-14 refer to the following memo.

To: All factory staff
From: Jacques Pineau, Operations Manager
Date: November 7
Re: Sealing equipment problem

Yesterday, it was noted that the ------- control knob on the equipment we use to seal our potato-
11.
chip packages is not working properly.

The sealer is actually cooler than the control knob setting indicates. -------.
12.

A technician is scheduled to come out this afternoon to take a look at the knob. In the meantime,

please ------- each package extra carefully before sending it to the shipping department. If a faulty
13.
seal is found, remove the product from the line and place it in ------- of the discard bins.
14.

---

11. (A) speed
(B) temperature
(C) timing
(D) pressure

12. (A) Turning it in this manner is not
recommended.
(B) The user manual explains how to
interpret this noise.
(C) Luckily, the sealer mechanism itself
appears to be functional.
(D) Therefore, the entire assembly line has
been shut down for now.

13. (A) are inspecting
(B) inspect
(C) to inspect
(D) inspected

14. (A) one
(B) most
(C) which
(D) anywhere

Unit | 07 수 일치

① 수 일치의 개념과 동사의 형태

■ 수 일치의 개념

현재 시제일 경우에 주어와 동사의 수를 일치시키는 것을 수 일치라고 해요.

■ 단수동사와 복수동사의 형태

❶ 일반동사

명사는 복수일 때 -(e)s를 붙이는 데 반해 동사는 단수일 때 -(e)s를 붙여요. 즉 단수동사는 동사원형에 -(e)s가 붙은 형태를 의미하고 복수동사는 동사원형이 됩니다.

Mr. Watson attends the conference every year. 왓슨 씨는 매년 그 학회에 참석한다.
　　단수주어　　　단수동사

Our employees **attend** the conference every year. 우리 직원들은 매년 그 학회에 참석한다.
　　복수주어　　　　복수동사

❷ be동사, do동사, have동사

	be동사	do동사	have동사
단수	is, am, was	does	has
복수	are, were	do	have

The festival is popular around the world.
그 축제는 전 세계적으로 인기가 있다.

Spanish festivals are popular around the world.
스페인의 축제들은 전 세계적으로 인기가 있다.

IGC Inc. does not produce heavy machinery.
IGC사는 중장비를 생산하지 않습니다.

They have not produced heavy machinery.
그들은 중장비를 생산한 적이 없습니다.

STEP 1

1. The library's e-mail system _____ notified patrons of the new hours of operation.
(A) has
(B) have

2. Our research _____ were published in the July issue of *Breakthrough*.
(A) result
(B) results

3. The manufacturer _____ the warranty on its latest camera models by twelve months.
(A) extend
(B) has extended

4. Second-quarter _____ were significantly above our expectations.
(A) earning
(B) earnings

STEP 2

5. Event organizers _____ an increase in the number of vendors at this year's art festival.
(A) anticipate
(B) anticipates
(C) anticipating
(D) to anticipate

6. Ms. Seon _____ to highlight earnings for the month of August at the upcoming board meeting.
(A) planning
(B) were planned
(C) plans
(D) plan

7. Our most important goal this year _____ to cut our expenses and save money.
(A) are
(B) is
(C) have
(D) do

8. Factory _____ have helped Zubiri Footwear to improve the design of its running shoes.
(A) test
(B) tests
(C) tested
(D) testing

어휘 | **1.** notify 공지하다 patron 고객, 이용자 operation 운영 **2.** publish 출판하다, 게재하다 issue (잡지의) 호 **3.** manufacturer 제조업자 warranty 품질 보증 latest 최근의, 최신의 **4.** significantly 상당히 expectation 기대 earnings 수익 **5.** organizer 기획자, 주최자 vendor 판매 업체 anticipate 기대하다 **6.** highlight 부각시키다, 강조하다 upcoming 다가오는 board meeting 이사진 회의 **7.** expense 비용 **8.** footwear 신발(류) improve 개선하다

② 주의해야 할 수 일치

주어를 수식하는 어구는
주어-동사 수 일치에
영향을 미치지 않아요.

The woman carrying many trays is Ms. Lee.

■ 수식어가 붙은 주어와 동사의 수 일치

주어와 동사 사이에 수식어가 있으면 주어와 동사의 사이가 멀어져 수 일치 여부를 판단하기가 쉽지 않아요. 이런 경우에는 전체 문장 구조를 파악해서 주어와 동사를 찾은 후에 수 일치를 판단하면 됩니다.

Each security camera (in the laboratories) **operates** 24 hours a day.
　　　　　　　　　　전치사구　　　　　　　operate
실험실에 있는 각각의 보안 카메라는 24시간 작동한다.

Each security camera (installed in the laboratories) **operates** 24 hours a day. (Unit 11 분사 참고)
　　　　　　　　　　분사구

Each security camera (that was installed in the laboratories) **operates** 24 hours a day. (Unit 13 관계사 참고)
　　　　　　　　　　관계대명사절

■ 주의해야 할 주어

❶ 고유명사나 동명사(-ing)로 시작하는 주어는 단수 취급

Acer Solutions (**offers** / ~~offer~~) effective accounting programs. 에이서 솔루션즈는 효율적인 회계 프로그램을 제공한다.

Taking pictures (**is** / ~~are~~) not allowed in the museum. 박물관에서 사진 촬영은 허용되지 않는다.

❷ a number of / the number of

A number of + 복수명사　~많은	+	복수 동사
= Many　주어		

The number of + 복수명사　~의 수	+	단수 동사
주어		

A number of **suitcases** (**were** / ~~was~~) missing. 많은 여행용 가방들이 없어졌다.

The number of tourists (**has** / ~~have~~) decreased. 여행객의 수가 감소했다.

❸ 부분을 나타내는 표현

most, some, half	of the + 단수 명사	+ 단수 동사
	of the + 복수 명사	+ 복수 동사

Most of the marketing staff members (**are** / ~~is~~) on vacation. 마케팅 팀원들은 대부분이 휴가 중이다.

STEP 1

1. Tedeschi Shoes _____ a discount to students of Brinkley University.
   (A) offer
   (B) offers

2. The number of smartphone users _____ expected to increase by 30% this year.
   (A) is
   (B) are

3. Sharing design ideas with co-workers _____ you to receive feedback from them.
   (A) enable
   (B) enables

4. Discount _____ for Thursday evening's jazz concert are available in Ms. Klein's office.
   (A) ticket
   (B) tickets

STEP 2

5. Everyone involved in the Greenfield project _____ in company housing.
   (A) reside
   (B) resides
   (C) residing
   (D) have resided

6. Most of the songs on Georgia Berne's latest CD _____ very popular with teenagers.
   (A) are
   (B) is
   (C) be
   (D) have

7. A number of vehicles _____ parked illegally every night despite the city's strict regulations.
   (A) being
   (B) been
   (C) is
   (D) are

8. The _____ provided by the consultant are supposed to improve staff productivity.
   (A) suggestion
   (B) suggest
   (C) suggestions
   (D) suggesting

어휘 | **1.** offer 제공하다 **2.** be expected to do ~할 것으로 예상되다 **3.** co-worker 동료 enable A to do A가 ~하는 것을 가능하게 하다 **4.** available 이용[구입] 가능한 **5.** involved in ~에 연관된 reside 살다, 거주하다 **6.** latest 최신의 **7.** illegally 불법적으로 despite ~에도 불구하고 strict 엄격한 regulation 규정, 규제 **8.** be supposed to ~하기로 되어 있다, ~ 할 것으로 추정되다 improve 향상시키다 productivity 생산성

1　Trains for Gruyville ------- at 9:00 A.M. Monday through Friday.
(A) depart
(B) is departed
(C) departs
(D) is departing

2　Royce Glass Company's free installation offer ------- from May 1 until August 31.
(A) extends
(B) extending
(C) extensive
(D) extensively

3　The deadline to sign up for one of the job-related courses ------- February 10.
(A) is
(B) are
(C) have been
(D) are being

4　The details of this report ------- a result of the discussion at the last business meeting.
(A) was
(B) being
(C) is
(D) are

5　The office complex ------- on the outskirts of the pedestrian shopping area.
(A) will be built
(B) built
(C) are building
(D) builder

6　The ------- for the MacNeill project is hanging on the wall in the first floor conference room.
(A) schedule
(B) scheduled
(C) schedules
(D) scheduler

7　This week only, spend over $200 and your order ------- for free overnight shipping.
(A) qualification
(B) qualifies
(C) qualify
(D) qualifying

8　The documents in the filing cabinet ------- to be organized alphabetically.
(A) need
(B) needs
(C) needing
(D) to need.

9　Tax laws passed recently ------- the majority of family-owned businesses in the province.
(A) has benefited
(B) have benefited
(C) having benefited
(D) has been benefited

10　The ------- given by author Michiko Hirota was received well by the employees of Ergan, Inc.
(A) addresses
(B) addressable
(C) addressed
(D) address

Questions 11-14 refer to the following letter.

Council Member Deborah Hsu
451 Forest Place, Ground Floor
Huxton, RI 02310

Dear Council Member Hsu,

I am writing on behalf of my fellow community members to request more bicycle lanes in our town. The development of new business facilities near residential areas ------- the distance we
11.
need to commute. The opening of a bicycle shop on Holleyhill Avenue attests to the increase in bicycle usage. In fact, the *Huxton Daily* made note of ------- in an article earlier in the year.
12.

I understand that the council approved plans on September 6 for bicycle lane development on Teasdale Street and Port Avenue. I fully support these -------. -------. Please improve the safety
13. **14.**
and efficiency of our roads by adding bicycle lanes.

Thank you.

Sincerely,

Gabriel Richards

11. (A) shorten
    (B) has shortened
    (C) shortening
    (D) to shorten

12. (A) this
    (B) which
    (C) few
    (D) them

13. (A) companies
    (B) groups
    (C) measures
    (D) factories

14. (A) In fact, more bicycle safety courses should be provided.
    (B) In addition, new bicycle shops have been opened.
    (C) In other words, riding a bicycle is good exercise.
    (D) Indeed, I feel that more bicycle lanes should follow.

Unit | 08 시제

① 현재/과거/미래 시제

과거 시점에 일어난 일은
과거 시제로 표현해요.

> They got
> married
> 35 years ago.

■ 현재 시제: 동사원형 또는 <동사원형+-(e)s>

현재의 상태, 반복되는 사건이나 습관, 일반적인 사실 등을 표현해요.

현재 시제와 함께 쓰는 말

always 항상	often/frequently 자주	usually 보통
sometimes 가끔	every week[month] 매주[매달]	regularly/periodically 정기적으로

We **hire** additional staff **every year**. 우리는 매년 직원을 추가로 채용한다.

■ 과거 시제: 동사원형+-(e)d

특정한 과거 시점에 일어난 일이나 과거의 상태를 표현해요.

과거 시제와 함께 쓰는 말

yesterday 어제	last week[month] 지난주[달]	previously 이전에
in+(과거) 연도 ~년에	시간 표현+ago ~ 전에	recently 최근에

Ms. Spencer **worked** for a bank **in 2010**. 스펜서 씨는 2010년에 은행에서 일했다.

Our sales **increased** by 10 percent **last year**. 우리의 매출은 지난해 10퍼센트 증가했다.

■ 미래 시제: will/be going to+동사원형

미래의 일에 대한 추측이나 의지를 표현해요.

미래 시제와 함께 쓰는 말

tomorrow 내일	next week[month] 다음 주[달]	this coming Monday 다가오는 월요일에
soon/shortly 곧	in the near future 가까운 미래에	as of/effective+미래 시점 ~부터

There **will be** a special event **tomorrow**. 내일 특별 행사가 있을 것이다.

Mr. Cohen **will resign** as president **next month**. 코헨 씨는 다음 달 사장직에서 물러날 것이다.

STEP 1

1. Mr. Kang _____ his printing business 25 years ago in Busan, South Korea.
(A) will start
(B) started

2. Zellacor Software, Inc., frequently _____ information technology specialists.
(A) hires
(B) hiring

3. The company dinner party _____ held this coming Saturday at Royal Hotel.
(A) will be
(B) has been

4. The award _____ to Hiroshi Suzuki at last night's dinner.
(A) was presented
(B) has presented

STEP 2

5. Businesses on Ellory Avenue _____ early yesterday to allow work crews to repave the street.
(A) are closed
(B) to close
(C) closing
(D) closed

6. The current system _____ users to access their online banking accounts by entering a password.
(A) allowed
(B) allow
(C) allows
(D) allowing

7. A new ordering process for all Engbert Appliance products _____ into effect as of next month.
(A) will come
(B) come
(C) came
(D) has come

8. Last year, the Hansford Automobile catalog _____ air-conditioning as a standard feature in all automobiles.
(A) listed
(B) list
(C) listing
(D) to list

어휘 │ **2.** technology 기술 specialist 전문가 hire 고용하다 **3.** be held 열리다 **4.** award 상 present 주다 **5.** work crew 작업반 repave (도로를) 재포장하다 **6.** access 접속하다 account 계좌 allow A to do A가 ~하는 것을 허락하다 **7.** process 절차, 과정 come into effect 시행되다 **8.** automobile 자동차 air-conditioning 에어컨 장치 feature 특징, 기능 list 리스트[목록]에 언급하다[포함시키다]

② 진행 시제

어떤 시점에 진행 중인 동작이나 사건은 진행 시제로 표현해요.

He is eating now.

■ 현재진행: am / is / are + -ing

'~하는 중이다'라고 해석되며 현재 시점에 진행 중인 일을 나타내요. 또한 미래를 의미하는 부사와 함께 쓰여서 가까운 미래에 예정된 일을 표현할 수도 있어요.

> 현재진행 시제와 함께 쓰는 말
>
> (right) now 지금   at the moment 지금   currently / presently 현재

The store clerk **is talking** with a customer **now**.   가게 점원은 지금 고객과 이야기하고 있다.

The board meeting **is starting** **soon**.   이사회가 곧 시작된다. (가까운 미래)

■ 과거진행: was / were + -ing

과거 특정 시점에 진행 중이던 동작이나 사건을 나타내요.

They **were discussing** the matter **at 9 last night**.   그들은 어젯밤 9시에 그 문제를 논의하고 있었다.

When I went in his office, he **was writing** an e-mail.   내가 그의 사무실에 갔을 때 그는 이메일을 쓰고 있었다.

■ 미래진행: will be + -ing

미래 특정 시점에 진행되고 있을 사건이나 동작을 나타내요.

I **will be staying** in New York **next week**.   나는 다음 주에 뉴욕에 머무르고 있을 것이다.

The technician **will be fixing** the heaters **this afternoon**.   그 기술자는 오늘 오후에 난방기들을 수리하고 있을 것이다.

T **실전 도움닫기** | 다음 문장의 빈칸에 들어갈 알맞은 말을 고르세요.   정답과 해설 p. 132

STEP 1

1. Due to overbooking, some Telco Bus passengers _____ now waiting over five hours.
(A) are
(B) were

2. Pohang residents will _____ to elect their new mayor this time next week.
(A) be voting
(B) voted

3. Ms. Yoon _____ from jet lag when she returned on Thursday.
(A) will suffer
(B) was suffering

4. The visitors _____ touring our production facilities at 10 A.M. tomorrow morning.
(A) were
(B) will be

STEP 2

5. A service engineer from PX Copytime _____ the broken copy machine at the moment.
(A) repair
(B) repairs
(C) will repair
(D) is repairing

6. The Brew Beverage Company _____ free samples in grocery stores next week.
(A) providing
(B) has been providing
(C) was providing
(D) will be providing

7. When Paxton Enterprises _____ its textile division, several middle managers were laid off.
(A) were restructured
(B) restructures
(C) was restructuring
(D) to restructure

8. Mornesse Hardware _____ free flashlights to the first 50 customers next Friday.
(A) is offering
(B) having offered
(C) was offered
(D) to offer

어휘 | **1.** due to ~ 때문에 overbooking 초과 예약 **2.** elect 선출하다 mayor 시장 vote 투표하다 **3.** jet lag 시차 return 되돌아오다 suffer (고통 등을) 겪다 **4.** visitor 방문객 production 생산 facilities 시설 **5.** broken 고장난 repair 수리하다 **6.** beverage 음료 sample 시음[시식] provide 제공하다 **7.** textile 직물, 피륙 restructure 구조 조정하다, 개혁하다 **8.** free 무료의 flashlight 손전등

RC
PART 5&6

Unit 08 시제 **181**

③ 완료 시제

> 과거의 어떤 시점을 기준으로
> 더 이전에 발생한 일은
> 과거완료 시제로 표현해요.

The train had left before she arrived.

■ 현재완료: have/has+p.p.

과거에 발생한 일이나 상태가 현재까지 계속되거나 영향을 미치고 있음을 나타내요. '~했다, ~해오고 있다, ~해본 적 있다' 등으로 해석됩니다.

┌─ 현재완료 시제와 함께 쓰는 말 ─────────────────────────────────┐
│ recently/lately 최근에   for+기간 ~ 동안   │
│ since+과거 시점 ~ 이래로   over[for/in] the last[past]+기간 지난 ~에 걸쳐[동안] │
└──┘

The business **has grown** significantly **since 2012**. 2012년 이후로 사업이 상당히 성장했다.

They **have worked** together **for the last two years**. 그들은 지난 2년 동안 함께 일했다.

> | 기본기 다지기 | 명확한 과거 시점과 함께 쓸 수 없는 현재완료 시제
> 현재완료 동사는 명확한 과거 시점을 나타내는 last+시점, ago, yesterday 등과 함께 쓸 수 없어요.
> The plant (**stopped** / ~~has stopped~~) operating **last week**. 공장은 지난주에 가동을 멈췄다.

■ 과거완료: had p.p.

과거의 어떤 시점을 기준으로 그보다 더 이전 과거에 일어난 일을 나타내요.

┌─ 과거완료 시제와 함께 쓰는 말 ─────────────────────────────────┐
│ before+주어+과거 동사 ~하기 전에   by the time+주어+과거 동사 ~ 했을 때 즈음에 │
└──┘

Many fans **had arrived** at the concert **before** the performance **started**.
공연이 시작하기 전에 많은 팬들이 콘서트장에 도착해 있었다.

■ 미래완료: will have p.p.

과거나 현재에 시작된 일이 미래까지 계속되거나 미래의 특정 시점에 완료될 것임을 나타내요.

┌─ 미래완료 시제와 함께 쓰는 말 ─────────────────────────────────┐
│ by the time+주어+현재 동사 ~ 할 때 즈음에   by+시점 ~ 까지   │
└──┘

I **will have left** the office **by the time** you **come**. 당신이 올 때 즈음에 나는 이미 퇴근하고 없을 것이다.

실전 도움닫기 | 다음 문장의 빈칸에 들어갈 알맞은 말을 고르세요. 정답과 해설 p. 132

STEP 1

1. Working conditions _____ greatly since the new CEO joined Loopa Investments.
(A) improved
(B) have improved

2. The two companies _____ an agreement on a merger plan one month ago.
(A) reached
(B) have reached

3. Mr. Imola's net profit rate _____ slightly risen for the last three quarters.
(A) has
(B) was

4. Several Tiger Gym health clubs _____ recently in the city center.
(A) have opened
(B) will have opened

STEP 2

5. More university students _____ in internships in the last five years than ever before.
(A) were participated
(B) have participated
(C) participating
(D) will participate

6. The 10:17 A.M. train _____ already left before Mr. Abaki's team arrived at the station.
(A) has
(B) had
(C) is
(D) will have

7. We _____ ten inquiries since the advertisement ran in last week's edition of the newspaper.
(A) receive
(B) have received
(C) will receive
(D) receiving

8. By the time Ms. Valspar retires, she _____ to increase the company's market share significantly.
(A) manages
(B) will have managed
(C) managed
(D) has been managing

어휘 | **1.** working conditions 근무 환경 greatly 대단히 **2.** agreement 합의, 계약서 merger 합병 **3.** net profit rate 순수익률 slightly 약간 quarter 사분기 **4.** city center 도심부 **5.** internship 인턴 프로그램 than ever before 과거 어느 때보다 participate in ~에 참가하다, 참여하다(= take part in) **6.** leave 떠나다 arrive 도착하다 station 역 **7.** inquiry 문의, 조회 advertisement 광고 **8.** retire 은퇴하다 market share 시장 점유율 significantly 상당히

1 Maggie Williams, the purchasing manager, currently ------- requested supplies at the end of each week.
(A) ordered
(B) orders
(C) order
(D) ordering

2 At the next staff meeting, Yoshihiro Miura ------- the most promising products under development.
(A) will discuss
(B) had discussed
(C) discussing
(D) to discuss

3 According to the Harton Fashion Chronicle, many designers ------ green and brown fabrics for their autumn collections this year.
(A) to use
(B) are using
(C) had been used
(D) were used

4 Polansky Data International ------- transportation for all employees attending the digital media conference in Liverpool next week.
(A) has arranged
(B) was arranged
(C) arranging
(D) arrangements

5 Dr. Suzuki arrived for the awards ceremony on time even though her train ------ twenty minutes late.
(A) is leaving
(B) will leave
(C) to leave
(D) had left

6 By the time the magazine article on home security devices ------ on the newsstands, the pricing information was already outdated.
(A) appears
(B) appeared
(C) will appear
(D) appearing

7 Real estate agents in Stranton anticipate that property values ------- in the coming year.
(A) increasingly
(B) increasing
(C) will increase
(D) to increase

8 The Salisbury Nature Club's treasurer ------ and suggested revisions to the budget for the next financial quarter.
(A) is examining
(B) has examined
(C) will examine
(D) to examine

9 Rachmann Industries disclosed that it will ------- be prepared to expand its manufacturing facilities in Helsinki.
(A) once
(B) recently
(C) soon
(D) newly

10 Because of a sudden decrease in sales, Mikkelsen Clothing suspended its current advertising campaign and ------- it substantially.
(A) to modify
(B) will be modifying
(C) having modified
(D) modifying

Questions 11-14 refer to the following e-mail.

To: kjackson@oldcornerjewelry.co.uk
From: mgmt@haverstrawwatches.ch
Subject: Order #445A2
Date: 1 February

Dear Mr. Jackson,

Please accept my apologies for not getting back to you sooner. I ------- to determine what
                11.

happened to your order. -------, it took the shipper two days to return my phone call. I was
           12.

informed that the delay was caused by a heavy snowstorm on the shipping route. As a result,

your two dozen watches should be ------- by 10 February. -------. Nevertheless, I'm certain your
         13.   **14.**

customers will appreciate the reliability and elegance of Haverstraw watches. Thank you for your

business and your patience.

Sincerely,

Julian Haverstraw

---

11. (A) am going to try
    (B) might try
    (C) am trying
    (D) have been trying

12. (A) Supposedly
    (B) Unfortunately
    (C) In the meantime
    (D) On the other hand

13. (A) sold
    (B) repaired
    (C) delivered
    (D) manufactured

14. (A) Again, I apologize for the delay.
    (B) Our Web page lists all of the features.
    (C) Snowstorms are common this time of
        year.
    (D) We will be relocating our headquarters
        soon.

Unit | 09 능동태와 수동태

① 수동태의 개념과 형태

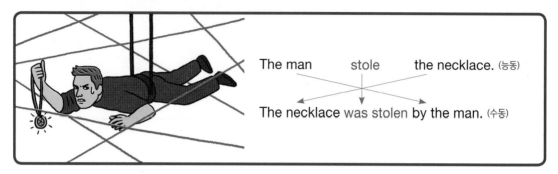

The man   stole   the necklace. (능동)

The necklace was stolen by the man. (수동)

■ 능동태와 수동태의 개념

영어는 주어가 어떤 행위를 직접 행하는 능동태와, 주어가 다른 대상으로부터 어떤 행위를 당하는 수동태로 구분할 수 있어요. 능동태는 '~하다'로, 수동태는 '~해지다, ~하게 되다'로 해석됩니다.

■ 수동태의 형태

기본 형태는 <be동사＋p.p.(과거분사)>입니다. 여기서 주어의 수와 시제에 따라 be동사의 형태가 달라져요.

현재 과거 미래	be＋p.p.	am/are/is＋p.p. was/were＋p.p. will be＋p.p.	The letter **is sent** by mail. 편지는 우편으로 전달된다. The letter **was sent** by mail. 편지는 우편으로 전달되었다. The letter **will be sent** by mail. 편지는 우편으로 전달될 것이다.
현재진행 과거진행 미래진행	be being ＋p.p.	am/are/is＋being＋p.p. was/were＋being＋p.p. will be＋being＋p.p.	All computers **are being repaired**. 모든 컴퓨터가 수리되고 있다. All computers **were being repaired**. 모든 컴퓨터가 수리되고 있었다. All computers **will be being repaired**. 모든 컴퓨터가 수리되고 있을 것이다.
현재완료 과거완료 미래완료	have been ＋p.p.	have/has＋been＋p.p. had＋been＋p.p. will have＋been＋p.p.	The plan **has been changed**. 계획이 변경되었다. The plan **had been changed**. 계획이 변경되어 있었다. The plan **will have been changed**. 계획이 변경되어 있을 것이다.

■ 수동태 문장의 형성

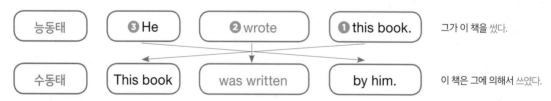

| 능동태 | ❸ He | ❷ wrote | ❶ this book. | 그가 이 책을 썼다. |

| 수동태 | This book | was written | by him. | 이 책은 그에 의해서 쓰였다. |

❶ 능동태의 목적어 this book이 주어 자리로 옵니다.

❷ 수동태 동사의 형태 <be＋p.p.>가 되도록 동사 wrote를 주어의 수와 시제에 맞게 was written으로 바꿔요.

❸ 능동태의 주어 He는 <by＋목적격>인 by him으로 바꿔요. 단, 이 부분은 생략 가능합니다.

➡ 능동태 문장의 목적어를 주어로 해서 만든 문장이 수동태이므로 목적어를 갖는 타동사만이 수동태가 될 수 있어요. 즉 뒤에 목적어가 오지 않는 rise와 같은 자동사는 수동태로 쓰이지 않아요.

STEP 1

1. Candidates for the position must _____ their applications by the end of the month.
(A) submit
(B) be submitted

2. A list of engineers nominated for a design award is _____ to this e-mail.
(A) attaching
(B) attached

3. The requested information should be _____ carefully in the space provided.
(A) writing
(B) written

4. The seminar will be attended _____ professionals in the food service industry.
(A) of
(B) by

STEP 2

5. Due to the airline strike, Mr. Jarvela _____ his plans to travel to Rome.
(A) postponing
(B) to postpone
(C) should be postponed
(D) had to postpone

6. Our quality control department tests all products before they are _____ to retailers.
(A) shipped
(B) shipment
(C) ships
(D) shipping

7. The report on the city's train system _____ to the public last Tuesday.
(A) to release
(B) have released
(C) is releasing
(D) was released

8. An updated list of job opportunities _____ on Island Hopper's Web page.
(A) is posted
(B) posting
(C) are posting
(D) post

어휘 | **1.** candidate 지원자, 후보자 application 지원서 **2.** nominate (후보로) 지명하다 award 상 attach 첨부하다 **3.** requested 요청된 carefully 신중하게 provided 제공된 **4.** professional 전문가 food service industry 외식산업 **5.** strike 파업 postpone 미루다 **6.** quality control 품질 검사 retailer 소매업자 ship 배송하다 **7.** public 일반인들, 대중 release 공개하다 **8.** opportunity 기회 post 게시하다

② 능동태와 수동태 구별하기

전치사와 함께 쓰이는 수동태 구문

He is equipped with arms.

■ 능동태와 수동태 구별하기

동사 자리가 능동태인지 수동태인지는 동사 뒤의 목적어 유무에 따라 결정돼요. 동사 자리 뒤에 목적어가 있으면 능동태, 동사 자리 뒤에 목적어가 없으면 수동태가 됩니다.

❶ 능동태: 빈칸 뒤에 한정사(관사, 소유격, 수량 형용사 등)가 있다면 그 뒤에 명사인 목적어가 있음을 알 수 있어요.

A famous architect (**built** / ~~was built~~) **the museum**.
유명한 건축가가 그 박물관을 건립했다.

Ablexar Co. (**is building** / ~~is being built~~) **its new plant**.
애블렉서 사는 새로운 공장을 짓고 있다.

❷ 수동태: 빈칸 뒤에 전치사나 부사가 왔거나 또는 문장이 빈칸으로 끝났다면 목적어가 없는 수동태 자리일 확률이 높아요.

Conference room B (**is being prepared** / ~~is preparing~~) **by Ms. Yoon**.
B회의실이 윤 씨에 의해 준비되고 있다.

The sales presentation (**will be prepared** / ~~will prepare~~) **soon**.
곧 영업 발표가 준비될 것이다.

■ 수동태+전치사 구문

in	be engaged in ~에 종사하다	be interested in ~에 관심이 있다	be involved in ~에 관련되다
to	be committed to ~에 전념하다 = be dedicated[devoted] to	be accustomed to ~에 익숙하다 = be used to	be exposed to ~에 노출되다 be related to ~와 관계가 있다
with	be satisfied with ~에 만족하다 be pleased with ~에 기뻐하다	be concerned with ~에 관련되다 be associated with ~와 관련되다	be equipped with ~을 갖추고 있다 be crowded with ~로 붐비다

Many people are interested in the seminar. 많은 사람들이 세미나에 관심이 있다.

The DX printer is equipped with a scanner. DX 프린터는 스캐너를 갖추고 있다.

Professor Lee is <u>committed</u> to teaching students. 이 교수는 학생들을 가르치는 일에 전념한다.
 = dedicated, devoted

STEP 1

1. The company handbook _____ the topics of compensation, bonuses, and overtime.
   (A) is covered
   (B) covers

2. The best trailer for small boats _____ by Tow-Well Manufacturing.
   (A) is made
   (B) is making

3. Better marketing strategies can always _____.
   (A) are developing
   (B) be developed

4. Both the designers and photographers are satisfied _____ the fall catalog.
   (A) for
   (B) with

STEP 2

5. Mr. Ling is _____ a revised schedule to the show's host as well as to the guest speakers.
   (A) distribute
   (B) distributing
   (C) distributes
   (D) distributed

6. A large number of team members are interested _____ the upcoming workshop.
   (A) in
   (B) of
   (C) to
   (D) for

7. Both the model number and the serial number _____ on the back of every watch.
   (A) were engraving
   (B) are engraved
   (C) to be engraved
   (D) engrave

8. Many problems with locks _____ by a simple repair or adjustment.
   (A) solved
   (B) could solve
   (C) can solve
   (D) can be solved

어휘 | **1.** compensation 보상, 보수 cover 다루다 **3.** strategy 전략 develop 개발하다 **5.** revised 수정된 as well as ~뿐만 아니라 distribute 나눠 주다, 분배하다 **6.** a number of 많은 upcoming 다가오는 **7.** serial number 일련 번호 engrave 새기다 **8.** lock 자물쇠 repair 수리; 수리하다 adjustment 조절, 조정

ETS 실전문제

1 Dave Minsent, a lawyer from Alsager, was
  ------- to serve on the town council.
  (A) election
  (B) electoral
  (C) elect
  (D) elected

2 The Silvau Division is now ------ a full line of
  steel products at a new modern facility just
  outside the city.
  (A) manufacturer
  (B) being manufactured
  (C) manufactured
  (D) manufacturing

3 All passengers ------- to stay seated while
  the bus is in motion.
  (A) can require
  (B) are required
  (C) are requiring
  (D) have required

4 Jae Kwon's collection of photographs
  ------- the subtle changes of light across the
  mountain landscape.
  (A) exposes
  (B) expose
  (C) is exposed
  (D) are exposing

5 The newly renovated laboratory is equipped
  ------- state-of-the-art research equipment
  and security cameras.
  (A) by
  (B) with
  (C) in
  (D) to

6 The technical manuals for the True Photo
  Printer ------ into Spanish by contractors
  from A-Language, Inc.
  (A) translation
  (B) were translated
  (C) translator
  (D) are translating

7 Graymont Grocery Store issues coupons
  that can be ------- for a variety of goods.
  (A) redeem
  (B) redeems
  (C) redeemed
  (D) redeeming

8 The various measures used to determine
  annual salary increases ------- to as the merit
  criteria.
  (A) are referred
  (B) referring
  (C) have referred
  (D) to refer

9 The winter agenda of the company's
  community service club ------- later this
  afternoon.
  (A) circulated
  (B) has circulated
  (C) has been circulating
  (D) will be circulated

10 Any requests to take a leave of absence
  must be ------- to a department supervisor at
  least two weeks in advance.
  (A) submitted
  (B) submit
  (C) submission
  (D) submitting

Questions 11-14 refer to the following guidelines.

The *Opalwood Tribune* welcomes letters from readers. Because space is limited, we cannot print

------- submissions we receive. We give priority to letters that provide a new perspective on issues
  11.

of local interest, particularly if the issue ------- in a recent article. We also prefer letters that do not
                 12.

exceed 200 words. -------.
       13.

Please be sure to include your name and contact information so the editors can notify you if your

letter is ------- for publication.
    14.

11. (A) any
    (B) total
    (C) all
    (D) original

12. (A) mentioned
    (B) has mentioned
    (C) being mentioned
    (D) was mentioned

13. (A) Therefore, we do not publish anonymous letters.
    (B) Submissions that are longer than that may be edited.
    (C) The use of such words is not allowed in our publication.
    (D) Please do not write us more frequently than this.

14. (A) selected
    (B) completed
    (C) opened
    (D) continued

to부정사와 동명사

① to부정사의 형태와 역할

to부정사는 문장에서
명사, 형용사, 부사 역할을 해요.

She studied
hard
to get a job.

■ to부정사의 형태

to부정사는 <to + 동사원형>의 형태로 대표적인 준동사 중 하나입니다. 준동사란 동사에서 비롯되었으나 동사가 아닌 다른 품사(명사, 형용사, 부사)로 쓰이는 것들을 말해요. to부정사, 동명사, 분사가 이에 해당되는데 동사처럼 부사의 꾸밈을 받을 수 있고, 목적어를 취할 수도 있어요.

Delemarke's profits are expected **to rise** <u>steadily</u>.   델레마케 사의 수익이 꾸준히 상승할 것으로 예상된다.
부사

The producers will meet **to arrange** <u>the schedule</u>.   제작자들이 일정을 짜기 위해 모일 것이다.
목적어

■ to부정사의 역할

to부정사는 문장에서 명사, 형용사, 부사의 역할을 해요.

❶ **명사 역할(~하는 것, ~하기):** 명사처럼 문장의 주어, 목적어, 보어 자리에 올 수 있어요.

주어   **To meet the deadline** is necessary.   반드시 마감일을 맞춰야 한다.

= **It** is necessary **to meet the deadline**.

→ 주어가 너무 길면 뒤로 보내고 그 자리에 가주어 it을 써요.

It is necessary **for him** to meet the deadline.   그는 반드시 마감일을 맞춰야 한다.

→ to부정사의 의미상 주어가 문장의 주어와 일치하지 않을 경우, <for + 목적격>의 형태로 표시해요.

목적어   The film producers **decided** to delay the release date.   영화 제작자들은 개봉일을 늦추기로 결정했다.

보어   Our goal **is** to develop cutting-edge technology.   우리의 목표는 최신 기술을 개발하는 것입니다.

❷ **형용사 역할(~할, ~하는):** 명사의 뒤에 위치해 앞에 나온 명사를 수식하는 형용사 역할을 할 수 있어요.

The government announced **a plan** to reduce traffic congestion.   정부는 교통 혼잡을 줄이기 위한 계획을 발표했다.

❸ **부사 역할(~하기 위하여):** 문장에서 목적을 나타내요.

The conference location was changed to accommodate 150 participants.
= in order to accommodate

150명의 참가자들을 수용하기 위해 회의 장소가 변경되었다.

STEP 1

1. The management team decided _____ the project because of budget constraints.
(A) cancel
(B) to cancel

2. One of your tasks as a computer programmer is _____ our Web site.
(A) update
(B) to update

3. Ms. Dodson has so many assignments _____ complete that she cannot take a day off.
(A) for
(B) to

4. _____ fine furniture, Mr. Taylor uses special wood that is not available in stores.
(A) To build
(B) To building

STEP 2

5. Rings on display in the jewelry case can be sized _____ fit any finger.
(A) to
(B) will
(C) so
(D) upon

6. To _____ clinic volunteers, Laradore Hospital administrators will provide refreshments.
(A) thankful
(B) thanks
(C) thanking
(D) thank

7. In order to _____ properly, this machine must be serviced at regular intervals.
(A) functions
(B) functional
(C) functioning
(D) function

8. _____ is possible for a robot to carry out several tasks at the same time.
(A) It
(B) This
(C) That
(D) There

어휘 | **1.** decide 결정하다 budget 예산 constraint 제약 **2.** task 업무 **3.** assignment 업무 complete 완료하다 take a day off 하루 쉬다 **4.** fine 질 좋은 **5.** size 치수를 바꾸다 fit 맞다 **6.** volunteer 자원봉사자 administrator 관계자, 관리자 refreshments 다과 **7.** properly 적절하게 service 정비하다 interval 간격 function 기능을 하다; 기능 **8.** possible 가능한 carry out 수행하다 at the same time 동시에

② 자주 출제되는 to부정사 표현

어떤 동사는 to부정사를 목적어로 취해요.

need
I want **to buy** a ring.
plan

■ 동사 + to부정사

want to부정사 ~하고 싶다
would like to부정사 ~하고 싶다
plan to부정사 ~할 계획이다
agree to부정사 ~하는 데 동의하다

decide to부정사 ~하기로 결정하다
need to부정사 ~해야 한다
expect to부정사 ~하기를 기대하다
fail to부정사 ~하지 못하다

tend to부정사 ~하는 경향이 있다
hope to부정사 ~하기를 바라다
try to부정사 ~하려고 노력하다
(= strive to부정사)

The personnel department **plans** to hold a retirement party. 인사과는 퇴직 기념 파티를 열 계획이다.

The local government **agreed** to protect the forest. 지방 정부는 숲을 보호하는 데 동의했다.

■ 명사 + to부정사

ability to부정사 ~할 능력
right to부정사 ~할 권리
way to부정사 ~할 방법

time to부정사 ~할 시간
chance to부정사 ~할 기회
opportunity to부정사 ~할 기회

effort to부정사 ~하려는 노력
failure to부정사 ~하지 못함
plan to부정사 ~할 계획

Moss & Co. is seeking a **way** to maximize profits. Moss & Co 사는 수익을 극대화할 방안을 모색하고 있다.

■ be동사 + 형용사 / 분사 + to부정사

be ready to부정사 ~할 준비가 되다
be allowed to부정사 ~하는 것이 허락되다
be able to부정사 ~할 수 있다
be expected to부정사 ~하리라 예상된다, ~할 것이다
be willing to부정사 기꺼이 ~하다
be asked to부정사 ~하도록 요청 받다

be pleased to부정사 ~하게 되어 기쁘다
be advised to부정사 ~하도록 권고 받다
be likely to부정사 ~할 것 같다
be designed to부정사 ~하도록 고안되다
be scheduled to부정사 ~할 예정이다
be required to부정사 ~하는 것이 필수적이다

We **were able** to find a replacement for Lydia Parry. 우리는 리디아 패리의 후임을 구할 수 있었다.

His flight **is expected** to arrive late. 그의 비행편이 늦게 도착할 것으로 예상된다.

STEP 1

1. Ms. Adrina hopes to _____ the deadline to finish her financial report.
   (A) extend
   (B) extending

2. Teachers are _____ to arrive early on Monday in order to meet the new students.
   (A) expectations
   (B) expected

3. Duncan Enterprise plans _____ its first store in Manila this year.
   (A) to open
   (B) opened

4. We are pleased _____ subscribers' letters on matters of interest to our readers.
   (A) to publish
   (B) publishing

STEP 2

5. We at TPG Financial Planning welcome the opportunity _____ you in your business.
   (A) assisting
   (B) to assist
   (C) assisted
   (D) assistant

6. National Bank officials have taken the necessary steps _____ another computer system failure.
   (A) prevented
   (B) to prevent
   (C) prevent
   (D) were prevented

7. The City Chorus is scheduled _____ at the dedication of the new library building.
   (A) is performing
   (B) will perform
   (C) to perform
   (D) performance

8. The board of Lee & Zhang, Inc. has concluded that it is time _____ the computer network.
   (A) upgrades
   (B) will upgrade
   (C) to upgrade
   (D) upgrading

어휘 | **1.** deadline 마감일 financial 재정의 extend 연장하다 **2.** expectation 기대, 예상 **4.** subscriber 구독자 matter of interest 관심사 publish 출판하다 **5.** welcome 환영하다 opportunity 기회 assist 돕다 **6.** official 공무원, 임원 take steps 조치를 취하다 failure 고장, 장애 prevent 막다, 방지하다 **7.** dedication 헌신; 개관식 perform 공연하다 **8.** board 이사회 conclude 결론 내리다

③ 동명사의 개념과 명사와의 차이점

어떤 동사는 동명사를 목적어로 취해요.

enjoy
I recommend **playing** golf.
suggest

■ 동명사의 개념과 역할

<동사원형+-ing>의 형태로 동사의 성격이 있지만 동사가 아니라 명사로 쓰이는 단어를 동명사라고 합니다. 명사처럼 문장에서 주어, 보어, 목적어 역할을 합니다.

주어 　 Boosting sales volume **is** our goal for this quarter. 　판매량을 올리는 것이 이번 분기 우리의 목표다.

보어 　 Our main concern **is** promoting our brand image. 　우리의 주 관심사는 브랜드 이미지를 제고하는 것이다.

목적어 　 The renovation project **includes** replacing floor tiles. 　수리 계획은 바닥 타일 교체하는 것을 포함한다.

┌─ **동명사를 목적어로 취하는 동사** ─────────────────────────────────

enjoy 즐기다 　　　 finish 마치다 　　　 postpone[delay] 미루다 　　 consider 고려하다 　　 recommend 추천하다

suggest 제안하다 　　 include 포함하다 　　 keep 계속하다 　　　　 avoid 피하다 　　　 give up 포기하다

■ 동명사와 명사의 차이

동사에서 파생된 동명사는 명사와 달리 뒤에 목적어를 취할 수 있고, 부사의 수식을 받을 수도 있어요. 전치사 뒤 목적어 자리 빈칸에는 명사 역할을 하는 단어(명사, 대명사, 동명사 등)가 들어가야 하는데, 빈칸 뒤에 명사가 있다면 그 빈칸은 동명사 자리가 될 수 있어요.

Wilson Fashion is famous for (**skillfully** / ~~skillful~~) making leather belts.
윌슨 패션은 가죽 벨트를 솜씨 있게 제작하는 것으로 유명하다.

This report is **about (improving** / ~~improvement~~) productivity. 　이 보고서는 생산성을 높이는 것에 관한 것이다.

→ 전치사와 명사 사이 빈칸은 동명사 자리일 확률이 높아요.

■ 동명사 관용 표현

spend 시간[돈] -ing ~하는 데 시간[돈]을 쓰다	in addition to (동)명사 ~뿐만 아니라
have trouble/difficulty -ing ~하는 데 어려움을 겪다	contribute to (동)명사 ~에 기여하다
be busy -ing ~하느라 바쁘다	look forward to (동)명사 ~을 기대하다
by -ing ~함으로써	be opposed to (동)명사 ~에 반대하다
on/upon -ing ~하자마자	be committed to (동)명사 ~에 헌신하다
play a role in -ing ~하는 데 역할을 하다	be subject to (동)명사 ~되기 쉽다

We are **looking forward to (meeting** / ~~meet~~) you soon. 　곧 당신을 만나기를 기대합니다.

STEP 1

1. To avoid _____ a late fee, you have to return the books by the due date.
(A) paying
(B) pay

2. _____ yourself to the audience is the first step of your presentation.
(A) Introduction
(B) Introducing

3. _____ arriving at the airport, take the free shuttle bus to the Hotel Marois.
(A) On
(B) From

4. The dieticians recommend _____ a well-balanced and healthy breakfast daily.
(A) eating
(B) eat

STEP 2

5. Personnel must sign the register before _____ any confidential papers from vaults.
(A) removed
(B) remover
(C) removal
(D) removing

6. Maga Electronics, Inc., spent over a million dollars _____ new mobile phones last year.
(A) develop
(B) developing
(C) is developed
(D) developed

7. Senior management has considered _____ a ban on the personal use of work computers.
(A) institute
(B) instituted
(C) institution
(D) instituting

8. Playo Construction plays a critical role _____ helping our company achieve its goals on every project.
(A) since
(B) though
(C) much
(D) in

어휘 | **1.** avoid 피하다 late fee 연체료 due date 마감일, 기일 **2.** audience 청중 **4.** dietician 영양사 well-balanced 균형 잡힌 healthy 건강한 daily 매일 **5.** personnel 직원 register 기록부 confidential 기밀의 vault 보관실, 금고 **6.** mobile phone 휴대폰 develop 개발하다 **7.** senior management 고위 경영진 ban 금지 personal 개인적인, 사적인 institute 제정하다, 설립하다, 실시하다; 협회 institution 제정, 설립, 기관 **8.** construction 건설, 공사 achieve 성취하다

1 The business consultant suggests ------- the
merger plan carefully before negotiations
begin.
(A) review
(B) reviews
(C) reviewing
(D) reviewed

2 ------- additional audio books is part of
the head librarian's plan to modernize the
library's collections.
(A) Purchases
(B) Purchasing
(C) Has purchased
(D) Will be purchasing

3 We at the Ribeiro Agency strive ------- all
communication with our clients clear and to
the point.
(A) to make
(B) making
(C) to be made
(D) having made

4 All employees of Future Styles Co. are
looking forward to ------- their new designers.
(A) meet
(B) met
(C) meeting
(D) have met

5 The entire sales team must meet the
annual target ------- qualify for performance
bonuses.
(A) in order to
(B) instead of
(C) even if
(D) so that

6 The publisher's goal is ------- the daily
circulation figure of 80,000 by next year.
(A) to surpass
(B) surpassed
(C) surpass
(D) surpassing

7 Mr. Jung will present the results of the
marketing study to the president after he has
had a chance ------- them.
(A) to review
(B) reviewer
(C) reviewed
(D) is reviewing

8 If you wish to pay for this computer
workshop by ------- your credit card, please
contact Linda Wagner at 555-4236.
(A) used
(B) using
(C) usage
(D) usable

9 It is important for companies -------
professional development opportunities in
order to retain qualified staff.
(A) offering
(B) offer
(C) to offer
(D) offered

10 Mercox Cosmetics hopes ------- its number
one ranking in consumer growth by
expanding its market.
(A) to defend
(B) defense
(C) defending
(D) defended

Questions 11-14 refer to the following information.

Rowes Atlantic Airways Baggage Policy

Each passenger ------- to carry one piece of hand baggage onto the plane without charge. The
      11.
carry-on item must not exceed the dimensions 56 cm x 45 cm x 25 cm, including the handle and

wheels. No carry-on bag should weigh more than 23 kg. Passengers should be ------- to lift bags
      12.
into the overhead storage bins unaided. These ------- do not apply to bags that are checked in at
      13.
the service desk.

A laptop computer bag, school backpack, or handbag may also be brought on board. -------.
      14.

---

11. (A) allowed
    (B) is allowed
    (C) allowing
    (D) had been allowed

12. (A) able
    (B) ably
    (C) abled
    (D) ability

13. (A) transfers
    (B) suggestions
    (C) duties
    (D) restrictions

14. (A) Please inquire at the service desk if it will
        be permitted on your flight.
    (B) It should be stored under the seats when
        not in use.
    (C) Thank you for becoming a member of
        the flight crew.
    (D) Therefore, they will be available for a
        small additional fee.

① 분사의 형태와 역할

분사에는 능동이나 진행을 의미하는 현재분사(-ing)와
수동이나 완료를 의미하는 과거분사(-ed)가 있어요.

a running man   fallen leaves

■ 분사의 형태와 의미

	형태	의미	예문
현재분사	동사원형+-ing	~한, ~하고 있는(능동, 진행)	falling leaves 떨어지는 잎사귀들
과거분사	동사원형+-ed	~된(수동, 완료)	fallen leaves (이미) 떨어진 잎사귀들

■ 분사의 역할

형용사처럼 명사를 수식하거나 보충하는 역할을 해요. 그리고 to부정사나 동명사와 마찬가지로 동사는 아니지만 동사의
성질이 있어서 뒤에 목적어가 올 수 있고 부사의 수식을 받을 수 있어요.

❶ 명사 앞에서 수식

All **damaged merchandise** should be returned within a week. 모든 손상된 제품은 일주일 이내에 반품되어야 한다.

❷ 명사 뒤에서 수식

Mr. Allen sent **an e-mail** accepting the job offer. 앨런 씨는 그 일자리 제안을 수락하는 이메일을 보냈다.

| 고득점 사다리 | 분사가 명사를 뒤에서 수식하는 경우 분사 뒤 목적어 유무로 능동/수동을 판단

대체로 분사 뒤에 목적어[명사]가 있으면 -ing, 뒤에 목적어가 없으면[전치사구나 부사가 있으면] -ed가 와요.

Dylan watched **a documentary** discussing Jazz. 딜런은 재즈를 다룬 다큐멘터리를 보았다.
~~discussed~~ 목적어

The records stored on the first floor are available now. 1층에 보관된 기록물들은 현재 열람할 수 있다.
~~storing~~ 전치사구

---

❸ 보어

The topic of the seminar **was** interesting. 세미나의 주제가 흥미로웠다.

Assistants should **keep** the items organized. 조수들은 물품들을 정돈되게 유지해야 한다.

→ 보어를 필요로 하는 동사는 Unit 1 문장의 구성 요소를 참고하세요.

STEP 1

1. The country's _____ exports have caused great concern among economic experts.
   (A) decrease
   (B) decreasing

2. The city's building codes have become very _____ to accommodate.
   (A) complicated
   (B) complicate

3. Any person _____ in a legal case is advised to consult a lawyer.
   (A) involving
   (B) involved

4. The discount offer is not valid on tickets _____ before publication of this advertisement.
   (A) purchased
   (B) purchases

STEP 2

5. Next week, the _____ candidates in the city council election will be on television.
   (A) distinguish
   (B) distinguished
   (C) distinguishing
   (D) distinguishes

6. Your personal digital files will remain _____ safely on our online server.
   (A) store
   (B) storage
   (C) stores
   (D) stored

7. The library contains many items _____ the history of the noted research facility.
   (A) document
   (B) documents
   (C) documentary
   (D) documenting

8. Mr. Vargas makes a point of including _____ notes in the welcome cards for new employees.
   (A) handwrite
   (B) to handwrite
   (C) handwrites
   (D) handwritten

어휘 | **1.** export 수출 cause 야기하다 concern 우려 expert 전문가 **2.** accommodate 수용하다 complicate 복잡하게 하다 legal case 소송 be advised to ~하도록 권고 받다 **4.** valid 유효한 publication 출판(물), 발표 **5.** candidate 입후보자 city council 시의회 election 선거 distinguish 구별하다 **6.** personal 개인적인, 사적인 remain ~한 상태로 있다 safely 안전하게, 무사히 stored 저장된, 축적된 **7.** contain 포함하다 noted 유명한 research facility 연구시설, 연구소 document 기록하다 **8.** make a point of -ing ~하는 것을 잊지 않다 handwrite 손으로 쓰다 handwritten 손으로 쓴

② 현재분사 vs. 과거분사

disappointing results

disappointed student

■ 현재분사

분사가 나타내는 행위를 명사가 직접 행하는 주체라면 '능동' 관계이므로 현재분사를 써요.

Online games enjoy **increasing** **popularity**. 온라인 게임은 늘어나는 인기를 누리고 있다.

The event **introducing** X-530 will be held next week. X-530을 소개하는 행사가 다음 주에 열릴 것이다.

■ 과거분사

분사가 나타내는 행위를 명사가 당하는 입장이면 '수동' 관계이므로 과거분사를 써요.

The **completed** **form** should be submitted by this Friday. 작성된 양식은 이번 주 금요일까지 제출되어야 한다.
~~completing~~

The discount offer is not valid on **tickets** **purchased** online. 온라인에서 판매된 티켓은 할인 혜택이 적용되지 않는다.
~~purchasing~~

■ 토익에 자주 출제되는 분사 표현

┌─ 현재분사 + 명사 ───

demanding task 힘든 일   missing luggage 분실 수하물   rewarding job 보람 있는 일

existing facility 기존 시설   outstanding speaker 뛰어난 연설가   upcoming festival 다가오는[곧 있을] 축제

lasting effect 지속되는 영향   remaining work 남은 일

└──

┌─ 과거분사 + 명사 ───

accomplished artist 뛰어난 예술가   designated area 지정 구역   preferred means 선호하는 수단

complicated system 복잡한 제도   detailed information 자세한 정보   experienced engineer 숙련된 기술자

damaged roads 파손된 도로   limited time 제한된 시간   proposed schedule 제안된 일정

└──

■ 감정 표현 분사

주로 감정을 유발하는 대상인 사물은 현재분사, 감정을 느끼는 사람은 과거분사와 어울려 쓰여요.

amazing 놀라게 하는	amazed 놀란	satisfying 만족시키는	satisfied 만족하는
exciting 흥분시키는	excited 신난	motivating 동기 부여하는	motivated 의욕적인
surprising 놀라게 하는	surprised 놀란	disappointing 실망시키는	disappointed 실망한
interesting 흥미롭게 하는	interested 흥미로워하는	confusing 혼란스럽게 하는	confused 혼란스러워하는
fascinating 매료시키는	fascinated 매료된	exhausting 지치게 하는	exhausted 지친

The new play received **disappointing** **reviews**. 새 연극은 실망스러운 평가를 받았다.

Passengers were **disappointed** with the poor service. 승객들은 형편없는 서비스에 실망했다.

STEP 1

1. To report lost or _____ baggage, please visit Nextrair's baggage services booth.
(A) damaged
(B) damaging

2. The government has published regulations _____ owners to provide recycling services for tenants.
(A) required
(B) requiring

3. In March, the city's orchestra will present an _____ opera by talented newcomer Maria Cruz.
(A) excited
(B) exciting

4. The sales representative is _____ in negative feedback from his customers.
(A) disappointing
(B) disappointed

STEP 2

5. Because of his experience _____ international accounts, Mr. Ito will take charge of the overseas office.
(A) supervisor
(B) supervising
(C) supervise
(D) supervised

6. Every day at Naupaka Cove Resort is filled with _____ activities.
(A) amusing
(B) amused
(C) amuse
(D) amuses

7. The plan _____ by the Ministry of Tourism to reduce unnecessary fees has been very well received.
(A) present
(B) presents
(C) presented
(D) presenting

8. The _____ edition of *Allen Business Monthly* will feature a story about changes to business models.
(A) nearest
(B) upcoming
(C) ahead
(D) forward

어휘 | **1.** lost 잃어버린 **2.** government 정부 publish 공표하다, 발행하다 regulation 규칙, 규정 tenant 세입자 require 요구하다
3. present 주다, 소개하다 talented 재능 있는 newcomer 신입 **4.** sales representative 판매사원 negative 부정적인
5. account 계정, 거래 고객 take charge of ~을 떠맡다 overseas 해외의, 해외에 supervise 감독하다 **6.** be filled with ~으로
가득하다 amusing 재미있는 amuse 즐겁게 하다 **7.** Ministry of Tourism 관광부 unnecessary 불필요한 fee 수수료, 요금
8. feature 특집으로 싣다 upcoming 다음의, 머지않아 발표할 ahead 앞서 forward 앞으로

③ 분사구문

분사구문이란 긴 부사절을 간단하게 축약해서
만든 구문을 말해요.

Reviewing the document,
Andy found an error.

■ 분사구문이란?

<접속사＋주어＋동사>로 이루어진 부사절을 분사가 포함된 형태의 부사구로 축약시킨 구문을 의미하며, 문장의 앞과 뒤에 모두 위치할 수 있어요.

■ 분사구문 만들기

① 부사절 접속사를 생략	① ~~While~~ he reviewed the contract, Andy found a significant error.
↓	↓
② 부사절의 주어가 주절의 주어와 같을 경우 부사절의 주어 생략	② ~~While he~~ reviewed the contract, Andy found a significant error.
↓	↓
③ 부사절의 동사를 분사(동사원형＋-ing)로 변경	③ ~~While he~~ <u>reviewed</u> the contract, Andy found a significant error.
	→ **Reviewing** the contract, Andy found a significant error.
	계약서를 검토하다가, 앤디는 중대한 오류를 발견했다.

| 고득점 사다리 | 정확한 의미 전달을 위해 접속사는 남겨 두기도 해요.

You must wear eye protection **when working** with tools.　도구로 작업할 때는 반드시 보안경을 착용해야 합니다.

As discussed over the phone, your order will be delivered soon.　전화로 논의된 대로, 귀하께서 주문하신 물품이 곧 도착할 겁니다.

→ <as＋p.p.>는 '~된 대로'라는 의미의 관용구로, as mentioned(언급된 대로), as stated(명시된 대로) 등도 자주 쓰여요.

■ 분사구문의 다양한 의미

시간　　**Arriving** at the hotel early, Ms. Lim had some time to prepare her speech.

　　　　= When she arrived at the hotel early, ~. 호텔에 일찍 도착하자, 임 씨는 연설을 준비할 시간이 있었다.

이유　　(**Being**) **upgraded** recently, the office computers were much faster.

　　　　= As they were upgraded recently, ~. 최근 업그레이드되어서 사무실 컴퓨터들이 훨씬 빨라졌다.

　　　　→ 수동태 분사구문에서 be동사는 being으로 바뀌는데, being은 생략될 수 있어서 p.p. 형태만 남을 수 있어요.

동시상황　**Watching** the fashion show, the audience filled out an evaluation form.

　　　　= As they watched the fashion show, ~. 패션쇼를 지켜보면서 관객들은 평가서를 작성했다.

STEP 1

1. _____ near one of the tourist attractions in the city, the hotel attracts a lot of travelers.
(A) Location
(B) Located

2. _____ the draft of the contract, Mr. Kelvin found some errors in it.
(A) Review
(B) Reviewing

3. _____ all electrical devices, the facility manager left for the day.
(A) Unplugging
(B) Unplugged

4. _____ three decades ago, the exhibition hall needs to be renovated.
(A) Constructing
(B) Constructed

STEP 2

5. _____ a leading industry report, executives have decided to increase the manufacture of truck tires.
(A) Citing
(B) Cite
(C) Cited
(D) Cites

6. _____ in plain language, the magazine on health and nutrition is easy to read.
(A) Written
(B) Writing
(C) Write
(D) Have written

7. JK Electronics, Inc., expanded into the Asian market, _____ its market share in the international market.
(A) increase
(B) being increase
(C) increasing
(D) increasingly

8. When _____ for the ZJA conference, you must provide your membership number.
(A) register
(B) registers
(C) registering
(D) was registered

어휘 | **1.** attract 끌어들이다 locate 위치시키다 **2.** draft 초안 contract 계약서 **3.** electrical device 전기 장치 leave for the day 퇴근하다 unplug 플러그를 뽑다 **4.** decade 10년 exhibition 전시 construct 건설하다 **5.** leading 주요한, 선두의 executive 중역, 임원 manufacture 생산, 제조 cite 인용하다 **6.** plain 쉬운 nutrition 영양 **7.** expand 넓히다 market share 시장 점유율 **8.** provide 제공하다 register for ~에 등록하다

1   New employees of Peachpower Software
    must attend a very ------- two-week training
    course when they are hired.
    (A) demands
    (B) demanded
    (C) demanding
    (D) demand

2   When hotel guests order room service,
    remember to inform them of the ------- time
    of delivery.
    (A) estimates
    (B) estimating
    (C) estimation
    (D) estimated

3   The advertising team made an -------
    recovery from a late start to finish the project
    a week ahead of schedule.
    (A) amaze
    (B) amazing
    (C) amazement
    (D) amazingly

4   Recent graduates apply for work at
    Harnum Corporation because it offers -------
    opportunities for advancement.
    (A) outstand
    (B) to be outstood
    (C) outstood
    (D) outstanding

5   When ------- in combination with a
    maintenance package, the Auto Tech
    Computer includes a three-year warranty.
    (A) was purchasing
    (B) purchased
    (C) is purchased
    (D) purchases

6   Stormy weather in Lorraine led to power
    outages last night, ------- some residents
    without electricity.
    (A) will leave
    (B) leaving
    (C) have left
    (D) leaves

7   While the cafeteria is closed for repairs,
    Osten Daily Gazette employees may take
    ------- lunch breaks to allow for travel off-site.
    (A) waiting
    (B) qualifying
    (C) extended
    (D) secured

8   Because the teams in Beijing and Lisbon
    must work together closely, e-mail is the
    ------- method of communication for
    this project.
    (A) prefer
    (B) preferred
    (C) preferably
    (D) preference

9   Because a flower market exists near the
    ------- site of a new Ayame Florist Shop,
    another location is being sought.
    (A) obliged
    (B) voluntary
    (C) deliberate
    (D) proposed

10 After nine ------- years at Kewlab, Inc., Ms.
    Rosen will resign as executive director to
    pursue a new business venture.
    (A) reward
    (B) rewards
    (C) rewarding
    (D) rewardingly

Questions 11-14 refer to the following e-mail.

From: Devray City History Museum via devrayupdates@d-museum.org
To: all members

Dear Member,

The Devray City History Museum is proud to unveil its new Digital Discovery Space, an interactive

online museum ------- to provide the community with free educational resources. To ------- the site,
         11.   **12.**
simply enter the main Web site, www.d-museum.org, and click "Enter Discovery Space." To view

the online museum's galleries, go to the menu and click "Explore our Collections". -------. You can
                                                                  13.
even get a close-up view of a particular exhibit by clicking the camera icon below it. What's more,

it's now possible to ------- all of our special exhibitions from the past five years by going to the
                        14.
site's archive section. We hope you enjoy all these features!

11. (A) creative
(B) creating
(C) created
(D) creates

12. (A) access
(B) close
(C) modify
(D) rate

13. (A) Member support funded those
renovations.
(B) You can then take a virtual museum tour.
(C) Photography is not allowed in any
gallery.
(D) Tickets for the event may sell out quickly.

14. (A) organize
(B) revisit
(C) plan
(D) donate

Unit | 12   전치사와 접속사

① 전치사의 개념과 역할

전치사의 뒤에는 항상 명사, 대명사, 동명사가 와요.

soccer.

I am interested **in** it.

playing soccer.

■ 전치사의 개념

전치사는 명사 앞에 위치하여 시간, 장소, 자격 등 다양한 의미를 더해주는 말이에요.

at 2 o'clock 2시에   **in** the building 건물 안에   **as** a lawyer 변호사로서

■ 전치사의 목적어

전치사 뒤에는 명사(구), 즉 명사, 대명사, 동명사 등이 위치하게 되는데 이들을 '전치사의 목적어'라고 해요. 동사는 전치사의 목적어가 될 수 없어요.

전치사 + 명사	This special offer is only **for our patrons**. 이 특가 행사는 우리의 단골 손님만을 위한 것이다.
전치사 + 대명사	Please report any problems **to me** by e-mail. 어떤 문제라도 제게 이메일로 말씀해 주세요.
전치사 + 동명사	Fill out the form completely **before submitting it**. 제출하기 전에 양식을 완벽하게 작성하세요.

■ 전치사의 역할

전치사와 명사(구)가 이루는 구를 전명구라고 하는데 문장에서 형용사, 부사의 역할을 해요.

형용사 역할	명사 수식	The producer **of the new play** is Emily Silva. 새 연극의 제작자는 에밀리 실바다.
	보어	Our staff is **on duty** 24 hours a day. 우리 직원들은 하루 24시간 근무 중이다. 보어
부사 역할	동사 수식	The equipment arrived **behind schedule**. 장비가 예정보다 늦게 도착했다.
	형용사 수식	Anita Shan is familiar **with the new system**. 아니타 샨은 새 시스템에 익숙하다.
	문장 수식	**In the end**, the two parties reached an agreement. 결국 양측은 합의에 이르렀다.

STEP 1

1. The volunteers are working hard _____ a successful fund-raising event.
   (A) for
   (B) together

2. Please provide the expiration date _____ your credit card.
   (A) of
   (B) has

3. Sales of the Moro Camera dropped by 3 percent _____ the last quarter.
   (A) well
   (B) during

4. All passengers are responsible for _____ proper travel documents.
   (A) obtain
   (B) obtaining

STEP 2

5. Three major market areas lie _____ a five-hundred-mile radius of our main production plant.
   (A) good
   (B) well
   (C) high
   (D) within

6. We have enclosed the damaged merchandise together _____ a written request for a full refund.
   (A) in
   (B) by
   (C) from
   (D) with

7. _____ signing any partnership agreement, thoroughly examine all options.
   (A) Before
   (B) Next
   (C) Whereas
   (D) Finally

8. Mr. Yamaguchi's train was delayed, forcing him to wait _____ the station for over two hours.
   (A) at
   (B) for
   (C) to
   (D) with

어휘 | **1.** volunteer 자원자 fund-raising 모금 **2.** provide 제공하다 expiration date 유효기간 **3.** drop 떨어지다, 하락하다
4. be responsible for ~에 책임이 있다 proper 적절한 obtain 획득하다 **5.** lie 놓여 있다 radius 반경, 범위 plant 공장
6. enclose 동봉하다 damaged 손상된, 파손된 merchandise 상품 refund 환불 **7.** partnership 협력 agreement 협약, 동의
thoroughly 철저히 examine 검토하다 **8.** delay 지연시키다, 지체시키다 force A to do A가 어쩔 수 없이 ~하게 만들다

② 전치사의 종류와 의미

전치사는 명사 앞에 위치하여
시간이나 장소, 수단, 목적 등 다양한 의미를 만들어요.

because of bad weather
= due to bad weather

■ 시간 전치사

시점	in + 월/계절/연도/morning on + 날짜/요일 at + 시각/noon	in the morning 아침에 on Friday 금요일에	in March 3월에 at four o'clock 4시에
	by (완료) ~까지 until (계속) ~까지	arrive by Friday 금요일까지 도착하다	stay until Friday 금요일까지 머무르다
	before = prior to ~전에 after ~후에	leave before 5 P.M. 5시 전에 떠나다	after the performance 공연 후에
기간	for + 숫자 during + 명사 ~동안	for three days 사흘 동안	during the presentation 발표 동안
	over the next[past] + 기간 다음[지난] ~에 걸쳐	over the past 5 years 지난 5년에 걸쳐	
	throughout + 명사 ~내내	throughout the summer 여름 내내	
	within + 기간 ~이내에	within a week 일주일 이내에	

■ 장소, 방향 전치사

장소	at + 지점 in + 공간 throughout + 장소 ~곳곳에, ~도처에	at the station 역에 in the city 도시에 throughout the building 건물 곳곳에	
	in front of ~ 앞에 behind ~ 뒤에	in front of the entrance 출입문 앞에	behind the seat 좌석 뒤에
	over = above ~ 위에	over the floor 바닥 위쪽에	above the bed 침대 위에
	next to = beside ~의 옆에	next to the printer 프린터 옆에	beside the road 길 옆에
	near ~근처에 around ~주변에	near the bus station 버스 정류장 근처에	around the building 건물 주변에
	between + 복수명사 (둘) 사이에 among + 복수명사 (셋 이상) 사이에	between two nations 두 국가 사이에 among the trees 나무 사이에	
방향	to ~로, ~에 toward ~을 향해	be open to ~에게 열려 있다	toward the bus 버스를 향해
	from ~로부터	permission from the supervisor 관리자의 승인	

■ 기타 전치사

수단	by ~함으로써 * by + 행위자 ~에 의해	by adjusting the volume 소리를 조절함으로써
	through + 추상 수단 ~를 통해	through the use of tools 도구의 사용을 통해
자격	as + 직업/자격 ~로서	known as a writer 작가로 알려져 있는
주제	about = on ~에 대해	an article about music 음악에 대한 기사
	= regarding, concerning	questions regarding the interview 면접에 관한 질문
제외	except (for) ~을 제외하고	every day except Sunday 일요일을 제외하고 매일
첨가	in addition to = besides ~뿐만 아니라	in addition to developing new products 신제품을 개발하는 것 이외에도
이유	because of = due to ~때문에	delay because of the weather 날씨 때문에 지연되다
양보	despite = in spite of ~에도 불구하고	resign despite many benefits 많은 혜택에도 불구하고 사임하다
목적	for + 목적/이유 ~를 위해/~해서	for further information 추가 정보를 위해서
소지	with ~와 함께, ~을 갖고 without ~없이	with care 주의 깊게 without any other help 다른 도움 없이

STEP 1

1. Please visit our Web site for more information _____ your new Brightstar camera.
   (A) about
   (B) of

2. Dalytown Hospital offers free classes on nutrition _____ adults and children.
   (A) by
   (B) to

3. Supervisors should review the confidential documents _____ the end of the month.
   (A) by
   (B) until

4. JHB Bank cannot process a loan application _____ the proper documentation.
   (A) without
   (B) along

STEP 2

5. Prices for items not on this list can be obtained directly _____ the vendors.
   (A) to
   (B) with
   (C) from
   (D) under

6. Goer, Inc., has been conducting a quality improvement campaign _____ the past six months.
   (A) by
   (B) at
   (C) for
   (D) along

7. The work environment is designed to encourage collaboration _____ coworkers.
   (A) among
   (B) throughout
   (C) until
   (D) besides

8. The city health department runs several free clinics for health professionals _____ the year.
   (A) concerning
   (B) throughout
   (C) before
   (D) around

어휘 | **2.** free 무료의 nutrition 영양 adult 성인 **3.** supervisor 관리자 confidential 기밀의 **4.** process 처리하다 loan application 대출 신청 documentation 서류 **5.** directly 직접 vendor 상인 **6.** conduct 행하다 quality improvement 품질 개선 **7.** environment 환경 encourage 촉진하다 collaboration 협업 coworker 동료 **8.** run 운영하다, 작동하다 clinic 병원, 강습 health professional 의료 종사자 concerning ~에 관한 throughout ~(기간) 내내, ~ 도처에

③ 등위접속사와 상관접속사

말과 말을 이어주는 접속사

love and money (등위접속사)

either love or money (상관접속사)

■ 등위접속사

서로 같은 성격의 단어와 단어, 구와 구, 절과 절을 대등하게 연결하는 말이에요.

| and 그리고 | or 또는 | but/yet 그러나 | so 그래서 |

The article is **interesting** and **informative**. 그 기사는 흥미롭고 유익하다.
　　　　　　　단어(형용사)　　　　단어(형용사)

You should make a payment **before** or **on** Thursday. 당신은 목요일 전 혹은 당일에 결제해야 한다.
　　　　　　　　　　　　　　단어(전치사)　　단어(전치사)

Dr. Dorin **is on vacation** but still **keeps busy**. 도린 박사는 휴가 중이지만 여전히 바쁘다.
　　　　　　동사구　　　　　　　　동사구

It is cold outside, so **you should wear a coat**. 밖이 추우니까 코트를 입는 게 좋겠다.
　　　　절　　　　　　　　　　　절
→ 접속사 so는 절과 절만 연결할 수 있고, 단어나 구를 연결하는 데는 쓸 수 없어요.

■ 상관접속사

두 단어 이상이 짝을 이루어 쓰이는 접속사를 상관접속사라고 해요.

| both A and B A와 B 둘 다 | neither A nor B A도 B도 아닌 | not A but B A가 아니라 B |
| either A or B A나 B 둘 중 하나 | B, but not A A가 아니라 B | not only A but (also) B A뿐만 아니라 B도 |

The lawyer finished **both** writing **and** proofreading the agreement.
변호사는 계약서 작성과 교정을 모두 마쳤다.

The company hopes to move their offices to **either** Hong Kong **or** Singapore.
그 회사는 사무실을 홍콩이나 싱가포르로 옮기고 싶어 한다.

Neither the shopkeeper **nor** the customer could remember the price.
가게 주인도, 손님도 가격을 기억할 수 없었다.

The soup **not only** tastes good **but** is good for your health as well.
그 수프는 맛있을 뿐 아니라 건강에도 좋다.

STEP 1

1. Ms. Ambani does not speak French, _____ she is fluent in Gujarati and Mandarin.
(A) or
(B) but

2. Mr. Yakamoto recommended _____ Mr. Ono and Ms. Simmons for promotions.
(A) both
(B) either

3. Successful candidates will be posted to either New York _____ Paris.
(A) or
(B) nor

4. Neither Mr. Tang _____ Ms. Tsuri attended the press conference on environmental policy.
(A) and
(B) nor

STEP 2

5. Ms. Choi is not only a good public speaker _____ also a talented writer.
(A) both
(B) if
(C) nor
(D) but

6. The career development seminars are open to both part-time _____ full-time employees.
(A) and
(B) or
(C) not
(D) to

7. Employees have the option of attending a training class _____ completing an online tutorial.
(A) except
(B) but
(C) or
(D) so

8. Your order is about to be shipped _____ can be canceled up until 2 P.M. today.
(A) however
(B) but
(C) still
(D) although

어휘 | **1.** fluent 유창한 Gujarati 구자라트어 Mandarin 중국어 **2.** recommend 추천하다 promotion 승진 **3.** successful candidate 합격자 post 배치하다, 게시하다 **4.** attend 참석하다 press conference 기자회견 environmental policy 환경 정책 **5.** public speaker 연설가 talented 재능 있는 **6.** career development 경력 개발 part-time 시간제의, 시간제 근무의 full-time 전임의 **7.** option 선택 사항 complete 완료하다 tutorial 개별 지도 **8.** be about to 막 ~하려고 하다 ship 배송하다

1 ------- a year of renovations to its facility, Bendell Department Store will celebrate its grand reopening on October 17.
(A) After
(B) Since
(C) Until
(D) During

2 Any Air-Fresh air conditioner will be repaired or replaced free of charge if it malfunctions ------- one year of the purchase date.
(A) beneath
(B) off
(C) within
(D) on

3 Ms. Jung has suggested that ------ Mr. Tesler or Ms. Sato attend the conference next month.
(A) both
(B) neither
(C) as
(D) either

4 One of Arca Corporation's primary goals is to promote individual professional development ------- its entire staff.
(A) since
(B) among
(C) during
(D) beside

5 The Lake District extends ------- the northern edge of the park right up to the foot of Rodger's Mountain.
(A) next
(B) through
(C) among
(D) besides

6 ------- the past two months, Ejime Theater attendance has increased dramatically.
(A) Into
(B) Behind
(C) Above
(D) During

7 Today, shareholders of Lewis Ridge Mining will approve ------- reject the sale of its copper division to Caxias Metals.
(A) and
(B) or
(C) as if
(D) neither

8 The Jonasson Library will not open until noon on Monday, February 4, ------ necessary building maintenance.
(A) due to
(B) instead of
(C) even though
(D) now that

9 Mr. Simmons, chairman of the board of directors, asks that all trustee nominations be submitted ------- 5:00 P.M. on Friday.
(A) within
(B) sooner
(C) before
(D) whenever

10 Fly Light's full line of luggage is both ------ and stylish.
(A) durable
(B) durability
(C) durably
(D) durableness

Questions 11-14 refer to the following e-mail.

Date: Friday, 22 June
To: Keith Oliver <koliver@allmail.ca>
From: Nira Scott <nscott@auxo.ca>
Subject: Order #CA203AL29

Dear Mr. Oliver,

Thank you for your recent vitamin purchase. The order you placed on Friday, 8 June, was

------- on Monday, 11 June. Our records show that it was delivered on Wednesday, 20 June. I am
  11.

writing to inform you that since your order ------- over $35.00, you were entitled to free shipping.
                12.

Unfortunately, ------- a clerical error, you were charged for shipping. -------. It should appear as a
      13.   **14.**

credit on your next bank statement. Please accept my apologies for this inconvenience.

Yours truly,

Nira Scott, Accounts Manager

---

11. (A) shipped
    (B) modified
    (C) canceled
    (D) misplaced

12. (A) total
    (B) totaling
    (C) totaled
    (D) to total

13. (A) as a result
    (B) after all
    (C) because of
    (D) whenever

14. (A) To correct this oversight, we are issuing
       a refund.
    (B) Please resolve this issue by visiting our
       Web site.
    (C) It is rare for our products to have a defect
       like this.
    (D) Thank you for notifying us of this
       mistake.

① 관계대명사의 개념과 종류

접속사 + 대명사 = 관계대명사

I watched a movie which is about space travel.
= and + it

■ 관계대명사의 개념

관계대명사는 두 개의 문장을 하나로 만들 때 <접속사+대명사> 기능을 하는 단어로, 관계대명사가 이끄는 절은 관계대명사 앞에 위치한 명사(선행사)를 수식하는 역할을 해요.

I watched a movie. + It is about space travel.   나는 영화를 보았다. 그것은 우주 여행에 관한 영화다.

→ I watched a movie and it is about space travel.   ➔ 두 개의 문장을 하나로 만들 때는 반드시 접속사가 필요해요.

→ I watched a movie which is about space travel.   나는 우주 여행에 관한 영화를 보았다.
　　　　　 선행사

■ 관계대명사의 종류

관계대명사절에서 관계대명사가 담당하는 역할(격)과 선행사의 종류에 따라 사용되는 관계대명사가 달라져요.

	주격: 바로 뒤에 동사가 옴	**소유격**: 바로 뒤에 오는 명사를 수식	**목적격**: 뒤에 <주어+동사>가 옴
사람 선행사	who, that	whose	who(m), that
사물 선행사	which, that	whose, of which	which, that

■ 주격 관계대명사

관계대명사가 관계대명사절에서 주어로 쓰이면 주격 관계대명사 who / which / that을 써요.

Mr. Han (who / ~~which~~) is the owner of the café plans to open a new store.

카페 주인인 한 씨는 새 가게를 열 계획이다.

➔ 선행사 Mr. Han이 사람이므로 who 또는 that을 써요. 그리고 관계대명사절의 동사는 선행사와 수를 일치시키는데 Mr. Han이 단수명사이므로 who 뒤에 단수동사(is)가 옵니다.

STEP 1

1. Many people _____ were interviewed felt that they did not need a larger car.
   (A) whom
   (B) who

2. Around 2,000 people went to the job fair _____ was held last month.
   (A) which
   (B) whose

3. These boots are made of synthetic leather _____ is durable and easy to clean.
   (A) that
   (B) whom

4. The customs agent _____ inspects passports is also authorized to issue visitors' visas.
   (A) whose
   (B) who

STEP 2

5. Ms. Reston and Mr. Parnthong were two of the senior partners _____ visited the clients last week.
   (A) who
   (B) when
   (C) what
   (D) whose

6. *Studio Ceramics Monthly* does not accept manuscripts _____ have previously appeared in print.
   (A) what
   (B) whose
   (C) they
   (D) that

7. Saturday's clearance sale will make room for next season's products, _____ will arrive very soon.
   (A) when
   (B) what
   (C) where
   (D) which

8. At the Podell Automotive plant, Ms. Krystle oversees workers who _____ rebuilt engines in vehicles.
   (A) installs
   (B) install
   (C) installment
   (D) installing

어휘 | **2.** job fair 취업 박람회 be held 열리다 **3.** be made of ~로 만들어지다 synthetic leather 합성피혁 durable 내구성 있는
4. customs 세관 inspect 검사하다 be authorized to ~할 수 있는 권한이 있다 issue 발행하다 **5.** senior partner (조합·합명 회사 따위의) 장, 사장 **6.** manuscript 원고 **7.** clearance sale 창고 정리 세일, 재고 정리 판매 make room for ~을 위한 공간을 마련하다 **8.** oversee 감독하다 vehicle 차량 install 설치하다

② 목적격 관계대명사와 소유격 관계대명사

관계대명사는 주격 외에도 소유격과 목적격이 있어요.

The information that you requested
is confidential. (목적격)

■ 목적격 관계대명사

관계대명사가 관계대명사절 안에서 목적어로 쓰이면 목적격 관계대명사 who(m)/which/that을 써요.

The information (which / ~~whom~~**) you requested** is confidential.

당신이 요구했던 정보는 기밀 사항입니다.

→ 타동사 requested의 목적어이자 선행사인 The information이 사물이므로 목적격 관계대명사 which나 that을 쓰면 돼요.

■ 소유격 관계대명사

선행사(관계대명사 앞의 명사)가 관계대명사 뒤에 오는 명사를 소유하는 관계일 때 소유격 관계대명사 whose를 써요.

People tend to buy **clothes (**whose / ~~which~~**) prices have decreased**.

사람들은 가격이 떨어진 옷을 사는 경향이 있다.

■ 관계대명사의 생략

① **<주격 관계대명사+be동사> 생략:** 주격 관계대명사 뒤에 <be+p.p.> 또는 <be+-ing> 형태가 오면 관계대명사와 be동사가 함께 생략될 수 있어요. 이런 경우, 분사가 명사를 뒤에서 수식하는 구조와 동일해져요.

Anyone **(who is)** interested in the seminar must sign up by noon.

세미나에 관심 있는 사람은 정오까지 신청해야 한다.

→ 선행사(Anyone) 뒤에 오는 -ing나 p.p.(interested)를 동사로 착각하지 않도록 주의해야 해요. 문장의 동사는 must sign up이에요.

② **목적격 관계대명사 생략**

The technician **(that)** we met yesterday is experienced.

우리가 어제 만났던 기술자는 경험이 많다.

→ 명사(technician) 뒤에 명사나 대명사(we)가 연달아 나온다면 중간에 목적격 관계대명사가 생략됐을 확률이 높아요.

1. The tasks _____ Ms. Ogawa must carry out are outlined in her employment agreement.
(A) who
(B) that

2. Refunds will be given to all customers _____ orders are damaged in shipping.
(A) which
(B) whose

3. The book _____ ordered yesterday will be delivered tomorrow morning.
(A) you
(B) your

4. The file _____ to this e-mail must be examined carefully.
(A) attaching
(B) attached

5. The applicant _____ the professor recommended will come for an interview soon.
(A) when
(B) which
(C) what
(D) that

6. Akira Tsukada's novel, _____ title hasn't been finalized yet, will be released next year.
(A) which
(B) that
(C) whose
(D) whom

7. Paula Coe has been contracted to inspect the area _____ the Crinside Hotel to ensure compliance with regulations.
(A) surround
(B) surrounds
(C) surrounded
(D) surrounding

8. The quality-control procedures _____ in the contract must be reviewed by the head of engineering.
(A) including
(B) includes
(C) included
(D) include

어휘 | **1.** task 업무 carry out 수행하다 outline 간략히 서술하다 **2.** damaged 파손된 **4.** examine 검사하다 attach 첨부하다
5. applicant 지원자 professor 교수 **6.** finalize 마무리 짓다 release 공개하다, 발표하다 **7.** contract (하청) 계약을 맺다
inspect 점검하다 compliance 준수 regulation 규정 surround 둘러싸다 **8.** procedure 절차

1 Many of the candidates ------- applied for the administrative assistant position at Ferber Systems were highly qualified.
(A) which
(B) what
(C) who
(D) when

2 Hemton House on Main Street, ------- served as Lunburgh's first schoolhouse, has been designated a historical landmark.
(A) who
(B) which
(C) where
(D) when

3 Factory personnel ------- job is to operate industrial machinery must attend a safety course once a year.
(A) whose
(B) they
(C) that
(D) these

4 Of all the business plans ------- by the marketing manager, Mr. Martin's idea is the most impressive.
(A) review
(B) reviewed
(C) are reviewed
(D) which reviewed

5 The Batami Financial Group provides expert consulting services ------- are based on economic research and analysis.
(A) also
(B) who
(C) that
(D) once

6 Skytown Airlines apologized to the passengers for the delays ------- experienced.
(A) they
(B) their
(C) them
(D) this

7 The keynote speaker was J. M. Lim, ------ research on wind power has helped shape the alternative energy industry.
(A) whose
(B) which
(C) from
(D) of

8 ZG Dental thanks all staff members who ------- marketing materials at last week's National Dentistry Expo in Pittsburgh.
(A) distribute
(B) distributes
(C) distributed
(D) distributing

9 Juanita is the most reliable employee ------- we have, so we can depend on her to handle this contract.
(A) which
(B) what
(C) that
(D) whose

10 The Cork County Council has approved an airport expansion project that ------- to better accommodate travelers.
(A) promising
(B) promises
(C) will be promised
(D) would have promised

Questions 11-14 refer to the following memo.

To: Geoffrey Zihan
From: Anne Meckel
Subject: Desk Hub Consultation

As noted during this week's briefing, our client Desk Hub has experienced a decrease in clients during the last three quarters. When the company first opened three years ago, it was the only one of its kind to offer temporary office space in Shanghai. Now it has several ------- in that
11.
market. As a result, Desk Hub has seen a steady decline in profits.

To help remedy the situation, I met with the marketing team this morning. -------. As a first step,
12.
we will conduct a market research study to better estimate the overall demand for office space.

-------, we discussed the idea of suggesting that Desk Hub enter the consulting field. In that area,
13.
we could line up corporate clients for them, many of ------- have already expressed an interest in
14.
creating alternative working spaces for their own employees.

I will keep you informed of developments.

---

11. (A) products
    (B) branches
    (C) employees
    (D) competitors

12. (A) We may consider raising the cost.
    (B) The team was late for the meeting.
    (C) The quality of service has improved.
    (D) Several ideas arose during the
        discussion.

13. (A) However
    (B) Therefore
    (C) In addition
    (D) On the contrary

14. (A) that
    (B) they
    (C) where
    (D) whom

명사절 접속사

① 명사절 접속사 that, whether, if

문장에서 명사 역할을 하는 절을 명사절이라고 하는데 that, if, whether는 명사절 접속사로 쓸 수 있어요.

I am wondering whether you are available tomorrow.

■ 명사절이란?

명사처럼 주어, 목적어(동사 뒤 또는 전치사 뒤), 보어 역할을 하는 절을 명사절이라고 하며, 문장에서 이런 명사절을 이 끄는 접속사를 명사절 접속사라고 합니다.

The notice says that the train will be 10 minutes late. 안내문에는 기차가 10분 연착된다고 게시되어 있다.

   문장의 동사 says의 목적어인 절(the train … late)을 that이 연결합니다.

■ that: ~라는[하는] 것

주어   **That** the play got disappointing reviews **is** true. 그 연극이 실망스러운 평가를 받은 것은 사실이다.

       = **It** is true that the play got disappointing reviews.

       → 주어가 that절처럼 긴 경우 주어를 뒤로 보내고 그 자리에 가주어 it을 대신 쓸 수 있어요.

보어   The problem **is that** we need more staff. 문제는 우리에게 더 많은 직원이 필요하다는 것이다.

목적어   **Ensure** that your work area is clean. 당신의 작업 공간을 깨끗하게 하세요.

┌─ that절을 목적어로 취하는 빈출 동사 ─────────────────────────

agree that ~에 동의하다   ensure that ~을 보장하다   announce that ~을 발표하다

indicate that ~을 나타내다   confirm that ~을 확인하다   note that ~을 유념하다

■ whether / if: ~인지 아닌지, ~할지 안 할지

불확실한 사실을 전달할 때 사용되는 whether는 종종 뒤에 'or not'과 함께 사용되며 whether 뒤에 주어를 생략하고 바로 to부정사를 쓸 수도 있어요. 같은 의미로 사용되는 if는 whether와 달리 동사 뒤에서 목적어절을 이끌 때만 써요.

(Whether / If) the city will widen the road hasn't been decided. 시가 도로를 확장할지는 결정되지 않았다.

Ms. Serena is considering (whether / if) to renew the contract. 세레나 씨는 계약을 갱신할지 말지를 고려 중이다.
                   = whether or not to renew the contract

The survey will determine (whether / if) the cost is important (or not). 설문조사는 비용이 중요한지를 판가름할 것이다.

STEP 1

1. The committee's opinion is _____ we have to build a day-care center.
   (A) that
   (B) whether

2. Gladsock employees do not know _____ they will receive a bonus this year.
   (A) if
   (B) and

3. Please note _____ a copy of the contract for you to sign is included with this letter.
   (A) which
   (B) that

4. Hahm Plastic Corporation is currently deciding _____ to open new offices in Jeju City.
   (A) whether
   (B) if

STEP 2

5. _____ the rival company will file a lawsuit against Trolman, Inc., remains to be seen.
   (A) Wherever
   (B) Which
   (C) Whether
   (D) What

6. Sales representatives know _____ they should reach their quarterly sales targets.
   (A) about
   (B) what
   (C) that
   (D) it

7. It is difficult to determine _____ Mr. Thomson is the best person to lead the project.
   (A) whether
   (B) what
   (C) so that
   (D) for

8. The company's decision on whether or not _____ a candidate will depend on reference checks.
   (A) hire
   (B) hiring
   (C) to hire
   (D) will hire

어휘 | **1.** committee 위원회 opinion 의견 day-care center 어린이집 **2.** receive 받다 **3.** note 유념하다 copy 사본; 한 부 contract 계약(서) include 포함하다 **4.** currently 현재 **5.** file a lawsuit 소송을 제기하다 remain to be seen 두고 볼 일이다 **6.** sales representative 영업 사원, 판매 직원 quarterly 분기별, 분기의 **7.** determine 결정하다 **8.** depend on ~에 달려 있다 reference 추천(서)

② 의문사 형태의 명사절 접속사

의문사(who, what, how 등)도
명사절 접속사로 쓸 수 있어요.

I know what will happen soon.

■ 의문사

who, what, which, when, where, how, why와 같은 의문사도 명사절 접속사로 쓰입니다.

주어   <u>Who will be in charge of the job</u> **is** everyone's concern.   누가 그 업무를 담당할 것인지가 모두의 관심사이다.
                문장의 주어 역할

목적어 The workers will **choose** <u>how they will receive payment</u>.   직원들은 급여를 어떻게 받을지 선택할 것이다.
                   동사 뒤 목적어 역할

         We will talk **about** <u>what is more important than the design</u>.   우리는 무엇이 디자인보다 더 중요한지에 대해
                      전치사 뒤 목적어 역할   논의할 것이다.

보어   Our main concern **is** <u>when we release the new product</u>.   우리의 주된 관심사는 언제 신제품을 출시하느냐이다.
                be동사 뒤 보어 역할

■ what vs. that

what과 that은 둘 다 '~하는 것'으로 해석될 수 있지만, what 뒤에는 불완전한 절(빠진 문장 요소가 있는 절), that 뒤에는 완전한 절이 와요.

The accountants provided <u>what the executives asked for.</u>   회계사들은 임원들이 요구하는 것을 제공했다.
                    that   불완전한 절

→ 전치사 for 뒤에 목적어가 없는 불완전한 절이 왔으므로 what을 써요.

The secretary confirmed <u>that the flight was reserved.</u>   비서는 비행기가 예약되었다는 것을 확인했다.
                  what   완전한 절

→ 참고로 명사절 접속사 that, if, whether, when, where, how, why 뒤에는 완전한 절이 오고, who, what, which 뒤에는 불완전한 절이 와요.

■ 의문사의 활용

❶ **의문사+to부정사**: 의문사 뒤에 주어와 동사 대신 간단히 to부정사가 나오는 형태가 문장에서 명사 역할을 하기도 해요.

The interns are learning **how to use** the software.   인턴들은 그 소프트웨어를 어떻게 쓰는지 배우는 중이다.

❷ **의문사+-ever**: 의문사 뒤에 -ever를 붙이면 '~(하)든지'라고 해석해요.

whoever 누가 ~든지	whenever 언제 ~든지	whatever 무엇을 ~든지
wherever 어디서 ~든지	however 어떻게/얼마나 ~든지	whichever 어느 것을 ~든지

Whoever wins the game will receive a big prize.   게임에서 우승하는 사람은 누구든지 큰 상을 받을 것이다.

STEP 1

1. The Personnel Manager has not
decided _____ will be transferred to
the Seoul office.
(A) who
(B) when

2. Most of the conference attendees do
not understand _____ the presenter
is saying now.
(A) what
(B) that

3. Free virus protection software is
available to _____ does not have it
yet.
(A) anyone
(B) whoever

4. At Neng Publishing Agency, clients
are encouraged to write _____ they
wish to express.
(A) however
(B) whatever

STEP 2

5. Tomorrow's session will train
participants on _____ to prepare
containers for overseas shipments.
(A) what
(B) how
(C) that
(D) then

6. The employee directory has a section
that tells users _____ can answer
questions about various departments.
(A) if
(B) how
(C) who
(D) he

7. Primo Publishing has not yet decided
_____ they will introduce their new
software's features.
(A) which
(B) who
(C) what
(D) when

8. _____ responding to the restaurant
survey will receive a $10 gift
certificate to the Rangely Café.
(A) Whoever
(B) Whose
(C) Someone
(D) Everyone

어휘 | **1.** personnel 인사부 decide 결정하다 transfer 옮기다 **2.** attendee 참석자 presenter 발표자 **3.** protection 보호 available
이용 가능한 **4.** be encouraged to do ~하도록 고무되다 express 표현하다 **5.** participant 참가자 overseas 해외의, 해외에
shipment 수송 **6.** directory 명부 section 부분, 부문 user 이용자 various 다양한, 여러 가지의 department 부서
7. introduce 소개하다, 도입하다 **8.** respond to ~에 응답하다 gift certificate 상품권

1 The study will determine ------- drilling new water wells in Nontock County will have a significant impact on groundwater levels.
(A) whatever
(B) while
(C) whichever
(D) whether

2 The instruction manual for the food processor indicates ------- it can be used for both grains and vegetables.
(A) but
(B) that
(C) while
(D) so

3 The board of directors is discussing ------- they will maintain their core technology.
(A) who
(B) which
(C) how
(D) what

4 The product development team cannot say ------- the new line of products will be released.
(A) which
(B) who
(C) what
(D) when

5 A report in the *Journal of the Agricultural Society* suggests that consumers are increasingly concerned about ------- their produce is grown.
(A) it
(B) where
(C) what
(D) that

6 *Jenkins Business Review* has asked thousands of people in a wide range of professions to describe ------- their jobs entail.
(A) what
(B) how
(C) when
(D) which

7 Mr. Nam inspects the landscaping work performed by our crews to determine ------- it conforms to company standards.
(A) because
(B) so
(C) whether
(D) while

8 ------- the parties involved in the negotiation agree with the terms or not is a crucially important matter.
(A) Where
(B) However
(C) Whether
(D) While

9 ------- arrives first to the grand opening of Dimkin's Ice Cream Shop will receive a free T-shirt.
(A) Who
(B) What
(C) Whoever
(D) That

10 The corporate officers have requested that Ms. Nguyen ------- all available options for reducing costs at the Hanoi factory.
(A) to investigate
(B) has investigated
(C) investigate
(D) is investigating

Questions 11-14 refer to the following press release.

FOR IMMEDIATE RELEASE   **November 18**

TREFFORD CITY — The City Waste Management Authority(CWMA) has teamed up with GDA

Waste Solutions, a local recycling facility, to collect electronic waste for recycling.

This ------- allows residents to drop off old devices, such as mobile phones and laptop computers,
           11.

for pickup at the Community Center on Fir Street. -------. Residents are asked not to leave items
                                                 12.

outside the center after it has closed. "The drop-off program is part of our new 'Clean City'

campaign," said CWMA Director Lloyd Ingram. "Now it's time for residents to decide ------- to
                                                                                     13.

promote this campaign." To that end, a public meeting --------- next Thursday at 7 P.M., in Room B
                                                        14.

of City Hall, to seek community input on promotion ideas.

More information: www.cwma-ewaste.org

---

11. (A) modification
 (B) partnership
 (C) separation
 (D) law

12. (A) These devices are not considered
     recyclable at this time.
 (B) The written estimate will include the total
     repair costs.
 (C) Items are accepted during the center's
     regular hours.
 (D) The company's new products are more
     energy-efficient.

13. (A) what
 (B) how
 (C) unless
 (D) whose

14. (A) was being held
 (B) will be held
 (C) has been held
 (D) would have been held

Unit | 15 부사절 접속사

① 시간·조건의 부사절 접속사

시간이나 조건 등을 의미하는 부사절 접속사로는 **before, since, if, as long as 등**이 있어요.

Stock prices have doubled
since the news was reported.

■ 부사절 접속사의 역할

<접속사＋주어＋동사> 덩어리가 문장 맨 앞이나 맨 뒤에서 수식어 역할을 하면 그것을 부사절이라고 하는데, 이런 부사절을 이끄는 접속사를 부사절 접속사라고 해요.

<u>All contracts must be reviewed thoroughly.</u> + <u>They(all contracts) are signed.</u>
　　　　　　　완전한 절　　　　　　　　　　　　　　　　　　완전한 절

All contracts must be reviewed thoroughly **before they are signed**.
모든 계약서들은 사인하기 전에 철저히 검토되어야 한다.　　　시간을 의미하는 부사절

= **Before they are signed**, all contracts must be reviewed thoroughly.

→ 부사절은 문장 앞과 뒤 어디든 위치할 수 있어요.

■ 시간을 나타내는 접속사

when/as ~할 때	while ~하는 동안에	before ~하기 전에	after ~한 후에
as soon as ~하자마자	until ~할 때까지	since ~이래로 (지금까지)	by the time ~할 즈음에

Audience members are not allowed to take photos **after the concert starts**.
관객들은 공연이 시작한 후에는 사진을 찍으면 안 된다.

Stock prices have doubled **since the news was reported**. 그 소식이 보도된 이후로 주가는 두 배가 되었다.

→ before, after, since, until은 같은 의미의 전치사로도 쓰여요.

■ 조건을 나타내는 접속사

if 만약 ~라면	unless(= if not) ~가 아니라면	once 일단 ~하면
in case ~의 경우에 (대비하여)	provided that ~라면	as long as ~하는 한

If you are interested, an insurance agent will help you. 만약 관심 있으시면, 보험 설계사가 도와드릴 것입니다.

The class will be canceled **unless three people or more sign up**. 세 명 이상이 등록하지 않으면 수업은 취소됩니다.
　　　　　　　　　　　　　= if three people or more don't sign up

STEP 1

1. _____ we have our next meeting, the project manager will thank everyone for their hard work.
   (A) When
   (B) That

2. The staff has been more productive _____ the new time-management software was installed.
   (A) if
   (B) since

3. Customers can write a check _____ they have two pieces of identification.
   (A) although
   (B) if

4. _____ you have registered with Select Software, you will receive a customer identification number.
   (A) Once
   (B) Next

STEP 2

5. _____ all the applications are received, the committee will determine a list of people to be interviewed.
   (A) About
   (B) Except
   (C) After
   (D) With

6. The Pentular desk cannot be shipped _____ a purchase order is signed by the manager.
   (A) despite
   (B) without
   (C) neither
   (D) unless

7. _____ the conference began, MOSA President Yolanda Gris announced the schedule of speakers.
   (A) Before
   (B) Still
   (C) During
   (D) Since

8. We will begin processing Mr. Vallejo's loan application _____ we receive the supporting documents.
   (A) just
   (B) once
   (C) upon
   (D) still

어휘 | **1.** hard work 노고 **2.** productive 생산적인 time-management 시간 관리 install 설치하다 **3.** identification 신분 증명(서) **4.** register 등록하다 receive 받다 identification number 식별 번호 **5.** application 지원서, 신청서 determine 확정하다, 결정하다 **6.** ship 수송하다 purchase order 구매 주문 manager 부장 **7.** conference 회의 announce 발표하다 **8.** process 처리하다 loan application 대출 신청 supporting 떠받치는, 지원하는 document 문서, 서류

② 이유 · 양보 · 기타의 부사절 접속사

이유나 양보, 목적은 because, although, so that 등으로 표현할 수 있어요.

Hansel left crumbs so that they can get back home.

■ 이유를 나타내는 접속사

because, as, since, now that ~하기 때문에

Dr. Logan was absent from the meeting **because his flight was delayed.**
로건 박사는 비행기가 연착하는 바람에 회의에 불참했다.

■ 양보 · 대조를 나타내는 접속사

though, although, even though, even if 비록 ~에도 불구하고   while, whereas ~인 반면에

Although he had plans for his trip, Mr. Kim was too busy.   김 씨는 여행 계획이 있었지만, 너무 바빴다.

The 1st floor offices handle customer service, **while the 2nd floor deals with marketing.**
2층은 마케팅을 다루는 반면에 1층 사무실은 고객 서비스를 취급한다.

■ 기타 접속사

so that, in order that + 주어 + (can) ~하기 위해서, ~할 수 있도록   so + 형용사/부사 + that 매우 ~해서 …하다

The company attended the job fair **so that they can find** competent applicants.

= **in order that they can find** competent applicants.

= **in order to find** competent applicants.

회사는 유능한 지원자를 찾기 위해서 취업 박람회에 참석했다.

The presentation was **so persuasive that** the clients signed another contract.
프레젠테이션이 아주 설득력 있어서 고객들은 다른 계약에도 서명했다.

■ 전치사 vs. 접속사

접속사 뒤에는 <주어 + 동사>가 오지만 전치사 뒤에는 명사(구)가 와요.

	접속사 + 주어 + 동사	전치사 + 명사(구) / 동명사(구)
이유 ~ 때문에	because, as, since	because of, due to
양보 ~에도 불구하고	although, though, even though, even if	despite, in spite of
시간 ~ 동안	while	during

The game was canceled (**because of** / ~~because~~) **the bad weather**.   궂은 날씨 때문에 경기가 취소되었다.

(**While** / ~~During~~) **you are** in the library, you must not eat.   도서관에 있는 동안, 먹으면 안 된다.

STEP 1

1. Mr. Jose has moved to the city _____ he is tired of the long commute to work.
(A) because
(B) whereas

2. _____ Ms. Tianen's team has been working diligently on the report, it is still not finished.
(A) Even though
(B) Only if

3. The product is _____ expensive that most shoppers are reluctant to buy it.
(A) so
(B) very

4. Aya Kodura maintained a rigorous practice schedule _____ her national tour.
(A) during
(B) while

STEP 2

5. _____ labor costs were significantly lower last quarter, Enex, Inc., still failed to show a profit.
(A) Even though
(B) In light of
(C) Nevertheless
(D) Therefore

6. The cancellation of Saturday's concert was _____ unexpected problems with the sound system.
(A) because
(B) as if
(C) due to
(D) unless

7. Mario D'Amico has been assigned to check the facts _____ Sean McCree types a draft of the report.
(A) also
(B) than
(C) moreover
(D) while

8. Physical files older than one year should be put in boxes _____ they can be moved to the storage facility.
(A) so that
(B) contrary to
(C) because of
(D) if so

어휘 | **1.** be tired of ~에 지치다 commute 통근(하다) **2.** diligently 부지런히 even though ~에도 불구하고 only if ~해야만 **3.** expensive 비싼 be reluctant to do ~하는 것을 꺼리다 **4.** maintain 유지하다, 관리하다 rigorous 엄격한, 정확한 **5.** labor cost 인건비 significantly 상당히 fail to do ~하지 못하다 profit 이윤 **6.** unexpected 예상치 못한 **7.** assign (업무를) 맡다, 할당하다 draft 초안 **8.** physical 실제의 storage 보관 facility 시설

1 ------- our chief financial officer is away on
   business, the budget meeting has been
   rescheduled for Monday.
   (A) Since
   (B) Either
   (C) How
   (D) That

2 Cosimo's Grocery offers customers practical
   cooking tips ------- they can make the most
   of the foods they purchase.
   (A) in addition
   (B) so that
   (C) just as
   (D) in case

3 Varangia Marketing Services has become a
   leader in corporate advertising, ------- they
   have only been in business for four years.
   (A) owing to
   (B) before
   (C) even though
   (D) instead

4 Tenants may play musical instruments ------
   the music does not disturb other residents in
   the building.
   (A) provided that
   (B) such as
   (C) in case of
   (D) owing to

5 Carpet cleaning is scheduled for this
   weekend, so please remove any items from
   the floor of your office ------- you leave today.
   (A) before
   (B) but
   (C) where
   (D) upon

6 ------- several ideas have been suggested to
   expand Carlston City's public transportation
   system, not one is within budget.
   (A) Why
   (B) Whether
   (C) Although
   (D) Unless

7 The personnel department revised the
   vacation policy ------- many employees found
   the old version confusing.
   (A) unless
   (B) because
   (C) until
   (D) thus

8 ------- the cleanup campaign has ended,
   the large trash bin will be removed from the
   work area.
   (A) Even so
   (B) In particular
   (C) Now that
   (D) For instance

9 Elmwood's commerce center provides
   support services to new shop owners ------
   their initial year of business.
   (A) since
   (B) though
   (C) during
   (D) while

10 ------- he arrives at the airport in the next ten
   minutes, Mr. Santini is going to have to take
   a later flight.
   (A) Regardless
   (B) While
   (C) Unless
   (D) Rather

Questions 11-14 refer to the following notice.

Attention Cleardale Apartments tenants:

Please be advised that the annual maintenance and cleaning of the boiler has been scheduled to take place on October 18. -------. The water supply for the entire building will be shut off during
11.
this time. -------, the laundry room will be closed.
12.

We apologize for any inconvenience this -------. Thank you in advance for your cooperation -------
13. **14.**
we complete this important work.

Louis Verella, Building Manager

---

11. (A) The project will last from 10:00 A.M. to approximately 1:00 P.M.
    (B) We are seeking a few volunteers to pick up trash on the grass.
    (C) All overdue rental payments must be submitted by this date.
    (D) The new machine will be more powerful and reliable.

12. (A) Nevertheless
    (B) Elsewhere
    (C) Consequently
    (D) Alternatively

13. (A) caused
    (B) should have caused
    (C) cause
    (D) may cause

14. (A) so
    (B) also
    (C) as
    (D) that

Unit | 16 비교구문

① 비교급과 원급

비교급 = -er + than

I am taller than you!

■ 비교급

두 대상을 비교해서 어느 한쪽의 정도가 더하거나 덜하다는 것을 나타낼 때 쓰는 비교급 구문은 <형용사/부사의 비교급 (-er/more/less) + than + 비교 대상>의 형태를 취해요. 따라서 문장에 than이 나오면 앞에 형용사나 부사의 비교급이 와야 해요.

The actual cost will be **higher than** the estimate. 실제 비용은 견적보다 더 높을 것이다.

The CEO has donated **more generously than** last year. CEO는 작년보다 더 후하게 기부했다.

Recycled paper is **less expensive than** new paper. 재생지는 새 종이보다 덜 비싸다.

> 비교급 강조 부사: 훨씬 더 ~한[하게] ─────────
> much, even, still, far, a lot

The department store was **much busier than** usual. 백화점은 평소보다 훨씬 더 부산했다.
~~very, more~~

■ 원급 비교

두 대상이 동등함을 나타내며 <as + 형용사/부사의 원형 + as A: A만큼 ~한>으로 표현해요.

Mobile games are **as popular as** computer games. 모바일 게임은 컴퓨터 게임만큼 인기 있다.
~~more popular, popularly~~

Your request will be addressed **as promptly as** possible. 귀하의 요청 사항이 가능한 신속하게 처리될 겁니다.
~~prompt~~

→ as ~ as 사이에 들어갈 품사를 고르는 문제는 앞의 as를 없애고 문장의 구조를 살펴서 빈칸에 적절한 품사를 고르면 돼요.

■ 비교급 관용 표현

no later than 늦어도 ~까지	no longer 더 이상 ~않다	as soon as possible 가능한 한 빨리
twice as ~ as 두 배 더 ~한	비교급+than expected 예상보다 더 ~한	more than ~이상
less than ~이하	rather than ~보다는 오히려	the 비교급 ~, the 비교급… ~하면 할수록 더 …하다

The nominations will be accepted **no later than** July 15. 늦어도 7월 15일까지만 후보 추천을 받을 것이다.

The new videos sold **better than expected**. 그 신작 비디오는 예상보다 더 잘 팔렸다.

STEP 1

1. The new antivirus software is more powerful _____ the old version.
(A) than
(B) with

2. Red Badge Corporation is now _____ famous as its competitor, Talo Security.
(A) very
(B) as

3. Plastic is now a _____ more versatile construction material than it was in the past.
(A) much
(B) very

4. Reimbursements for medical expenses will be paid as _____ as possible.
(A) quickly
(B) quicker

STEP 2

5. Professional experience is _____ important as educational credentials for the editorial position.
(A) as
(B) so
(C) much
(D) more

6. Tomorrow's training is intended for employees who have been with the company for _____ one year.
(A) rather than
(B) less than
(C) no longer
(D) by far

7. Surveyed consumers responded even _____ to the product's new packaging than expected.
(A) favorably
(B) most favorable
(C) more favorably
(D) favorable

8. Seats will be assigned on a first-come, first-served basis, so it would be best to arrive no _____ than 11:00 A.M.
(A) later
(B) latest
(C) lateness
(D) late

어휘 | **1.** antivirus 바이러스 방지 **2.** competitor 경쟁자 **3.** versatile 다용도의 construction material 건축 자재 past 과거
4. reimbursement 상환, 변제 medical expenses 의료비 **5.** educational credential 학력 editorial 편집의 **6.** be intended for ~을 위해[대상으로] 마련되다 **7.** survey 설문조사; 설문조사를 하다 consumer 소비자 respond 반응하다, 응답하다
8. assign 배정하다, 할당하다 on a first-come, first-served basis 선착순으로

② 최상급

최상급 = the + most / -est

Snow White is the most beautiful girl in the world.

■ 최상급의 의미와 단서 표현

셋 이상의 대상들 중에서 정도나 수준이 가장 높다는 것을 나타낼 때 최상급을 써요. 형용사나 부사의 뒤에 -est를 붙이거나 앞에 most를 쓰는데, 형용사일 경우에는 최상급 앞에 the나 소유격이 와요.

❶ 최상급 + in + 장소/분야/시간: ~에서 가장 …한

Fairheed Inc. is one of the oldest companies **in the industry**.
~~the most oldest~~

페어히드 사는 업계에서 가장 오래된 기업 중 하나이다.

❷ 최상급 + of/among + 복수명사: ~중에서 가장 …한

Yu Shang is the most experienced **of all the managers**.

유 생 씨는 전체 매니저들 중 가장 경험이 많은 사람이다.

❸ 최상급 + that + 주어 + have (ever) p.p.: 지금까지 ~한 중에서 가장 …한

This is the biggest change **that we have ever experienced**.

이것은 우리가 이제껏 경험한 것 중에 가장 큰 변화이다.

> **| 고득점 사다리 |** 품사 문제는 항상 자리부터 확인하자.
> 보기에 형용사나 부사의 비교급, 최상급, 원급 등이 함께 나오더라도, 빈칸이 형용사 자리인지 부사 자리인지부터 먼저 확인해야 해요.
> It rains (**frequently** / ~~frequent~~ / ~~more frequent~~) these days.   요즘음 비가 자주 온다.

■ 주의할 비교급, 최상급 형태

원급	비교급	최상급
good / well 좋은/잘	better 더 좋은/더 잘	best 최상의/가장 잘
bad 나쁜	worse 더 나쁜	worst 최악의
many / much 많은	more 더 많은	most 가장 많은
little 적은	less 더 적은	least 가장 적은

STEP 1

1. The NX 2016 model from AC Autos is one of the _____ cars in the world.
   (A) fast
   (B) fastest

2. Yesterday's festival featured some of the _____ performances that the Palace Theater has ever hosted.
   (A) most lively
   (B) lively

3. Among the candidates the manager has interviewed, Ms. Porwit is the _____ highly qualified.
   (A) so
   (B) most

4. Of the three presentations that were given, the one made by the Shanti Group was the _____.
   (A) impression
   (B) most impressive

STEP 2

5. Sorin's Lakeview Grill is the _____ restaurant that we've ever been to in the city of Swensen.
   (A) large
   (B) larger
   (C) largely
   (D) largest

6. Sunnydec Resort is reviewing proposals from several businesses, and it will choose the _____ bid.
   (A) most affordable
   (B) more affordable
   (C) affordably
   (D) affordability

7. Of all the entries for the advertising campaign, Mr. Andrew's design is the _____.
   (A) most creative
   (B) most creatively
   (C) creatively
   (D) creative

8. Edwards & Sons Plumbing earned the _____ ratings for customer satisfaction in this year's survey.
   (A) higher
   (B) highest
   (C) more highly
   (D) most highly

어휘 | **2.** feature ~을 특징으로 하다 host 주최하다 lively 활기찬 **3.** among ~ 중에서 candidate 후보자 highly 매우 qualified 적임의, 자격이 있는 **6.** proposal 제안(서) bid 입찰 (가격) affordable 가격이 적당한 **7.** entry 출품작 creative 창의적인 **8.** earn (명성·평판 등을) 얻다 rating 순위, 평가 customer satisfaction 고객 만족

Unit 16 비교구문 **237**

1 E-mailing the technology assistance office generally gets a ------- response than calling does.
(A) quick
(B) quicker
(C) quickest
(D) quickly

2 The general contractor expects Mountain Office Park to be ready for occupancy no ------- than next month.
(A) late
(B) later
(C) latest
(D) lately

3 Please contact Ms. Shridhar as ------- as possible about planning the spring clothing sale.
(A) long
(B) soon
(C) highly
(D) stated

4 Although no additional workers were scheduled, the inventory review was completed ------- than expected.
(A) most rapidly
(B) rapid
(C) rapidly
(D) more rapidly

5 Once the most recent update is installed, the phone's platform will ------- longer support this application.
(A) not
(B) none
(C) no
(D) nowhere

6 Architects' models of the proposed bridge are ------- easier to understand than their drawings alone.
(A) very
(B) much
(C) so
(D) too

7 ------- the three candidates for art director at CCAR, Mr. Shaw has the most experience.
(A) Of
(B) At
(C) Yet
(D) So

8 In your search for an architect, you could not hope to find a ------- designer than Ms. Lopez.
(A) more accurately
(B) most accurately
(C) more accurate
(D) most accurate

9 According to annual employee surveys, morale at the Juntasa Toy factory has become ------- better over the last five years.
(A) progresses
(B) progressive
(C) progressing
(D) progressively

10 The newly released Nivido mobile phone is almost ------- as expensive as the company's other models.
(A) double
(B) two
(C) second
(D) twice

Questions 11-14 refer to the following advertisement.

If you are planning a party, conference, or any social event, use Inviting Designs. ------- We are
11.

------- to use than other card companies because of our extensive collection of premade
12.

invitations. Planners in a rush can choose from these invitation ------- that are perfectly suited to
13.

dozens of different occasions. Or, if you need a ------- touch, we can create a customized package
14.

just for you. Whatever you need, call today and order Inviting Designs invitations that your guests

won't be able to ignore!

---

11. (A) We can help you invite all your guests
with style.
(B) A party is the best time to tell others
about our service.
(C) All of our invitations are made specifically
for you.
(D) We offer all the supplies you need to
prepare for any event.

12. (A) easy
(B) easier
(C) easing
(D) easiest

13. (A) templates
(B) fonts
(C) designers
(D) enhancements

14. (A) typical
(B) specialized
(C) reusable
(D) sensitive

기출 어휘 - 동사 1

accelerate
속도를 높이다, 가속화하다
파 acceleration
표현 accelerate the company's growth
회사 성장 속도를 높이다

accept
수락하다, 인정하다
파 acceptance 수락
표현 accept a position
직책을 수락하다

access
접근하다, 접속하다; 접근, 접속
파 accessible 접근 가능한
표현 access restricted areas
제한 구역에 접근하다

accommodate
수용하다
파 accommodation 숙박, 수용
표현 accommodate your request
당신의 요청사항을 수용하다

accompany
동행하다
표현 be accompanied by
~와 동행하다

address
연설하다, 처리하다
동 handle, deal with 다루다
표현 address the audience
청중에게 연설하다
address a complaint
불만 사항을 처리하다

assess
평가하다, 산정하다
파 assessment 평가, 과세
표현 assess the team's performance
팀 실적을 평가하다

assign
맡기다, 할당하다
파 assignment 과제, 임무
표현 assigned task 할당된 업무

attach
첨부하다
파 attachment 첨부 (파일)
표현 attach a sample form
샘플 양식을 첨부하다

award
(상을) 주다, 수여하다; 상
파 award-winning 상을 받은, 수상한
표현 award first prize to
~에게 일등상을 수여하다

apply
지원하다, 신청하다; (크림 등을) 바르다
파 application 지원, 신청
applicant 지원자
표현 apply for a job
일자리에 지원하다

attend
참석하다, 관심을 두다
파 attendance 참석
attention 주의, 주목
표현 attend a seminar
세미나에 참석하다

collaborate
협력하다, 공동 작업하다
파 collaborative 공동의
표현 collaborate to achieve a goal
목표를 달성하기 위해 협력하다

commend
칭찬하다, 기리다
파 commendation 칭찬, 찬사
표현 be highly commended
높이 칭찬받다

comply
따르다, 준수하다
파 compliance (법령의) 준수, 따름
표현 comply with regulations
규정을 따르다

confirm
확인하다
파 confirmation 승인, 확인
표현 confirm a reservation
예약을 확인하다

cooperate
협동하다
파 cooperative 협조적인
cooperation 협동
표현 cooperate with each other
서로 협동하다

create
창조하다, 만들어 내다
파 creative 창조적인, 창의적인
creation 창조, 창작(물)
표현 create a protective barrier
보호막을 만들다

deliver
배달하다, 배송하다
파 delivery 배달, 배송
표현 deliver products with care
제품을 주의해서 배달하다

encourage
격려하다, 고무하다
파 encouragement 격려
encouraging 격려의, 유망한
표현 encourage employees
직원들을 격려하다

enclose
동봉하다
파 enclosed 동봉된
표현 the document is enclosed
문서가 동봉되다

STEP 1

1. The mayor will _____ the issue of road improvement in today's speech.
   (A) educate
   (B) address

2. Employees who wish to _____ the sales exposition in London next month should let their managers know.
   (A) participate
   (B) attend

3. Executives from the two firms may soon be ready to _____ the terms of the proposed merger.
   (A) confirm
   (B) collaborate

4. Croydon Transport will always _____ your parcel on time.
   (A) exceed
   (B) deliver

STEP 2

5. Skaghill Fisheries have been _____ by local authorities for exceeding workplace safety guidelines.
   (A) proposed
   (B) commended
   (C) perceived
   (D) asserted

6. The initial model produced by our contractors failed to _____ with the specifications we provided them.
   (A) adhere
   (B) comply
   (C) belong
   (D) approach

7. Pawel Ltd. has _____ more than fifteen educational scholarships to local high school students this year.
   (A) entitled
   (B) allowed
   (C) awarded
   (D) appointed

8. How to _____ production of furniture at the Linderwood plant is the topic of the next supervisors' meeting.
   (A) appeal
   (B) notify
   (C) accelerate
   (D) subscribe

어휘 | **1.** mayor 시장 improvement 개선 **2.** employee 직원 exposition 전시회, 박람회 participate (in) 참가하다 attend 참석하다 **3.** executive 임원 firm 회사 terms 조건 merger 합병 collaborate 협력하다 **4.** parcel 소포 on time 제시간에 exceed 초과하다 deliver 배송하다 **5.** fishery 수산 회사 authority 당국 exceed 초과하다 propose 제안하다 commend 칭찬하다 perceive 인지하다 assert 주장하다 **6.** initial 초기의 contractor 하청업자 fail to do ~하지 못하다 specification 명세 사항 **7.** scholarship 장학금 entitle 자격을 주다 award 수여하다 appoint 임명하다 **8.** supervisor 감독 notify 통보하다 accelerate 속도를 높이다

기출 어휘 – 동사 2

evolve
발전하다, 발달하다
- 명 evolution 진화, 발전
- 표현 evolve into a big city
  대도시로 발전하다

expand
확장하다, 확대하다
- 명 expansion 확장
- 표현 expand business
  사업을 확장하다

implement
시행하다, 이행하다
- 명 implementation 시행, 이행
- 표현 implement the new policies
  새로운 정책을 실시하다

improve
개선되다, 향상시키다
- 명 improvement 향상, 개선
- 표현 improve productivity
  생산성을 향상시키다

issue
발행하다; 쟁점, 호
- 표현 issue an invitation
  초대장을 발행하다
  social issues
  사회 문제

notify
알리다, 통보하다
- 명 notification 통지
- 표현 notify Ms. Suh of her promotion
  서 씨에게 승진을 통보하다

offer
제안하다, 제공하다; 제안, 제공
- 표현 offer a variety of appetizers
  다양한 애피타이저를 제공하다
  receive a job offer
  일자리 제의를 받다

operate
작동하다, 운영하다
- 명 operation 작동, 운영
- 표현 operate new machinery
  새 장비를 작동하다
  be operated by a large
  corporation 대기업에 의해 운영되다

perform
수행하다, 공연하다
- 명 performance 실적, 공연
- 표현 perform a task
  업무를 수행하다
  job performance
  업무 능력, 직무 수행

permit
허락하다, 허용하다; 허가증
- 명 permission 허락
- 표현 photography is not permitted
  사진촬영은 허용되지 않는다
  obtain a building permit
  건축 허가를 받다

present
제시하다, 소개하다; 현재의
- 동 give 제시하다
  introduce 소개하다
- 표현 present a boarding pass
  탑승권을 제시하다

prevent
막다, 예방하다
- 명 prevention 예방
- 표현 prevent staff from accessing the
  file
  직원들이 그 파일을 열 수 없도록 막다

provide
제공하다
- 동 supply 공급하다
- 표현 provide a replacement
  교체품을 제공하다

reach
이르다, 닿다; 연락을 취하다
- 표현 reach our destination
  우리 목적지에 닿다
  reach him by e-mail
  그에게 이메일로 연락하다

register
등록하다, 기록하다
- 명 registration 등록
- 동 sign up, enroll 등록하다
- 표현 register for a workshop
  워크숍에 등록하다

release
출시하다, 개봉하다
- 표현 release new products
  신제품을 출시하다
  release a film
  영화를 개봉하다

reserve
예약하다, 보류하다
- 명 reserved 예약된
- 동 book 예약하다
- 표현 reserve a meeting room
  회의실을 예약하다

return
돌아오다; 반송[반납]하다
- 표현 complete and return the form
  양식을 작성하여 반송하다

sign
서명하다; 표지판, 간판
- 표현 sign a contract
  계약서에 서명하다
  traffic sign
  교통 표지판

support
지지[지원]하다, 후원하다
- 명 supportive 지원하는
- 표현 support a proposal
  제안을 지지하다

undergo
겪다, 경험하다
- 동 experience, go through 경험하다
- 표현 undergo changes
  변화를 겪다

STEP 1

1. Forming international partnerships is an effective way for a company to _____ its market.
   (A) expand
   (B) include

2. Meran Investments has _____ an agreement to purchase new headquarters.
   (A) labeled
   (B) signed

3. Leeworth's coffee subsidiary will _____ under the name of Genus Beans.
   (A) conduct
   (B) operate

4. The CEO of Argall Enterprises is expected to _____ a statement to the press later this week.
   (A) speak
   (B) issue

STEP 2

5. We require all visitors to _____ photo identification prior to entering the building.
   (A) notify
   (B) assign
   (C) permit
   (D) present

6. Team leaders should try to _____ workshop attendees from repeating one another's comments.
   (A) ignore
   (B) present
   (C) organize
   (D) prevent

7. To _____ the hotel fitness center, please use the staircase at the back of the main lobby.
   (A) feature
   (B) invite
   (C) incline
   (D) reach

8. While all the programmers _____ well in their job interviews, Susan Trafford stood out from the rest.
   (A) treated
   (B) revealed
   (C) handled
   (D) performed

어휘 | **1.** form 형성하다 international 국제적인 effective 효과적인 **2.** investment 투자 agreement 계약 purchase 매입하다 headquarters 본사 label 라벨을 붙이다 sign an agreement 계약을 체결하다 **3.** subsidiary 자회사 conduct 이행하다 operate 운영하다 **4.** statement 성명(서) press 언론 **5.** require 요구하다 photo identification 사진이 있는 신분증 prior to ~ 전에 **6.** attendee 참석자 ignore 무시하다 present 제시하다 organize 조직하다 prevent 막다 **8.** stand out 돋보이다 rest 나머지 perform 수행하다

appointment
약속, 임명

동 appoint 임명하다

표현 make an appointment
약속을 잡다

appointment for an interview
면접 약속

approval
인정, 승인

동 approve 인정하다, 승인하다

표현 receive approval 승인을 받다

authority
권한; 당국

동 authorize
인가하다, 권한을 부여하다

표현 have the authority to
~할 권한이 있다

badge
신분증, 배지

표현 company identification badge
사원증

benefit
혜택, 이익; 이익을 주다

표현 membership benefits 회원 혜택

benefit the environment
환경을 이롭게 하다

candidate
지원자, 후보자

명 candidacy 출마, 후보 (자격)

표현 qualified candidates
자격을 갖춘 지원자들

capacity
용량, 수용력

표현 at full capacity 완전 가동하여

consideration
고려, 배려

동 consider 고려하다

표현 Thank you for your
consideration.
고려해 주셔서 감사합니다.

concern
관심사, 걱정, 근심

형 concerned 걱정하는
concerning ~에 관한

표현 have concerns about
~에 대해 걱정하다

contract
계약(서); 계약하다

표현 win a contract
계약을 따내다[수주하다]

contract to build a bridge
교량 공사를 계약하다

contribution
공헌, 기부(금)

동 contribute
공헌하다, 기여하다

표현 contribution to the company
회사에 대한 기여

debate
논의하다, 토론하다; 토론, 논의

표현 after lengthy debate
긴 논의 후에

debate the proposal
제안서에 대해 논의하다

defect
결함, 결점

형 defective 결함 있는
동 flaw 결함, 결점

표현 eliminate defects 결함을 제거하다

demand
요구, 수요; 요구하다

표현 demand for organic food
유기농 식품에 대한 수요

description
묘사, 설명

동 describe 묘사하다

표현 a brief description of the problem
문제에 대한 간단한 설명

development
개발

동 develop 개발하다

표현 research and development
연구 개발(R&D)

distribution
유통, 분배, 배부

동 distribute 분배하다, 나눠주다

표현 an overseas distribution system
해외 유통 시스템

district
지역, 지구, 구역

표현 the financial district
금융 지구

directions
길 안내; 사용법

동 direct 길을 안내하다; 지시하다

표현 directions to the branch
지사로 가는 길 (안내)

estimate
견적(서); 견적을 내다

형 estimated 추정되는

표현 a free estimate
무료 견적

expiration
(기한 등의) 만료, 종료

동 expire 만료되다

표현 expiration date 유효기간

T **실전 도움닫기** | 다음 문장의 빈칸에 들어갈 알맞은 말을 고르세요.   정답과 해설 p.161

STEP 1

1. Dietrich Dentistry asks patients to provide 24-hour notice to cancel a scheduled _____.
   (A) appointment
   (B) investment

2. The assistant statistician's job _____ includes data collection, coding, and statistical analysis.
   (A) topic
   (B) description

3. _____ about the actual cost of the project have delayed the plans for expanding the arena.
   (A) Additions
   (B) Concerns

4. Kweon Accounting and Sunwoo Cleaning Services will renegotiate their current ------ before it expires.
   (A) authority
   (B) contract

STEP 2

5. All items shipped by Howeland Manufacturing are carefully inspected for possible _____.
   (A) inquiry
   (B) signs
   (C) scarcity
   (D) defects

6. For _____ to Pavella Testing Lab's corporate office, as well as a map, click on the link below.
   (A) experiments
   (B) directions
   (C) reviews
   (D) situations

7. Please thank the team at the Southfield office for their continued _____ to the Dewan merger project.
   (A) demonstrations
   (B) contributions
   (C) professions
   (D) ambitions

8. Ndori Industries received all the necessary _____ from the town council for the proposed construction project.
   (A) certainties
   (B) activities
   (C) intentions
   (D) approvals

어휘 | **1.** patient 환자 notice 통보, 알림 cancel 취소하다 **2.** statistician 통계학자 collection 수집 statistical analysis 통계 분석 job description 업무 명세 **3.** actual 실제의 arena 경기장 addition 추가(물) **4.** renegotiate 재협상하다 current 현재의 expire 만료되다 authority 당국 contract 계약(서) **5.** inspect 검사하다 possible 가능한 defect 결함 **6.** corporate 회사의 experiment 실험 directions 길 안내 situation 상황 **7.** continued 계속된 demonstration 설명, 입증 profession 직업 ambition 야망 **8.** receive 받다 necessary 필요한 proposed 제안된 certainty 확실성 intention 의도 approval 승인

forecast
예상[예측], 예보; 예상[예보]하다

표현 economic forecasts 경제 전망
forecast a heavy snowfall
폭설을 예보하다

gain
증가, 이득; 얻다

동 increase, rise 증가

표현 financial gains 금전적 이득
gain work experience
업무 경험을 쌓다

industry
산업, 공업

파 industrial 산업의, 공업의
industrialize 산업화하다, 공업화하다

표현 work in the food industry
음식업계에서 일하다

inspection
검사, 점검, 검열

파 inspector 검사관, 조사관
inspect 점검하다

표현 pass a safety inspection
안전 검사를 통과하다

instruction
설명(서), 지시 (사항)

파 instruct 지시하다, 가르치다

표현 follow the instructions
설명서대로 따르다

investment
투자(물)

파 invest 투자하다
investor 투자자

표현 initial investment
초기 투자

malfunction
오작동; 오작동하다

표현 computer malfunction
컴퓨터 오작동

measure
조치, 정책; 측정하다

표현 effective measures
효과적인 조치
safety measures
안전 조치

negotiation
협상, 협의

파 negotiate 협상하다

표현 contract negotiation
계약 협상

objection
이의, 반대

파 object 반대하다

표현 the main objection to the plan
계획에 반대하는 주된 이유

option
선택(권), 옵션

파 opt 선택하다

표현 a wide range of options
폭넓은 선택권

participation
참여, 참가

파 participate 참여[참가]하다
participant 참가자

표현 participation in the survey
설문 조사 참여

preference
선호, 우선권

파 prefer 선호하다
preferably 되도록이면

표현 food preference 음식 선호도

priority
우선 사항, 우선 순위

파 prior to ~전에

표현 top priority 최우선 사항

promotion
승진, 홍보, 촉진

파 promote 승진시키다, 홍보하다
promotional 홍보용의

표현 promotion to Sales Manager
영업 부장으로의 승진

purchase
구입, 구매; 구입하다, 구매하다

파 purchaser 구입자, 구매자

표현 all cosmetic purchases
모든 화장품 구매

replacement
교체(품), 후임자

파 replace 대신하다, 대체하다

표현 replacement parts 교체 부품
train my replacement
후임자를 교육시키다

reputation
명성, 평판

동 renown, fame 명성

표현 build a reputation
명성을 쌓다

requirement
필요 조건

파 require 요구하다, 필요로 하다

표현 meet the requirements
필수조건을 충족시키다

responsibility
책임(감), 책무

파 responsible 책임이 있는

표현 primary responsibilities
주요 책무

submission
제출, 제출물

파 submit 제출하다

표현 review the submissions
제출물을 검토하다

STEP 1

1. Zumorito Tile Company offers a free DVD that provides step-by-step installation _____.
   (A) destinations
   (B) instructions

2. The study found that the biotechnology _____ is growing faster than other related fields.
   (A) equipment
   (B) industry

3. In yesterday's third-quarter financial statement, Vargas Industries reported a 15 percent _____ in value.
   (A) gain
   (B) advantage

4. Norhaven Associates, Inc., provides clients with expert market _____ for a three-year period.
   (A) industries
   (B) forecasts

STEP 2

5. Stafford Cable offers several payment _____, so customers can choose the most convenient way to pay their bills.
   (A) outcomes
   (B) effects
   (C) options
   (D) passages

6. Divard, Inc., is a small public relations firm dedicated to the _____ of promising new musicians.
   (A) promotion
   (B) application
   (C) exception
   (D) suggestion

7. _____ that are out of compliance with contest rules will be automatically disqualified.
   (A) Credentials
   (B) Acknowledgements
   (C) Submissions
   (D) Consequences

8. Conference fees and travel costs will be paid by Direxco, but dining expenses are the participants' _____.
   (A) requirement
   (B) necessity
   (C) responsibility
   (D) commitment

어휘 | **1.** installation 설치 destination 목적지 instruction 지침 **2.** related 관련된 equipment 장비 industry 산업
3. financial statement 재무제표 value 가치 advantage 유리한 점, 이점 **4.** expert 전문적인 forecast 전망 **5.** payment
결제 convenient 편리한 outcome 결과 effect 영향 passage 통과 **6.** public relations 홍보 dedicated to ~에 전념하는
promising 유망한 promotion 홍보 application 지원, 신청 exception 예외 suggestion 제안 **7.** compliance 준수
automatically 자동으로 disqualify 실격시키다 credential 신임장 acknowledgement 인정 submission 출품작, 제출물
consequence 결과 **8.** expense 지출, 경비 participant 참가자 requirement 요구, 요구조건 commitment 헌신, 약속

기출 어휘 - 형용사

additional
추가적인
- 파 add 추가하다
  addition 추가(물)
- 표현 additional workers 추가 직원들

alternative
대안의; 대안
- 파 alternatively 그렇지 않으면
  alternate 번갈아 하다
- 표현 alternative energy 대체 에너지

appropriate
적절한
- 파 appropriately 적절하게
- 표현 wear appropriate gear
  적절한 장비를 착용하다

available
이용 가능한
- 파 availability 이용할 수 있음
- 표현 available for rental
  임대 가능한

aware
알고 있는
- 파 awareness 인식
- 파 unaware 알지 못하는
- 표현 be aware of customer needs
  고객의 욕구를 알다

critical
비평의; 비판적인; 극히 중요한, 중대한
- 표현 receive critical acclaim 호평을 받다
  critical issues 중대한 문제

competitive
경쟁적인, 경쟁의
- 파 compete 경쟁하다
  competition 경쟁
- 표현 competitive prices 경쟁력 있는 가격

complimentary
무료의, 칭찬의
- 파 compliment 칭찬(하다)
- 표현 complimentary tickets
  무료 티켓

confidential
기밀의, 비밀의
- 파 confidentiality 기밀성
- 표현 confidential information
  기밀 정보

dedicated
헌신적인, 전념하는
- 파 dedication 헌신, 공헌
- 표현 dedicated employees
  헌신적인 직원들

detailed
세부적인, 자세한
- 파 details 세부사항
- 표현 detailed information
  자세한 정보

eligible
자격이 있는, 적임의
- 동 entitled, qualified 자격이 있는
- 표현 be eligible for promotion
  승진할 자격이 있다

extensive
광범위한
- 파 extend 연장하다, 늘리다
  extension 연장, 내선 전화
- 표현 extensive experience
  광범위한 경험

innovative
혁신적인
- 파 innovate 혁신하다
  innovation 혁신
- 표현 an innovative product
  혁신적인 제품

potential
잠재적인; 잠재력
- 파 potentially 잠재적으로
- 표현 potential customers
  잠재 고객들

punctual
시간을 지키는[엄수하는]
- 파 punctually 시간대로, 엄수하여
- 표현 a punctual start at 9 o'clock
  9시에 정확히 맞춘 시작

reliable
믿을 만한, 신뢰할 수 있는
- 파 rely 믿다, 의지하다
- 표현 reliable transportation
  믿을 만한 교통 수단

significant
중요한, 상당한
- 파 significantly 상당하게
- 표현 significant changes
  상당한 변화

stable
안정된, 안정적인
- 파 stability 안정(감)
- 표현 stable prices
  안정적인 물가

thorough
철저한
- 파 thoroughly 철저하게
- 표현 thorough inspection
  철저한 검사

valid
유효한
- 동 effective 유효한
- 파 invalid 유효하지 않은
- 표현 valid form of ID 유효한 신분증

T 실전 도움닫기 | 다음 문장의 빈칸에 들어갈 알맞은 말을 고르세요. 정답과 해설 p.162

STEP 1

1. The entertainment complex is _____ for private functions every weekend.
   (A) attractive
   (B) available

2. Your selection will arrive in seven to ten days and will be followed by _____ deliveries every six weeks.
   (A) thorough
   (B) additional

3. The street guide to Tompkinsville has been compiled from _____ national and local maps.
   (A) dependent
   (B) detailed

4. Edith Kozik's corporation guarantees that even temporary employees are _____ for paid holidays.
   (A) eligible
   (B) flexible

STEP 2

5. It is _____ that laboratory employees follow the instructions in this manual exactly as written.
   (A) particular
   (B) critical
   (C) substantial
   (D) immediate

6. *Global Flyways* is a _____ magazine provided as a courtesy to Olan Airlines passengers.
   (A) complimentary
   (B) variable
   (C) perpetual
   (D) subsequent

7. JQT Corporation's business goals cannot be fulfilled without _____ market research.
   (A) contented
   (B) convinced
   (C) reliable
   (D) right

8. Tomorrow's seminar begins at 9:00 A.M. sharp, so attendees should try to be _____.
   (A) punctual
   (B) advanced
   (C) instant
   (D) sudden

어휘 | **1.** private 사적인 function 기능, 행사; 기능을 하다 attractive 매력적인 **3.** compile 편집하다, 편찬하다 national 국가의, 전국의 local 지역의 dependent 의존적인 **4.** corporation 기업 guarantee 보장하다 even 심지어 temporary 임시의, 일시적인 flexible 유연한 **5.** laboratory 실험실 instruction 지침 exactly 정확하게 particular 특별한 critical 극히 중요한 substantial 상당한 immediate 즉각적인 **6.** courtesy 서비스, 배려 passenger 승객 complimentary 무료의 variable 변하는 perpetual 끊임없이 계속되는 subsequent 차후의 **7.** fulfill 달성하다 contented 만족하는 convinced 확신하는 reliable 신뢰할 수 있는 right 옳은 **8.** sharp 정각에 attendee 참석자 punctual 시간을 지키는 advanced 앞선 instant 즉시의 sudden 갑작스러운

기출 어휘 – 부사

accurately
정확하게
- 형 accurate 정확한
- 표현 describe accurately
  정확하게 묘사하다

automatically
자동적으로, 기계적으로
- 형 automatic 자동의
- 표현 download automatically
  자동으로 다운로드하다

briefly
잠시, 간략하게
- 형 brief 간략한; 간략히 보고하다
- 표현 visit briefly 잠시 방문하다

closely
면밀히, 밀접하게
- 형 close 가까운, 가까이에
- 표현 be monitored closely
  면밀히 감시되다

completely
완전히
- 형 complete 완전한; 완료하다
- 표현 completely new
  완전히 새로운

consistently
지속적으로, 일관되게
- 형 consistent 지속적인
- 표현 consistently positive reviews
  지속적으로 긍정적인 평가

diligently
부지런히, 열심히, 애써
- 형 diligent 부지런한, 근면한
  diligence 근면, 성실
- 표현 work diligently 부지런히 일하다

exclusively
독점적으로, 오로지
- 형 exclude 제외하다
  exclusive 독점적인, 배타적인
- 표현 exclusively available
  독점적으로 이용 가능한

finally
마침내, 최종적으로
- 형 final 마지막의, 최종적인
- 표현 finally finish the report
  마침내 보고서를 완성하다

formally
정식으로, 공식적으로
- 형 formal 정식의, 공식적인
- 표현 formally announce the merger
  합병을 공식 발표하다

frequently
종종, 자주
- 형 frequent 잦은, 빈번한
- 표현 be frequently delayed
  자주 지연되다

generally
일반적으로, 대개, 보통
- 형 general 일반적인
  generalize 일반화하다
- 표현 generally free on Wednesdays
  일반적으로 수요일에 한가한

immediately
즉시
- 형 immediate 즉각적인, 직접의
- 표현 immediately after purchase
  구매 직후에

increasingly
점점
- 형 increase 증가하다
  increasing 증가하는
- 표현 become increasingly popular
  점점 더 인기 있어지다

intentionally
의도적으로, 고의로
- 통 on purpose 고의로
- 형 intentional 의도적인, 고의로 한
- 표현 intentionally omit the information
  의도적으로 정보를 삭제하다

particularly
특히
- 형 particular 특정한
- 표현 particularly busy in winter
  겨울에 특히 바쁜

previously
이전에, 미리
- 형 previous 이전의
- 표현 as previously scheduled
  이전에 정해진 대로

primarily
주로
- 형 primary 주요한
- 표현 focus primarily on marketing
  strategies 주로 마케팅 전략에 집중하다

rapidly
빠르게, 신속하게
- 형 rapid 신속한
- 표현 grow rapidly
  급속히 성장하다

recently
최근에
- 형 recent 최근의
- 표현 recently renovated
  최근에 보수된

specifically
특별히, 명확하게
- 형 specific 구체적인
- 표현 parking space specifically
  designated for the staff
  직원들에게 특별히 지정 할당된 주차 공간

실전 도움닫기 | 다음 문장의 빈칸에 들어갈 알맞은 말을 고르세요. 정답과 해설 p.163

STEP 1

1. Tyradex assembly-line workers are expected to do their jobs _____ but accurately.
   (A) fortunately
   (B) rapidly

2. The revised work plan is scheduled to begin _____ and will be in effect for at least three months.
   (A) immediately
   (B) closely

3. The _____ formed client advisory division of the Mantar Corporation is now hiring financial specialists.
   (A) currently
   (B) recently

4. Requests for new office equipment ------ take one month to process.
   (A) totally
   (B) generally

STEP 2

5. Mr. Loren worked for Kloss Fibers for one week before he was _____ introduced to his division manager.
   (A) primarily
   (B) currently
   (C) substantially
   (D) formally

6. Employees at Tihomir Toys work _____ to ensure the quality of the company's merchandise.
   (A) extremely
   (B) enormously
   (C) seemingly
   (D) diligently

7. Please make sure that all sections of the form are filled out _____ for quick processing.
   (A) moderately
   (B) hardly
   (C) completely
   (D) highly

8. Customers who make cash withdrawals _____ may be interested in our new online banking service.
   (A) totally
   (B) hugely
   (C) greatly
   (D) frequently

어휘 | **1.** assembly 조립 fortunately 운 좋게 **2.** be in effect 효력이 있다[발생하다] **3.** advisory 자문의 specialist 전문가 currently 현재 **4.** equipment 장비 process 처리하다 totally 완전히 generally 보통 **5.** division manager 부서장 primarily 주로 substantially 상당히 formally 정식으로, 공식적으로 **6.** ensure 확보하다 merchandise 상품 extremely 극도로 enormously 엄청나게 seemingly 겉보기에는 diligently 부지런히 **7.** section 부분, 부문 form 양식 fill out 작성하다 moderately 적당하게 hardly 거의 ~않다 **8.** cash withdrawal 현금 인출 totally 완전히, 전적으로 hugely 엄청나게, 크게

1. Anyone interested in mentoring a summer intern should ------- Sharmila Kumar in the human resources department.
   (A) acquaint
   (B) notify
   (C) respond
   (D) explain

2. Because of its ------- for outstanding customer service, Mei's Hair Salon is the most popular business of its kind in the area.
   (A) approval
   (B) estimation
   (C) probability
   (D) reputation

3. ------- savings on the cost of building materials contributed to a growth in Minbrough Construction's revenue.
   (A) Virtual
   (B) Tentative
   (C) Observant
   (D) Significant

4. The flash on the Yinkam camera activates -------, so the photographer does not need to turn it on.
   (A) potentially
   (B) ultimately
   (C) automatically
   (D) simultaneously

5. Pinet City Council has ------- a plan to build a shopping center near the bus station next spring.
   (A) approved
   (B) cooperated
   (C) treated
   (D) connected

6. On Thursday, the CEO held a press conference ------- plans to merge with Remini Financial Services.
   (A) except
   (B) versus
   (C) along
   (D) concerning

7. Neltin Corporation takes ------- security measures to safeguard all customer data from unauthorized access.
   (A) appropriate
   (B) dependent
   (C) receptive
   (D) concerned

8. The latest digital edition of *Silvina Business Law* has an online review section that was not available -------.
   (A) professionally
   (B) previously
   (C) mainly
   (D) thoughtfully

9. Eating establishments in the city are frequently ------- by inspectors to verify compliance with health and safety standards.
(A) invested
(B) assessed
(C) conducted
(D) conveyed

10. Officials attribute the ------- in service to a software upgrade that makes the system run faster.
(A) exchange
(B) relief
(C) improvement
(D) lift

11. Workshop participants may choose any seat in the auditorium except those in the front row, which are ------ for the presenters.
(A) chaired
(B) reserved
(C) substituted
(D) performed

12. Dr. Saito's research project has been discontinued because it became ------ time-consuming and financially taxing.
(A) poorly
(B) thickly
(C) increasingly
(D) differently

13. To be chosen as the building contractor for the new museum, Rappert Construction must first ------- against several other construction firms.
(A) contribute
(B) decide
(C) compete
(D) associate

14. Thanks to his fifteen years at Dulesse Tech, Mr. Duvarre has a ------- understanding of company policies.
(A) thorough
(B) distracting
(C) prepared
(D) last

15. The Minabet County Forestry Service has the ------- to close recreational areas early when necessary.
(A) authority
(B) consequence
(C) significance
(D) reaction

16. This year alone, the V1X Auto Industry Awards will be given ------- to manufacturers of energy-efficient vehicles.
(A) exceptionally
(B) routinely
(C) traditionally
(D) exclusively

17. To receive reimbursement for any business travel, employees must submit expense reports within 30 days of ------- from their trip.
(A) working
(B) flying
(C) returning
(D) conducting

18. Marsden Manufacturing, Inc., is hiring temporary workers to address the present ------- for greater personnel resources.
(A) measure
(B) denial
(C) demand
(D) claim

19. Applicants for the dental assistant position must possess a license that is ------- in the state of New York.
(A) respectful
(B) actual
(C) skillful
(D) valid

20. Through the years, Glenview Laboratory has ------- provided quality, cost-effective services to its customers.
(A) broadly
(B) formerly
(C) consistently
(D) repetitiously

21. The computer technicians ------- sales representatives with detailed instructions for accessing the client database.
(A) offer
(B) arrange
(C) contribute
(D) provide

22. Because Legolos Company recognizes the importance of protecting customer information, it has made data privacy a high -------.
(A) conformity
(B) liability
(C) priority
(D) seniority

23. Analysts characterize Westonville Financial as a ------- company because it has a long record of sustained profitability.
(A) whole
(B) total
(C) stable
(D) routine

24. To save time during Sunday's session, the roundtable discussion was ------- omitted from the conference schedule.
(A) intentionally
(B) arguably
(C) commonly
(D) vitally

25. Metta Electronics, Inc., has not sold its old building because it is waiting for an ------ that meets the asking price.
(A) offer
(B) expense
(C) addition
(D) incident

26. Residents who have ------- to the plan for the community center's renovation can present their concerns at Monday night's meeting.
(A) decisions
(B) offenses
(C) objections
(D) installments

27. Trade magazine writers remain largely ------- of Airita's new technology and how it could drastically affect the market.
(A) severe
(B) indicative
(C) subtle
(D) unaware

28. Developed last December, Speedy Print's new emission-reduction strategy will ------- be implemented next month.
(A) finally
(B) recently
(C) lastly
(D) exactly

29. Senior management ------- employees to submit ideas for increasing workplace satisfaction to the human resources department.
(A) responds
(B) excels
(C) maintains
(D) encourages

30. Teklind, Inc., implements strict security ------ to prevent unauthorized users from gaining access to confidential information.
(A) consents
(B) measures
(C) angles
(D) distances

31. The information you provide on this questionnaire is strictly ------- and will not be shared with any other vendors.
(A) potential
(B) concentrated
(C) dedicated
(D) confidential

32. Volunteers are needed to take pictures at the company banquet, ------- those who have experience in event photography.
(A) gradually
(B) accordingly
(C) constantly
(D) specifically

Part

독해

7

Part 7은 제시된 지문을 읽고 그에 따른 문제를 푸는 유형으로, Part 7은 단일 지문이 총 29문항, 복수 지문이 총 25문항 출제돼요.

■ Part 7의 빈출 지문 유형과 질문을 익혀두자

1 **지문 유형:** 편지, 이메일, 광고, 회람, 공지, 기사, 정보문, 기타 양식
2 **질문 유형:** 주제·목적 찾기, 세부 내용 파악, Not/True, 추론, 문장 삽입, 동의어 찾기, 연계 추론

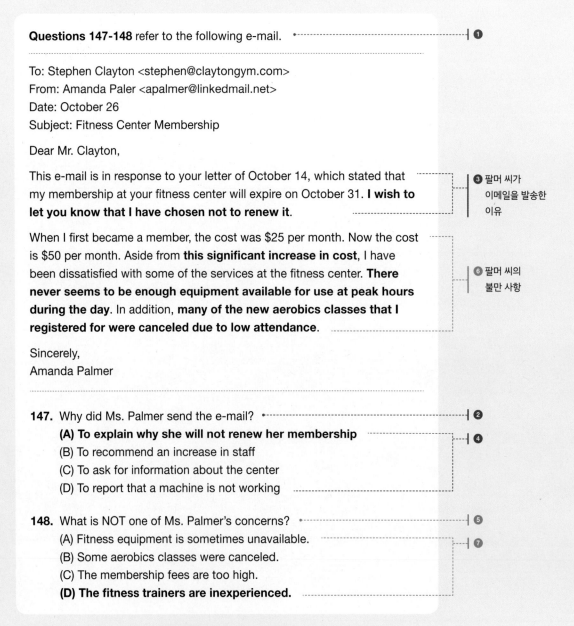

Questions 147-148 refer to the following e-mail. •----------------| ❶

To: Stephen Clayton <stephen@claytongym.com>
From: Amanda Paler <apalmer@linkedmail.net>
Date: October 26
Subject: Fitness Center Membership

Dear Mr. Clayton,

This e-mail is in response to your letter of October 14, which stated that   ❸ 팔머 씨가
my membership at your fitness center will expire on October 31. **I wish to**   이메일을 발송한
let you know that I have chosen not to renew it.   이유

When I first became a member, the cost was $25 per month. Now the cost
is $50 per month. Aside from **this significant increase in cost**, I have
been dissatisfied with some of the services at the fitness center. **There**   ❻ 팔머 씨의
never seems to be enough equipment available for use at peak hours   불만 사항
during the day. In addition, **many of the new aerobics classes that I**
registered for were canceled due to low attendance.

Sincerely,
Amanda Palmer

147. Why did Ms. Palmer send the e-mail? •-------------------| ❷
    (A) To explain why she will not renew her membership ----| ❹
    (B) To recommend an increase in staff
    (C) To ask for information about the center
    (D) To report that a machine is not working

148. What is NOT one of Ms. Palmer's concerns? •-------------| ❺
    (A) Fitness equipment is sometimes unavailable. -----| ❼
    (B) Some aerobics classes were canceled.
    (C) The membership fees are too high.
    (D) The fitness trainers are inexperienced.

❶ 지문의 종류를 읽는다.

이 글은 이메일이므로, 누가 누구에게 어떤 목적으로 보낸 이메일인지를 염두에 두고 문제 풀이에 임해야 해요.

→ 아만다 팔머 씨가 스티븐 클레이튼 씨에게 보낸 이메일로, 제목(Subject: Fitness Center Membership)을 통해 헬스 클럽 회원권에 관련해 보낸 이메일임을 예상할 수 있어요.

❷ 문제를 파악한다.

팔머 씨가 이메일을 보낸 이유는 무엇인가?

→ Why did ~ send the e-mail? / What is the purpose of the e-mail? / Why was the e-mail written? 등은 이메일을 보낸 목적을 묻는 문제예요.

❸ 본문을 처음부터 읽는다.

문제 포인트와 관련된 내용이 나올 때까지 요약하며 읽어요.

→ 팔머 씨는 자신의 회원권이 10월 31일자로 만료되는데, 회원권을 갱신하지 않기로 결정했다고 했어요.

❹ 답이 나올 때까지 읽고 답한다.

(A) 회원권을 갱신하지 않는 이유를 설명하려고

→ 팔머 씨는 회원권을 갱신하지 않겠다고 했으니, (A)가 정답이에요.

❺ 다음 문제를 읽는다.

팔머 씨의 불만 사항이 아닌 것은 무엇인가?

→ NOT 문제이므로, 지문에 언급된 내용과 선택지의 내용을 하나씩 대조해 가면서 문제를 풀어야 한다는 것을 예상할 수 있어요.

❻ 본문을 이어서 읽는다.

두 번째 단락에 팔머 씨의 불만 사항이 조목조목 열거되어 있어요.

→ 팔머 씨는 한 달에 25달러에서 50달러로 인상된 회비, 피크 시간대에는 이용할 수 없는 부족한 장비, 저조한 출석률로 인해 취소된 강좌에 대해 불만을 토로하고 있어요.

❼ 답이 나올 때까지 읽고 답한다.

(D) 헬스 트레이너들의 경험이 부족하다.

→ 헬스 트레이너에 대한 언급은 없으므로 (D)가 정답이에요.

RC

PART 7

편지 / 이메일

출제 포인트 1 사내 편지/이메일에서는 업무 제안, 수리 및 행사 일정 등의 주제가 주로 다뤄지고 회사-외부인 편지/이메일에서는 감사, 불만, 제품 문의, 예약 확인 같은 내용이 자주 나와요.

출제 포인트 2 글의 흐름은 주제 · 목적 → 세부사항 → 요청/제안사항의 순서로 전개되는 것이 일반적이에요.

■ 빈출 질문

목적	• What is the purpose of the letter?	이 편지를 쓴 목적은 무엇인가?
목적	• Why was the e-mail written?	이메일은 왜 쓰였는가?
요청사항	• What are employees asked to do?	직원들이 무엇을 하도록 요청 받는가?
첨부사항	• What was sent with the letter?	편지와 함께 발송된 것은 무엇인가?

■ 지문의 흐름 및 문제풀이 전략

정답과 해설 p.167

받는 사람   Dear Mr. Osborn:

문제점   Aphrodite Sporting Goods (ASG) recently mailed you a copy of our summer catalogue, using the address we have on file for you. Unfortunately, the item was returned, marked "Undeliverable."

목적   We would like to get the catalogue to you. Given your order history, you might be interested in our new line of tennis equipment. If you could provide me your current mailing address, I will resend the catalogue along with some valuable coupons.

추가적인 세부 사항   We have also made improvements to our mail order service. We now provide online order tracking and no longer charge shipping on orders over $50.
We hope to hear from you.

보낸 사람   Trang Minh Pham

STEP ❷ 단서 찾기
→ 글의 목적은 주로 초반부에 제시되는 경우가 많지만, 글 전반에 걸쳐 제시되는 경우도 있으니 유의하세요.

목적을 담고 있는 빈출 표현
- I am writing (in regard to) ~
- I would like to ~
- This is to remind you that ~
- I'm pleased to ~
- Please ~

STEP ❶ 질문 파악: 목적 문제
→ What is the (main) purpose of ~? / Why was ~ sent? / Why was ~ written? 등은 목적을 묻는 문제예요.

Q What is **the purpose** of the e-mail?
(A) To explain how to get a refund
(B) To offer a gift card
(C) To obtain contact information
(D) To provide details about an order

STEP ❸ 정답 찾기
→ 쿠폰과 함께 카탈로그를 받을 수 있는 주소를 요청하고 있으므로, 정답은 (C)입니다.

어휘 | equipment 장비 online order tracking 온라인 주문 추적 서비스 no longer 더 이상 ~않다 charge 청구하다

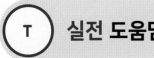
1.   E-mail

To: warren.cluett@reva.org
From: delia.kwon@reva.org
Subject: Shipment arrival

Hi Warren,

We will be receiving a shipment of bricks tomorrow morning. The manufacturer has informed me that the truck will be arriving at 7:30 A.M. When the truck arrives, please take inventory as the shipment is unloaded and verify that the quantities on the receipt are accurate. In addition, please make sure that the bricks are stacked no more than three bricks high.

Delia Kwon

What is the purpose of the e-mail?
(A) To provide instructions to an employee
(B) To address a mistake with a shipment

2.   Letter

Dear Ms. Gomez:

We anticipate an opening for a bilingual customer service associate in our sales department starting next month. Your application was retained from last year's search for our bilingual clerical pool. We are interested in learning whether you still have an interest and might be available to work full-time this year. If so, please contact me at 604 555-0009 by Friday, May 15th and I can supply you with further details.

Sincerely,

Pamela Finch

What qualification is required for the position?
(A) Experience in sales
(B) Fluency in two languages

어휘 | **1.** shipment 선적물, 배송품 brick 벽돌 take inventory 재고 조사를 하다 unload (짐을) 내리다 verify 확인하다 quantity 수량 receipt 영수증, 인수증 accurate 정확한 stack 쌓다
2. bilingual 두 개 언어를 구사하는 application 지원(서) retain 보관하다, 유지하다 clerical 사무직의 pool 이용 가능한 인력 further details 추가 상세 사항 fluency 유창함

Questions 1-2 refer to the following e-mail.

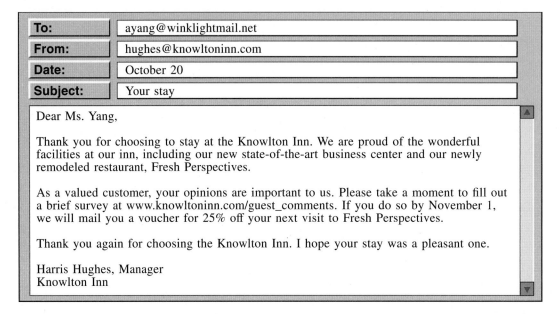

To:	ayang@winklightmail.net
From:	hughes@knowltoninn.com
Date:	October 20
Subject:	Your stay

Dear Ms. Yang,

Thank you for choosing to stay at the Knowlton Inn. We are proud of the wonderful facilities at our inn, including our new state-of-the-art business center and our newly remodeled restaurant, Fresh Perspectives.

As a valued customer, your opinions are important to us. Please take a moment to fill out a brief survey at www.knowltoninn.com/guest_comments. If you do so by November 1, we will mail you a voucher for 25% off your next visit to Fresh Perspectives.

Thank you again for choosing the Knowlton Inn. I hope your stay was a pleasant one.

Harris Hughes, Manager
Knowlton Inn

1. Why did Mr. Hughes send the e-mail?

(A) To confirm a reservation
(B) To request feedback from a customer
(C) To respond to a customer's complaint
(D) To ask that payment be made

2. What is suggested about the Knowlton Inn?

(A) It is located in a city's historic district.
(B) Its Web site will soon be redesigned.
(C) It has recently undergone changes.
(D) It is noted for its reasonable pricing.

어휘 | facility 시설 state-of-the-art 첨단의 newly 최근 valued 귀중한 opinion 의견 important 중요한 fill out 작성하다 survey 설문조사 voucher 쿠폰

Questions 3-4 refer to the following letter.

May 26

Ken Izumu
Westlake Marching Band
5443 Wells Point Blvd.
Kingsland, Missouri 64160

Dear Mr. Izumu,

Congratulations! Your marching band has been selected to perform in the Kingsland summer parade. The parade will begin at 2:00 P.M. on Saturday, June 20. Please tell your musicians to arrive at the convention center no later than 1:30 P.M. Performers will gather near the south gate of the convention center to start and then head west on Main Street, past city hall, and toward the Joplin Bridge. The festivities will end at Perrywood Park, where shuttle buses back to the convention center will be available.

We look forward to seeing you there!

Sincerely,

Maryann Jones
Maryann Jones
Event Coordinator

3. Who most likely is Mr. Izumu?

(A) A band leader
(B) A bus driver
(C) A convention center employee
(D) A parade organizer

4. Where will the parade begin?

(A) At city hall
(B) Under the Joplin Bridge
(C) In Perrywood Park
(D) At the convention center

어휘 | perform 연주[공연]하다 no later than 늦어도 ~까지 head 향하다 past ~을 지나서

Questions 5-7 refer to the following e-mail.

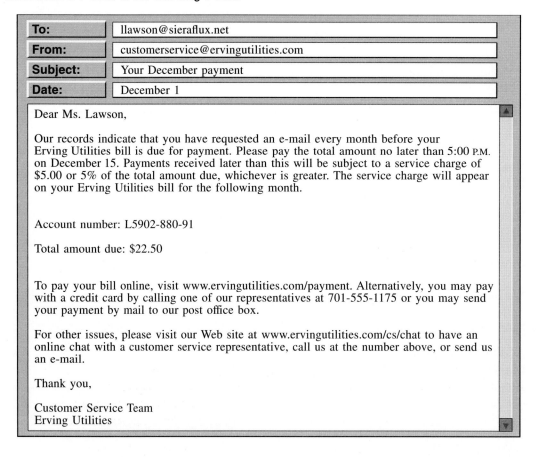

To:	llawson@sieraflux.net
From:	customerservice@ervingutilities.com
Subject:	Your December payment
Date:	December 1

Dear Ms. Lawson,

Our records indicate that you have requested an e-mail every month before your Erving Utilities bill is due for payment. Please pay the total amount no later than 5:00 P.M. on December 15. Payments received later than this will be subject to a service charge of $5.00 or 5% of the total amount due, whichever is greater. The service charge will appear on your Erving Utilities bill for the following month.

Account number: L5902-880-91

Total amount due: $22.50

To pay your bill online, visit www.ervingutilities.com/payment. Alternatively, you may pay with a credit card by calling one of our representatives at 701-555-1175 or you may send your payment by mail to our post office box.

For other issues, please visit our Web site at www.ervingutilities.com/cs/chat to have an online chat with a customer service representative, call us at the number above, or send us an e-mail.

Thank you,

Customer Service Team
Erving Utilities

5. Why was the e-mail sent to Ms. Lawson?

(A) To announce changes to a policy
(B) To issue a payment reminder
(C) To correct a billing error
(D) To request account information

6. What is indicated about the service charge?

(A) It applies to late payments.
(B) It will be eliminated on December 15.
(C) It is the same amount every month.
(D) It must be paid immediately.

7. What is NOT a suggested way to contact the company about service issues?

(A) By postcard
(B) By online chat
(C) By phone
(D) By e-mail

어휘 | due 지불 기일이 된 payment 납부 amount 액수 no later than 늦어도 ~까지 be subject to ~의 대상이다 alternatively 그렇지 않으면 representative 직원 post office box 사서함

To:	<Undisclosed Recipients>
From:	Ivana Robbins
Date:	February 6, 1:00 P.M.
Subject:	Help Desk ticket #4456A

Hello everyone,

Kevin Gilmore, supervisor of the Computer Help Desk, has reported that employees in our branch offices are having difficulty today accessing the Internet and the e-mail system. His technicians have been working on the problem all morning and hope to have it resolved by 5:00 P.M. Though none of us here at corporate headquarters seem to be affected by this problem, it does affect everyone in payroll as well as our sales department in Loughlin. If you need to contact anyone in these departments, you can reach them by telephone. I will let you know as soon as I hear from Mr. Gilmore that our colleagues are back online.

Best,

Ivana Robbins
Administrative Assistant

8. Who most likely received the e-mail?

(A) Employees at corporate headquarters
(B) Sales representatives in Loughlin
(C) Supervisors in branch offices
(D) Employees in the payroll department

9. According to the e-mail, what is
Mr. Gilmore's staff trying to do?

(A) Make a purchasing decision
(B) Restore Internet connections
(C) Reorganize computer help documents
(D) Confirm a contact list

10. What are recipients of the e-mail advised to do?

(A) Report technical problems to Mr. Gilmore
(B) Pick up their paychecks in person
(C) Work at a different computer temporarily
(D) Use a different method of communication

어휘 | undisclosed 비공개의 recipient 수신자 help desk (컴퓨터 관련) 업무지원부 supervisor 관리자 have difficulty -ing ~하는 데 어려움을 겪다 access 접속하다 resolve 해결하다 affect 영향을 미치다 payroll department 급여부 colleague 동료

Questions 11-13 refer to the following e-mail.

From:	Alisa Koertig
To:	Dancosti Circulation Dept.
Date:	2 May
Subject:	Subscription

I am writing about my *Dancosti Magazine* subscription. — [1] —. Specifically, the last two issues were sent to my old address in Chesterton. Fortunately, the postal service was helpful in tracking down the two issues in question and forwarding them to my new address in Batesville. Moving forward, however, I would like to have the problem corrected and the magazines sent to me directly. — [2] —.

Please note that immediately after moving into my new apartment in February, I added the new address to my online user account on your Web site, following your instructions for subscribers. — [3] —. Could you please check to make sure that your distribution division has my new address? — [4] —.

Sincerely,

Alisa Koertig

11. What is the purpose of the e-mail?

(A) To cancel a subscription
(B) To report delivery problems
(C) To inquire about a special offer
(D) To request access to a Web site

12. Why did Ms. Koertig access her online account in February?

(A) To submit a payment
(B) To request missing issues
(C) To contact customer service
(D) To update personal information

13. In which of the positions marked [1], [2], [3], and [4] does the following sentence best belong?

"However, I am not sure I did it correctly."

(A) [1]
(B) [2]
(C) [3]
(D) [4]

어휘 | circulation 배포, 유통 subscription 구독 specifically 구체적으로 issue (잡지) 호 fortunately 다행히 forward 전달하다 correct 바로잡다 directly 직접 immediately after ~ 직후 instruction 지침 subscriber 구독자 distribution 배포, 유통

Questions 14-17 refer to the following letter.

The McTierney Foundation

4553 Avenue of the Americas
New York, NY 10036

June 16

Ms. Diana Santoso
Utami Health Centre
Jalan Kober 16, Cipete
Jakarta Selatan, Indonesia 12150

Dear Ms. Santoso,

I first learned of your hospital network at the Southeast Asia Health Initiative conference last year and have been following the progress of your work closely since then. Your expansion of the network is extraordinary.

Our foundation has recently been asked to take over a project to develop a similar network of hospitals and clinics in the Philippines. The project's goal will be to integrate several new hospitals and existing care providers into one coherent network like yours. Until now, our foundation's work has been primarily with individual hospitals and clinics in North America. Thus, it is important for us to learn as much as we can from organizations like yours and managers like you who have worked on multiple-hospital projects.

As a consequence, I am writing to ask whether it might be possible to arrange a fact-finding trip to meet with you and your staff and to see your hospitals. Specifically, I wish to learn more about managing a hospital network formed by incorporating several rural hospitals and clinics, as you have done. Ideally, I'd like to make the trip sometime in the next three months, at your convenience. Please let me know if this is possible and the best time for me to come. Thank you in advance for considering this unusual request for your time and help with our new endeavor.

Sincerely,

John Shaker
John Shaker, M.D., M.P.H.

RC

PART 7

14. What is a purpose of the letter?

(A) To invite Ms. Santoso to apply for a grant
(B) To request that Ms. Santoso share her expertise
(C) To ask if Ms. Santoso can complete a report sooner than expected
(D) To offer Ms. Santoso a full-time job

15. The word "following" in paragraph 1, line 2 is closest in meaning to

(A) obeying
(B) accomplishing
(C) participating in
(D) paying attention to

16. What does Dr. Shaker point out about his foundation's new project?

(A) It involves coordinating the work of multiple institutions.
(B) It will require building specialized hospitals in North America.
(C) It is being funded by the Indonesian government.
(D) It has been nominated for an award.

17. According to the letter, what does Dr. Shaker want to do within three months?

(A) Expand his foundation's staff
(B) Travel abroad for research purposes
(C) Visit a new hospital in New York
(D) Find a new source of funding for his foundation

어휘 | foundation 재단 extraordinary 놀라운, 비범한 take over 인계받다 integrate 통합하다 existing 기존의 as a consequence 따라서, 결과로 specifically 구체적으로, 분명히 convenience 편의, 편리 in advance 미리, 사전에 endeavor 노력

■ 빈출 질문

주제	• What is being announced?	무엇이 발표되고 있는가?
목적	• What is the purpose of the notice?	공지의 목적은 무엇인가?
요청사항	• What are the employees asked to do?	직원들이 요청 받는 것은 무엇인가?
세부사항	• What is NOT a requirement?	필수 자격요건이 아닌 것은 무엇인가?
일정	• When will the policy change take effect?	변경된 정책은 언제부터 효력이 있는가?

■ 지문의 흐름 및 문제풀이 전략

정답과 해설 p. 171

Mantero City Community Center
Summer Cooking Classes

공지 목적 | The Mantero City Community Center will offer the following cooking classes this summer:

Class	Date	Time	Cost
Soups and Appetizers	July 9	4:00 P.M.-6:00 P.M.	$20
Poultry and Meat Dishes	July 11	1:00 P.M.-3:00 P.M.	$35
Quick Pasta Dishes	July 13	9:00 A.M.-11:00 A.M.	$25

세부 사항 | Classes will be held at the Mantero City Community Center, 3535 Springdale Boulevard, Mantero City. Registration will begin on July 1. To reserve a place, visit the administration office. Alternatively, you may send your information to Rosa Morales by fax at 928-555-0198 or by e-mail at rmorales@manterocc.net. Please include your name, the name of the class you wish to attend, and a telephone number.

Q In what way are readers **NOT** instructed to respond?
(A) By e-mail
(B) By telephone
(C) By fax
(D) In person

STEP ❷ 단서 찾기
→ 지문에 언급된 내용과 보기를 하나씩 확인해 봅니다. 보기에서는 지문의 내용을 다른 표현으로 바꾸어 제시하는 경우가 많으므로 주의해야 해요.

• visit the administration office
  → (D) In person
• by fax at 928-555-0198
  → (C) By fax
• by e-mail at rmorales@manterocc.net
  → (A) By e-mail

STEP ❶ 질문 파악: Not / True 문제
→ (What is) NOT ~? / What is true about ~? / What is mentioned ~? 등은 사실 관계를 확인하는 문제예요.

STEP ❸ 정답 찾기
→ 지문에 전화번호는 언급되어 있지 않으므로, 정답은 (B)입니다.

어휘 | poultry 가금류 registration 등록 reserve 예약하다 administration office 행정실 alternatively 그 대신에, 그렇지 않으면

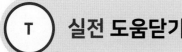
1.

Advertisement

The Coastal Palate
Is your office hosting a party? Let us help!

The Coastal Palate can provide delicious dishes for any occasion, from a simple office party to a formal dinner. We specialize in French, Italian, and Spanish cuisines with an emphasis on sea food dishes.

Visit our shop at 5600 Piedmont Avenue to talk to one of our specialists and taste items from our menu at no cost whatsoever. See why we are the top choice of business executives for a spectacular dining experience!

What kind of business is being advertised?
(A) A kitchen supply store
(B) A food preparation service

2.

Memo

From: Eun Mi Ha, CEO
To: All Employees
Subject: January 10 Meeting
Date: January 13

We will be changing the regular work hours for most employees as part of our initiative to reduce energy costs. Since our energy costs are generally higher in the late afternoon, it will be to our advantage to perform more work in the morning. Therefore, beginning on Monday, February 24, the workday will officially start at 8:00 A.M. instead of 9:00 A.M., and it will end at 4:00 P.M. instead of 5:00 P.M. The last day of the old schedule will be Friday, February 21.

What are employees asked to do?
(A) Adjust their typical work schedules
(B) Switch to energy-efficient light bulbs

어휘 | **1.** cuisine 요리 emphasis 중점 executive 간부
2. regular 통상의, 일상의 initiative (문제 해결을 위한 독창적인) 계획, 전략 to one's advantage ~에게 유리하게 workday (하루의) 근무 시간, 평일 officially 공식적으로 adjust 조정하다, 맞추다 typical 전형적인, 일반적인 energy-efficient 연료[에너지]가 적게 드는 light bulb 전구

Questions 1-2 refer to the following advertisement.

WPI
WILSON-PRICE INSTITUTE
Chicago/Dallas/New York

Become a Certified Pharmacy Technician

Pharmacy technicians assist registered pharmacists with:
➢ Accepting and checking prescriptions
➢ Assembling medications for dispensing
➢ Maintaining patient records

At Wilson-Price, you can qualify to be a CPT in one year!

Classes begin in September and January.

Call (872) 555-0143 or
e-mail info@wilsonprice.com today!

---

1. What is indicated about the Wilson-Price Institute?

   (A) It offers online classes.
   (B) It trains registered pharmacists.
   (C) It has more than one location.
   (D) It enrolls students just once a year.

2. What is NOT mentioned as a task performed by certified pharmacy technicians?

   (A) Reviewing prescriptions
   (B) Preparing packages of medicine
   (C) Contacting patients
   (D) Keeping records

어휘 | pharmacy technician 약사 보조 registered pharmacist 등록 약사 prescription 처방전 medication 약 dispense 조제하다
patient 환자 qualify 자격을 얻다

RC

PART 7

Questions 3-5 refer to the following memo.

To: All staff
From: Stuart Wentworth, Vice President of Operations
Date: Monday, January 26
Subject: Winter storm

Because of the impending snowstorm, Zelman Architects will be closed tomorrow. The county Department of Transportation has requested that all nonemergency vehicles stay off the roads.

Employees are expected to work on assignments at home during regular business hours and to stay in touch with their department managers by e-mail. Managers should note that all end-of-month deadlines remain in effect.

The storm is expected to stop early Wednesday morning. To give the snowplow crews enough time to clear the parking areas, employees are asked to arrive no earlier than 10:30 A.M. on Wednesday. The usual Wednesday morning staff meetings will be moved to later in the day.

Thank you for your cooperation.

---

3. What is the purpose of the memo?

   (A) To explain a new policy
   (B) To remind staff about a new deadline
   (C) To request that employees work extended hours
   (D) To notify employees about an office closing

4. What are managers expected to do on Tuesday, January 27?

   (A) Attend a staff meeting in the afternoon
   (B) Arrive at work later than usual
   (C) Contact Mr. Wentworth about revised schedules
   (D) Maintain e-mail communication with staff

5. What is suggested about Zelman Architects?

   (A) It has a contract with the Department of Transportation.
   (B) It has several office locations.
   (C) It employs many people who commute by car.
   (D) It has had to postpone a special company event.

어휘 | impending 임박한 nonemergency 긴급하지 않은 vehicle 차량 be expected to ~해야 한다, ~하리라 예상된다 assignment 업무, 과제 effect 유효한 snowplow 제설 no earlier than ~ 이후에

Questions 6-7 refer to the following advertisement.

Are you a business owner looking to expand your customer base?

Alcove, Inc., provides everything you need to build a Web site that promotes your business and increases sales. Our service puts you in control with easy-to-use design tools. Using our point-and-click editing features, you can choose from our hundreds of Web design templates and stock photo images to create your own look. You can maintain your Web site with tracking tools that show you exactly how your site is performing for you. Customer service technicians are always available to help during any step of the process to ensure your products and services are reaching a larger audience. Let Alcove take your business to the next level. Visit www.alcoveinc.com to learn more!

Alcove, Inc.

---

6. What is being advertised?

   (A) A photography business
   (B) An employment agency
   (C) A Web site design service
   (D) A sale on computers

7. What is indicated about Alcove, Inc.?

   (A) It provides photographs for customer use.
   (B) It is hiring new customer service technicians.
   (C) It offers a discount on large orders.
   (D) It has recently expanded its Web site.

어휘 | expand 확장하다 promote 홍보하다 increase 올리다 feature 기능 template 견본 perform 수행하다 process 절차 reach 닿다 audience 청중

North County Department of Transportation Career Opportunities

North County Department of Transportation (NCDT) is recruiting talented engineers to meet the demand for its expanding services. — [1] —. Applications are currently being accepted for transportation engineering supervisor, development engineering assistant, and highway project manager. — [2] —.

NCDT is a mid-sized government department with staff members who have experience and expertise in roadway, bridge, and light rail construction and maintenance. — [3] —.

We offer excellent benefits, a great workplace environment, and opportunity for professional development. — [4] —. For more information and to apply for one of these positions, please visit www.ncdt.gov/jobs. The deadline for application is March 31.

8. What is the purpose of the notice?

(A) To present updates to a Web site
(B) To introduce county employees
(C) To announce job openings
(D) To summarize a new service plan

9. What is indicated about NCDT?

(A) It is a small division.
(B) Its volume of work is increasing.
(C) Its budget was recently approved.
(D) It works only on road projects.

10. In which of the positions marked [1], [2], [3], and [4] does the following sentence best belong?

"The team's additional skills include transportation planning and surveying."

(A) [1]
(B) [2]
(C) [3]
(D) [4]

어휘 | transportation 교통 demand 수요 expand 확대하다 application 지원(서) expertise 전문지식 maintenance 정비 benefits 수당 workplace environment 근무환경

Questions 11-13 refer to the following memo.

To: All staff
From: Neil Halderan, CEO, Halderan Financial, Inc.
Date: January 25
Subject: Job Search

As many of you are aware, we have recently conducted a thorough search for a new vice president of Halderan Financial, Inc. We are pleased to announce that Ms. Chieko Sakai has been appointed to the position.

Ms. Sakai served as the managing director of BRI Investment Group for the last five years. Before that, she was a senior sales representative at Welton Insurance Ltd. for three years; she attained the senior position after serving for two years as a junior sales representative for the same company. She has a bachelor of science degree in business and a master of business administration, both from Northmont University.

To welcome Ms. Sakai to Halderan Financial, we will be holding a reception at the Round House Restaurant on Broad Street between 5 and 7 P.M. on Friday, February 4, which all employees are invited to attend. Ms. Sakai assumed her new position today.

---

11. Why was the memo sent?

(A) To explain a marketing plan

(B) To announce a job opening

(C) To arrange an employee orientation

(D) To introduce a new employee

12. What is Ms. Sakai's current title?

(A) Vice president

(B) Managing director

(C) Senior sales representative

(D) Junior sales representative

13. What will happen on February 4?

(A) A job interview will be conducted.

(B) A university course will begin.

(C) A gathering will be held.

(D) A company will be sold.

어휘 | recently 최근에 thorough 수고를 다하는 appoint 임명하다 attain 이르다 bachelor of science degree 학사 학위 master 석사 business administration 경영학 assume 맡다

Business Leaders to Be Honored

By Jane Chadwick, *Metro Daily* Staff

ALFREDVILLE (March 4)—Leaders and innovators from the business world will be honored during the Innovative Technology Committee (ITC) Annual Business Awards Dinner on Wednesday, April 24, at the Sakolsky Hotel. The dinner, originally established by ITC president Kei Kan, includes awards such as the Best New Consumer Electronic Product and the highly coveted Innovator of the Year, presented to the leader of the year's most innovative company.

According to an ITC spokesperson, three finalists have been chosen from the numerous candidates nominated for the Innovator of the Year award. The finalists for this year's award are Martha Wilder, creator of the online advertising company Stylen DX; Maxwell Bernard, who founded the Web-site design service Ipictix; and a finalist from our last dinner, Victor Rocha, whose popular Web site, Cookdemoz, offers free cooking tutorial videos. As usual, the Innovator of the Year award will be presented by the ITC president.

Guests do not need to be members of the ITC in order to attend the gala. Nonmembers can purchase tickets for $50. ITC members, however, can purchase tickets at the reduced price of $30. Tickets may be ordered by calling 972-555-0136 or visiting www.itc.com. "Anyone interested in technology should really become a member this year. It only costs $40 to join, and there are so many benefits associated with being a member," urges ITC spokesperson Clara O'Brien. All guests will be entered into a drawing to win prizes, including a two-night trip to the Gallus Sea Resort.

14. What is suggested about the ITC Annual Business Awards Dinner?

(A) It is open to ITC members only.
(B) It is being held in a new location this year.
(C) It will be broadcast on the Internet.
(D) It honors innovators from multiple industries.

15. The word "last" in paragraph 2, line 9, is closest in meaning to

(A) final
(B) current
(C) previous
(D) following

16. Who will present the Innovator of the Year award?

(A) Ms. Kan
(B) Mr. Bernard
(C) Mr. Rocha
(D) Ms. Wilder

17. What recommendation does Ms. O'Brien make?

(A) To call the Gallus Sea Resort
(B) To pay for a membership
(C) To nominate candidates
(D) To try a new product

어휘 | honor 상을 주다 innovator 혁신가 coveted 탐내는 spokesperson 대변인 numerous 수많은 candidate 후보자 found 설립하다 tutorial 지도하는 reduced 할인된 benefit 혜택 associated with ~와 관련된 urge 강조하다

출제 포인트 1 양식 지문은 단편 정보들로 구성되는 경우가 많으며, 비교적 단시간에 풀 수 있는 쉬운 유형이에요. 문제에서 요구하는 정보 위주로 검색하면서 푸는 것이 좋아요.

출제 포인트 2 문자 메시지/온라인 채팅은 신속한 업무 처리를 위해 즉석에서 주고받는 정보나 의견 전달이 주를 이뤄요.

■ 빈출 질문

일정	• What is scheduled for June 8?	6월 8일에는 무슨 일정이 잡혀 있는가?
이유	• Why did Ms. Alden receive free shipping?	알덴 씨는 왜 무료로 배송 받았는가?
의도 파악	• At 10:08, what does Lopez mean when she writes, "Absolutely"?	10시 8분에 로페즈가 "물론이죠"라고 쓴 것은 무슨 의미인가?

■ 지문의 흐름 및 문제풀이 전략

정답과 해설 **p. 175**

말론 씨의 문제점	**Paula Malone** **January 23, 8:53 A.M.** Can you do me a favor? I'm scheduled to teach my exercise class at the gym at 9:00, and I'm going to be late. The train I'm on had a mechanical problem and left the station about 15 minutes behind schedule.

Martin Bileck   **January 23, 8:54 A.M.**
That's too bad. How can I help you?

> **STEP ❷ 단서 찾기**
> → 제시문의 주변 상황을 통해 문맥을 파악해야 해요.
>
> **말론 씨:** 수업을 취소하거나 학생들에게 자신이 9시 15분쯤에 도착할 것임을 알려 달라고 요청
>
> **빌렉 씨:** 수키와 바꿔 수업 시간 변경 제안

말론 씨의 요청

Paula Malone   **January 23, 8:55 A.M.**
Would you either cancel the class or let the students know that I'll be there about 9:15?

Martin Bileck   **January 23, 8:57 A.M.**
Most of your students are already here, so I hate to cancel. Suki is also working today and is here early.

빌렉 씨의 제안

I'll ask her to switch class with you, and you can teach the 10:00 class.

Paula Malone   **January 23, 8:58 A.M.**
That works out perfectly. Thanks.

> **STEP ❶ 질문 파악: 의도 파악 문제**
> → 문제를 읽고 지문에서 제시문의 위치를 확인해요.

Q At 8:58 A.M., what does Ms. Malone most likely mean when she writes, "**That works out perfectly**"?

  (A) She likes Mr. Bileck's idea.
  (B) She likes exercising in the morning.
  (C) She is excited about her new job.
  (D) She is happy that she has the day off.

> **STEP ❸ 정답 찾기**
> → 수업 시간을 변경하여 10시에 수업을 할 수 있을 것이라는 빌렉 씨의 아이디어가 좋다는 의미이므로, 정답은 (A)예요.

어휘 | gym 체육관 mechanical problem 기계적인 문제 behind schedule 예정보다 늦게 switch 바꾸다

1. Sign

> ## Tintern on Cherwell
>
> *Antique furniture, lighting, glassware, ceramics, rugs, and other home decor items*
> Open Monday–Thursday 9 A.M.–6 P.M., Saturday Noon–5 P.M.
> Inquire within about our antique furniture reupholstery and repair service.
> Michael Grasmere, Proprietor
> 13 Norham Mews, Oxford • Telephone: (0306) 999 0164 • www.tinternoncherwell.co.uk

What type of business is Tintern on Cherwell?

(A) An architectural firm

(B) A home furnishings shop

2. Form

> ### *Aunt Amelia's Cakes*
> Home-style cakes, tarts, and more!
>
> Thank you for your purchase. We value our customers' feedback. Please take the time to fill out the enclosed survey and return in the addressed, postage-paid envelope we have provided. In return, we will send you a coupon for 20 percent off the price of your next purchase.
>
> Rate the following on a scale of 1 to 5, with 5 being "excellent" and 1 being "poor."

Taste	1	2	3	4	(5)
Texture	1	2	3	4	(5)
Decoration (if applicable)	(1)	2	3	4	5
Overall appearance	(1)	2	3	4	5

What are customers asked to do?

(A) Pick up a cake

(B) Mail a form

어휘 | **1.** antique furniture 고가구 ceramics 도자기류 decor (실내) 장식 reupholstery 재장식
2. value 소중히 여기다 fill out (서식을) 기입하다 addressed 주소가 적힌 postage-paid envelope 우편요금 지급필 반송용 봉투 mail (우편으로) 보내다 form 서식, 양식

Questions 1-2 refer to the following card.

**Custom-fitted replacement windows designed
for tropical and subtropical climates**

Serving Residential and Commercial Needs

Free estimates

Visit our showroom at
447 Holomua Street, Hilo, HI 96720
Monday through Saturday, 10:00 A.M.–6:00 P.M.
Joseph Kalani
Product Consultant

---

1. In what field is Mr. Kalani employed?

(A) Insurance
(B) Cleaning and maintenance
(C) Commercial advertising
(D) Retail sales

2. What is indicated about Rainbow Windows?

(A) It is hiring new technicians.
(B) It has just renovated a showroom.
(C) It serves homeowners and businesses.
(D) It has just moved to Holomua Street.

어휘 | custom-fitted 맞춤형의 replacement 교체 residential 주거의 commercial 상업의 estimate 견적(서)

Questions 3-4 refer to the following form.

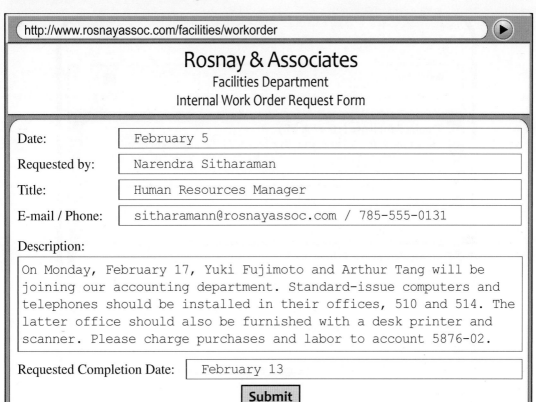

http://www.rosnayassoc.com/facilities/workorder

Rosnay & Associates
Facilities Department
Internal Work Order Request Form

Date: February 5

Requested by: Narendra Sitharaman

Title: Human Resources Manager

E-mail / Phone: sitharamann@rosnayassoc.com / 785-555-0131

Description:

On Monday, February 17, Yuki Fujimoto and Arthur Tang will be joining our accounting department. Standard-issue computers and telephones should be installed in their offices, 510 and 514. The latter office should also be furnished with a desk printer and scanner. Please charge purchases and labor to account 5876-02.

Requested Completion Date: February 13

Submit

3. What most likely did Rosnay & Associates recently do?

   (A) They merged with an accounting firm.
   (B) They upgraded their computer system.
   (C) They hired additional employees.
   (D) They changed their purchasing process.

4. What is the order for?

   (A) Equipment setup
   (B) Furniture assembly
   (C) Printer repairs
   (D) Office cleaning

어휘 | description 설명 install 설치하다 latter 후자의 furnish 비치하다 purchase 구매(품) labor 일, 노동

Questions 5-6 refer to the following text-message chain.

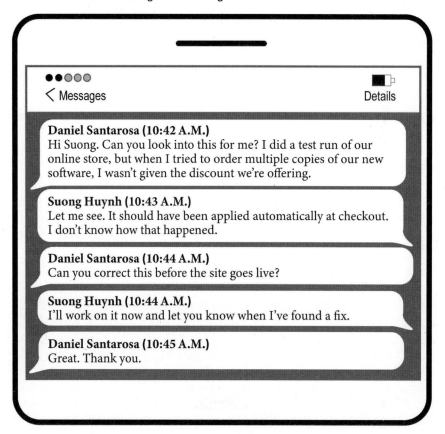

Daniel Santarosa (10:42 A.M.)
Hi Suong. Can you look into this for me? I did a test run of our online store, but when I tried to order multiple copies of our new software, I wasn't given the discount we're offering.

Suong Huynh (10:43 A.M.)
Let me see. It should have been applied automatically at checkout. I don't know how that happened.

Daniel Santarosa (10:44 A.M.)
Can you correct this before the site goes live?

Suong Huynh (10:44 A.M.)
I'll work on it now and let you know when I've found a fix.

Daniel Santarosa (10:45 A.M.)
Great. Thank you.

5. What is suggested about Mr. Santarosa?

(A) He works for a shipping company.
(B) He works in the software industry.
(C) He has corrected an issue.
(D) He has developed a new product.

6. At 10:43 A.M., what does Ms. Huynh mean when she writes "Let me see"?

(A) She will investigate a problem.
(B) She will determine a discount.
(C) She is helping Mr. Santarosa's customer to place an order.
(D) She wants Mr. Santarosa to show her a particular Web page.

어휘 | automatically 자동으로 correct 고치다 fix 해법

From:
Calden Company
5 Extension Road
Mobile, Alabama 36606
T: 251-555-0152

Calden Company

To:
Landers Restaurant
71 W. Charles Street
Chapel Hill, NC 27515

Item Number	Description	Quantity	Unit Price	Subtotals
121-B	Salad plates (12/case)	4	$25.59	_____
782-A	Engraved soup spoons (12/pack)	4	$5.78	$23.12
78-K	Soup bowls (48/case)	1	$58.19	$58.19
59-C	Cloth napkins (12/pack)	8	$13.29	$106.32
193-W	5-quart stainless steel sauté pan with lid	3	$46.31	$138.93

			Total Cost	**$326.56**
			Shipping	**$17.92**
			Amount Due	**$344.48**

Note: The engraved spoons you ordered will be shipped separately, directly from one of our retail locations. The salad plates you ordered are currently out of stock and will not be available for 2–3 weeks. You will not be charged for that item until it is shipped, and the shipping charge for that item will be reduced by 50 percent. We apologize for any inconvenience.

7. What most likely is Calden Company?

(A) A regional catering service
(B) An interstate shipping company
(C) A chain of kitchen goods stores
(D) An exclusive restaurant

8. What is indicated about Item 782-A?

(A) It was mislabeled in the catalog.
(B) It arrived damaged.
(C) It is not available in the color requested.
(D) It is being sent from a retail store.

9. What is indicated about the shipment of the items?

(A) One item will be shipped at a discount.
(B) One item could not be shipped due to bad weather.
(C) Some items will be shipped overnight.
(D) Some items were shipped to the wrong address.

어휘 | engrave 조각하다 separately 별도로 retail 소매의 currently 현재 out of stock 재고가 없는 reduce 할인하다 apologize for ~에 대해 사과하다 inconvenience 불편

Questions 10-12 refer to the following information on a Web page.

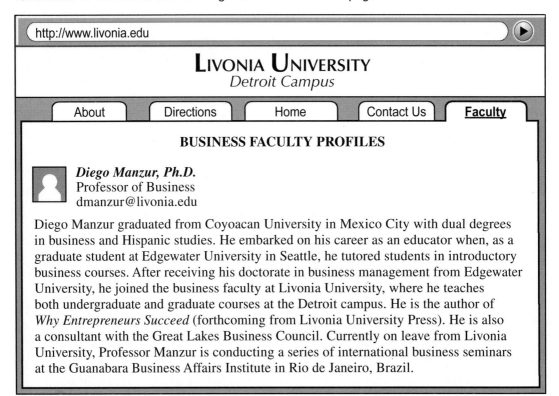

10. What is the purpose of the information?

(A) To advertise a business seminar
(B) To publicize facts about an employee
(C) To invite entrepreneurs to purchase a book
(D) To provide details for a job application

11. Where did Professor Manzur begin his teaching career?

(A) In Seattle
(B) In Detroit
(C) In Mexico City
(D) In Rio de Janeiro

12. What is indicated about Professor Manzur?

(A) He is a professor of Hispanic studies at the moment.
(B) He used to work for the Great Lakes Business Council.
(C) He is working temporarily in Brazil.
(D) He owns a business.

어휘 | faculty 교수진 embark 시작하다 tutor 가르치다 introductory 입문의 doctorate 박사학위 undergraduate 학부의 graduate 대학원생의 entrepreneur 기업인 forthcoming 다가오는 on leave 휴가 중인

Sarah Lo [9:38 A.M.]	Hi all. I'd like your input. Jovita Wilson in sales just told me that her client, Mr. Tran, wants us to deliver his order a week early. Can we do that?
Alex Ralston [9:40 A.M.]	If we rush, we can assemble the hardwood frames in two days.
Riko Kimura [9:41 A.M.]	And my department needs just a day to print and cut the fabric to cover the cushion seating.
Mia Ochoa [9:42 A.M.]	But initially you need the designs, right? My team can finish that by end of day today.
Sarah Lo [9:43 A.M.]	OK. Then we'll be ready for the finishing steps by end of day on Wednesday. Alex, once you have the fabric, how long will it take to build the cushions, stuff them, and attach them to the frames?
Alex Ralston [9:45 A.M.]	That will take two days—if my group can set aside regular work to do that.
Sarah Lo [9:46 A.M.]	I can authorize that. Bill, how long will it take your department to package the order and ship it?
Bill Belmore [9:48 A.M.]	We can complete that on Monday morning.
Sarah Lo [9:49 A.M.]	Great. Thanks all. I'll let Jovita know so she can inform the client.

SEND

RC

PART 7

---

13. At 9:38 A.M., what does Ms. Lo mean when she writes, "I'd like your input"?

(A) She needs some numerical data.
(B) She needs some financial contributions.
(C) She wants to develop some projects.
(D) She wants to gather some opinions.

14. For what type of company does Ms. Lo most likely work?

(A) A package delivery business
(B) A furniture manufacturer
(C) An art supply store
(D) A construction firm

15. According to the discussion, whose department must complete their work first?

(A) Mr. Belmore's department
(B) Ms. Kimura's department
(C) Ms. Ochoa's department
(D) Mr. Ralston's department

16. What will Ms. Wilson most likely tell Mr. Tran?

(A) That she can meet his request for rush work
(B) That there will be an extra charge for completing his order
(C) That his order will be ready for delivery on Friday
(D) That she will meet him at her office next Monday

어휘 | input 의견, 생각 order 주문(품) assemble 조립하다 hardwood 경재, 단단한 나무 frame 틀, 뼈대 print 날염하다 fabric 천, 직물 seating (의자, 쿠션 등의) 속 initially 처음에 finishing step 마무리 단계 stuff 속을 채우다 attach A to B A를 B에 부착하다 set aside ~을 따로 떼어놓다, 고려하지 않다 authorize 허가하다, 권한을 부여하다 package 포장하다; 소포 ship 배송하다

출제 포인트 1 복수 지문은 편지/이메일이 포함된 구성이 가장 일반적이에요.
출제 포인트 2 문제를 풀기 전에 지문의 종류, 수신인/발신인 등을 훑으면서 각 지문들 간의 관계를 파악하는 것이 좋아요.

■ 지문의 흐름 및 문제풀이 전략

정답과 해설 p.179

Calling all artists!

Are you an amateur or professional graphic artist? Relling Transit (RT) Center is holding its first ever logo contest. Logos that are related to bus or train travel will be accepted from August 2 to 22 at the RT Central Office, located at Relling Terminal. Thirty Finalists will be selected for display in the alcove at Union Street Station. From September 1 to 30, the public will be able to cast a ballot and vote on their favorite logo. Four prizes will be awarded.

First place: *Yellow pass.* Good for unlimited rides on the RT local train or bus for five days

Second place: *Blue pass.* Good for unlimited rides on the RT local train for three days.

Third place: *Green pass.* Good for one round-trip ticket to any destination on the RT express train

Fourth place: *Red pass.* Good for one round-trip ticket to any destination on an RT express bus.

> **STEP ❸ 두 지문 간의 연결 고리 찾기**
> → 5일간 유효한 패스는 옐로 패스예요.

Dear Ms. Ivankova:

Congratulations on winning Relling Transit Center's Logo Contest. Enclosed is your prize. Please note that the pass does not have a definite start date. It is valid for any five-day period, beginning whenever you wish.

On behalf of Relling Transit Center, I would like to thank you for your contribution.

Sincerely,

Rita Rajwal
Community Relations Manager, Relling Transit Center

> **STEP ❷ 단서 찾기**
> → 이반코바 씨가 부상으로 받은 것은 5일짜리 패스입니다.

> **STEP ❶ 질문 파악**
> → 이반코바 씨가 받은 것을 묻는 문제예요.

Q What did Ms. Ivankova receive?

(A) A yellow pass

(B) A blue pass

(C) A green pass

(D) A red pass

> **STEP ❹ 정답 찾기**
> → 이반코바 씨가 부상으로 받은 것은 5일짜리 패스라는 것과, 옐로 패스가 5일간 유효하다는 두 단서를 조합해 보면, 이반코바 씨가 받은 것은 옐로 패스이므로 정답은 (A)예요.

어휘 | alcove 벽감(벽면을 들어가게 해서 만든 공간) cast a ballot 투표를 하다 valid 유효한 on behalf of ~를 대신하여

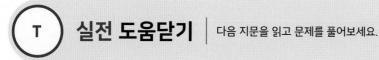
Questions 1-2

Advertisement + Notice

Anderson Productions is offering an opportunity for a student of journalism to work as an intern at Anderson's local television studios in Odessa. The intern will be paid on an hourly basis for the two months of July and August and will assist in the production of sports news programs for the recently launched Spanish-language channel, Lesco TV.

Applications listing relevant courses completed and any awards received will be accepted between May 1 and May 15 by the human resources office on the first floor of Avery Hall, next to the advertising office. Applications and résumés can also be sent by e-mail to openings@hr.andersonproductions.org with "Internship" in the subject line. Interviews will be held on May 25 in rooms E30 and E67 on the second floor.

The internship will be granted to a qualified candidate who is fluent in English and Spanish. Computer and Internet research skills are required. Please no telephone calls about this opening.

Remodeling

The human resources office and the advertising office in Avery Hall will be closed for remodeling from May 10 to May 15. The human resources office will temporarily operate in Room D20, and the advertising office in room D22 of Avery Hall. We do not expect any of the regular operations of these departments to be affected by this change. Thank you for your patience in this matter as we strive to make Anderson Productions a state-of-the-art facility.

Fatima Chouaba, Director of Operations
Anderson Productions

1. What is indicated about Anderson Productions?
   (A) It covers mainly local events.
   (B) It has started a new channel.

2. What is suggested about the remodeling?
   (A) It will take place on the first floor.
   (B) It will require a building to be closed.

어휘 | on an hourly basis 시간 단위로 launch 시작하다 relevant 관련된, 연관된 grant 수여하다, 주다 qualified 자격 있는
temporarily 임시로 operate 운영하다 operation 운영 affect 영향을 미치다 patience 인내 state-of-the-art 최신식의

RC

PART 7

Questions 1-5 refer to the following notice and e-mail.

This Week on "Book Talk"

Tune in on Wednesday, February 7, at 1:00 P.M., for *Book Talk*, KNAE-FM's weekly radio show celebrating books and authors. On this week's program, *Book Talk* host Pablo Araya talks with Anne Kindall about her latest novel, *Feliz Blue*.

While traveling in Brazil, Ms. Kindall was inspired to create and research a story about musicians vacationing there who find themselves drawn to the various styles of Brazilian music. They soon begin to help one of the characters, a young artist, record his debut album. You will hear some of Ms. Kindall's recordings of Brazilian music and learn about her long-standing fascination with South American culture, which started when she was an exchange student in Peru.

Listen to KNAE-FM's *Book Talk* every Wednesday at 1:00 P.M.

E-mail	

Date:	February 21
To:	Anne Kindall <akindall@burland.edu>
From:	Pablo Araya <pablo.araya@knae-fm.com>
Re:	Upcoming call-in show

Dear Anne,

Judging from the e-mail response, our recent interview on *Book Talk* generated a lot of interest from listeners. I expect we will have plenty of people phoning in and texting questions when you are here for our first ever live *Book Talk* show on March 14. Please be at the radio station at noon so we have time to set up for the broadcast, which, as always, will be transmitted over the air and simultaneously streamed on our Web site.

By the way, I saw that *Feliz Blue* received a glowing review in *Publishers Magazine*. Congratulations! I hope it stays on the best-seller list even longer than your first novel did.

Yours,

Pablo

1. Who is Mr. Araya?

   (A) A writer
   (B) An exchange student
   (C) A musician
   (D) A radio host

2. What is indicated about *Feliz Blue*?

   (A) It was written in Peru.
   (B) It takes place in Brazil.
   (C) It was advertised on a television show.
   (D) Its main character is a sculptor.

3. What does Mr. Araya ask Ms. Kindall to do?

   (A) Send him a copy of her book
   (B) Provide photographs from her travels
   (C) Give advice about writing novels
   (D) Arrive early to prepare for a broadcast

4. What did NOT happen during the *Book Talk* show on February 7?

   (A) An author discussed one of her works.
   (B) The program was aired on the Internet.
   (C) Listeners called in to ask questions.
   (D) Recordings of music were broadcast.

5. What can be inferred about Ms. Kindall's first novel?

   (A) It was read by many people.
   (B) It required extensive research.
   (C) It was published in South America.
   (D) It described her experiences in school.

RC

PART 7

어휘 | inspire 영감을 주다 long-standing 오래 지속되는 fascination 매혹 call-in show 시청자 전화 참여 프로그램 generate 만들어 내다 plenty of 많은 transmit 전송하다 simultaneously 동시에 glowing 극찬하는

Questions 6-10 refer to the following advertisement and e-mail.

Vaughn Vacations

Book your getaway today! Vaughn Vacations is offering 30 percent off the price of the following packages.

Relaxing Escape: Want to get out of town? Book a relaxing weekend at the Snow Peaks Hotel and Spa in Vermont. Our package includes a large suite and a guided hike in the mountains. Award-winning restaurant on site.

Winter Paradise: Enjoy the beaches of Puerto Rico. Our weeklong package includes beautiful beachside accommodations at the Aguas Bonitas Hotel, water sports lessons, and nighttime entertainment. Perfect weather year-round. Group rates available!

Family Fun: Looking for a great trip for the whole family? Enjoy activities and excursions for parents and children with our four-day trip to the Briarsfield Hotel and Amusement Park in beautiful Colorado. Food vendors are available throughout the park.

Sun-Filled Delight: Enjoy five days, four nights by the crystal blue waters of the Caribbean. Package includes daily excursions, gourmet meals, a deluxe room, and outstanding service at Sunshine Villas in Saint Thomas.

Offer valid for travel from December 1 until January 31. Book by October 31 to receive a free travel guide for your destination and a tote bag. Visit our office in Sanders Square, call (518) 555-0133, or e-mail info@vaughnvacations.net. For specific pricing details, visit our Web site at http://www.vaughnvacations.com.

From:	AllisonGelden@ridgeford_hospital.org
To:	info@vaughnvacations.net
Date:	December 4
Subject:	Getaway Dec 17 through Dec 19

Good morning,

A colleague of mine noted that you are offering promotions on a number of vacation packages. I know this is short notice, but I wondered if it might still be possible to book one of your promotional vacations from the evening of Friday, December 17, to Sunday, December 19? My husband and I would really like to get away soon, but we are both physicians, and that is the only weekend we are not working or attending a conference. We would prefer to visit a quiet spot in the mountains, if possible. Please let me know if you have anything available.

Thanks,

Dr. Allison Gelden, Neurologist
Ridgeford Hospital

6. What is included only with the Sun-Filled Delight vacation package?

(A) Excursions
(B) Meals
(C) Entertainment
(D) Child care

7. What most likely can be found in Sanders Square?

(A) A medical clinic
(B) A hotel
(C) A restaurant
(D) A travel agency

8. Why do the Geldens want to travel from December 17 to 19?

(A) It is the only time they are free.
(B) The weather is forecasted to be pleasant.
(C) They are presenting at a conference.
(D) They are attending the opening of a hospital.

9. Where will the Geldens most likely go?

(A) To Vermont
(B) To Puerto Rico
(C) To Colorado
(D) To Saint Thomas

10. What will Dr. Gelden receive if she books a vacation package?

(A) A tote bag and travel guide
(B) Tickets to an event
(C) A discount
(D) Coupons for future travel

RC

PART 7

어휘 | getaway 휴양(지) on site 부지 내에, 현장에 accommodations 숙박 시설 excursion (짧은) 유람 vendor 노점 gourmet 미식가 outstanding 탁월한 valid 유효한 destination 목적지 promotion 판촉 short notice 촉박한 통지 physician 의사 neurologist 신경과 전문의

Questions 11-15 refer to the following e-mail, Web site, and schedule.

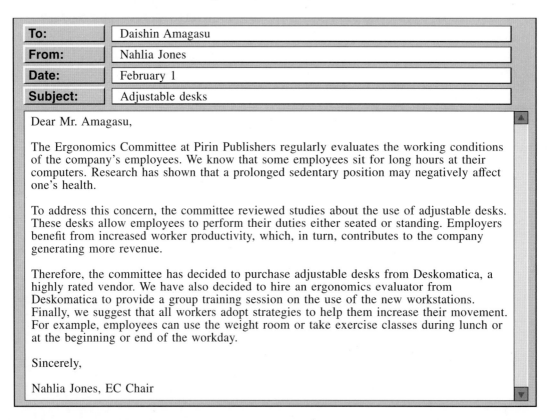

To: Daishin Amagasu
From: Nahlia Jones
Date: February 1
Subject: Adjustable desks

Dear Mr. Amagasu,

The Ergonomics Committee at Pirin Publishers regularly evaluates the working conditions of the company's employees. We know that some employees sit for long hours at their computers. Research has shown that a prolonged sedentary position may negatively affect one's health.

To address this concern, the committee reviewed studies about the use of adjustable desks. These desks allow employees to perform their duties either seated or standing. Employers benefit from increased worker productivity, which, in turn, contributes to the company generating more revenue.

Therefore, the committee has decided to purchase adjustable desks from Deskomatica, a highly rated vendor. We have also decided to hire an ergonomics evaluator from Deskomatica to provide a group training session on the use of the new workstations. Finally, we suggest that all workers adopt strategies to help them increase their movement. For example, employees can use the weight room or take exercise classes during lunch or at the beginning or end of the workday.

Sincerely,

Nahlia Jones, EC Chair

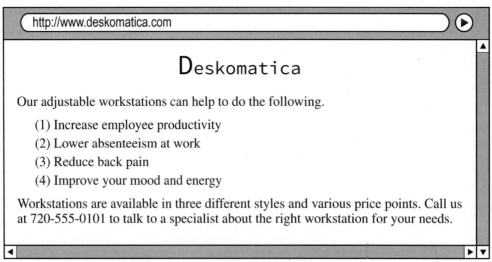

http://www.deskomatica.com

Deskomatica

Our adjustable workstations can help to do the following.

(1) Increase employee productivity

(2) Lower absenteeism at work

(3) Reduce back pain

(4) Improve your mood and energy

Workstations are available in three different styles and various price points. Call us at 720-555-0101 to talk to a specialist about the right workstation for your needs.

Pirin Publishers
Training Sessions with Mr. Xavier of Deskomatica

Monday, February 25	
9:00–10:00 A.M.	Accounting Department—Room 438
10:15–11:15 A.M.	Translating Department—Room 323
12:00–1:00 P.M.	Copyedit Department—Room 102

Tuesday, February 26	
10:30–11:30 A.M.	Payroll Department—Room 216
12:00–1:00 P.M.	Art Department—Room 112

11. What is one purpose of the e-mail?

(A) To justify a policy change
(B) To ask for participants in a study
(C) To explain a purchase
(D) To report an increase in revenue

12. What does the committee suggest
employees do?

(A) Contact the management team
(B) Participate in athletic activities
(C) Visit the Deskomatica Web site
(D) Request ergonomic keyboards

13. What benefit of adjustable desks is noted both
in Ms. Jones's e-mail and on the Web page?

(A) Their impact on workers' absence
(B) Their improvement of users' concentration
(C) Their effect on employees' productivity
(D) Their influence on workers' moods

14. What is suggested about Mr. Xavier?

(A) He is a publisher at Pirin Publishers.
(B) He resolved a conflict in his schedule.
(C) He recently started a new career.
(D) He provides training to employees.

15. With what department will Mr. Xavier meet on
Tuesday morning?

(A) Accounting
(B) Copyedit
(C) Payroll
(D) Art

어휘 | adjustable desk (높낮이) 조절 가능한 책상 ergonomics 인체공학 prolonged 장기의 sedentary 앉아 있는 affect 영향을
미치다 address 해결하다 benefit 이득을 얻다 productivity 생산성 in turn 결국 contribute 기여하다 generate 창출하다
revenue 수익 adopt 채택하다 weight room 체력단련실 absenteeism 잦은 결근 price point 기준 소매가격

Questions 16-20 refer to the following e-mails and invoice.

From:	Todd Goodwin <t.goodwin@ossieofficesupply.com>
To:	OOS Management Team <management@ossieofficesupply.com>
Date:	July 2
Subject:	Team meeting agenda
Attachment:	⬚Kurminoff article

Hi, team.

Here is the agenda for today's management meeting. See you at 1 P.M.!

1. New-employee training schedule. Karen Park was hired this week and will begin training on July 8. Please look at your schedules before the meeting and come prepared to take a training shift.

2. Second quarter sales results. Julio Gomez will review our in-store sales. I will discuss our online sales.

3. Online sales. Please read the attached article about boosting online sales and come to the meeting prepared to discuss its ideas. We need to boost online sales, so I think we should consider offering free shipping or returns, a buy-one-get-one-free special, or a 10 percent loyalty discount for return customers.

4. Progress on finding a new shipping company. Last month on June 14, I presented on the results of a customer survey, which showed that customers want to be able to track their packages. They also want lower shipping rates. Julie Lindt will present on a few shipping companies for us to consider.

Todd Goodwin
Ossie Office Supply General Manager

From:	Ossie Office Supply <invoice@ossieofficesupply.com>
To:	Seema Shah <s.shah@gopromail.com>
Date:	August 18
Subject:	Invoice #08912

Thank you for your purchase from Ossie Office Supply! Please see your invoice below.

Item	Quantity	Unit Price	Total Price
Black Ballpoint Pens (8 pack)	10	$2.99	$29.90
Red Ballpoint Pens (8 Pack)	2	$2.99	$5.98
White printer paper (500 sheets)	20	$4.29	$85.80
		Subtotal	$121.68
		Discount: (10% off)	$12.17
		Tax: (5%)	$6.08
		Shipping: (express)	$10.00
		Pay this amount:	**$125.59**

Your online order can be revised or canceled up until it ships. If you need to make a change, please call (413) 555-0130. The progress of your shipment can be tracked on Zip Ship's Website using tracking number 0008971 (zipship.com/trackmypackage).

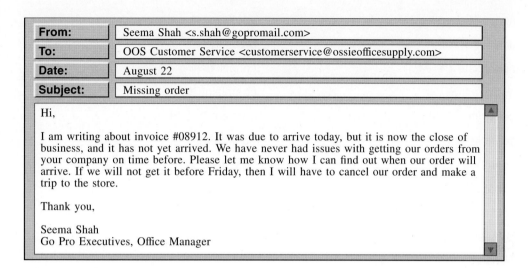

From:	Seema Shah <s.shah@gopromail.com>
To:	OOS Customer Service <customerservice@ossieofficesupply.com>
Date:	August 22
Subject:	Missing order

Hi,

I am writing about invoice #08912. It was due to arrive today, but it is now the close of business, and it has not yet arrived. We have never had issues with getting our orders from your company on time before. Please let me know how I can find out when our order will arrive. If we will not get it before Friday, then I will have to cancel our order and make a trip to the store.

Thank you,

Seema Shah
Go Pro Executives, Office Manager

16. What does Mr. Goodwin ask members of the management team to do?

(A) Help to train a new employee
(B) Submit their teams' sales results
(C) Make edits to an article
(D) Review a return policy

17. Who will present on shipping companies?

(A) Ms. Park
(B) Ms. Lindt
(C) Mr. Goodwin
(D) Mr. Gomez

18. Which of Mr. Goodwin's suggestions did the group most likely approve?

(A) Free shipping
(B) Free returns
(C) A buy-one-get-one-free special
(D) A loyalty discount

19. What will a customer support representative most likely ask Ms. Shah to do?

(A) Visit Zip Ship's Web site
(B) Cancel an order
(C) Visit an Ossie Office Supply store
(D) Call the customer service number

20. When was Ms. Shah's delivery supposed to arrive?

(A) On June 14
(B) On July 2
(C) On August 18
(D) On August 22

어휘 | agenda 안건 buy-one-get-one-free 원플러스원 return customer 재구매 고객 progress 진행 track 추적하다 shipping rate 배송비 revise 수정하다 due to ~하기로 예정된

■ 감사 / 축하

accomplished 뛰어난

achieve 달성하다

appreciate 감사히 여기다

award 수여하다

celebrate 축하하다

commitment 헌신, 약속

contribute 공헌하다

donation 기부

hold 열다, 개최하다

impressed 감명 받은

pleased 즐거운(=delighted, glad)

reason 이유

■ 문제 / 사과

apology 사과

breakage 파손

cancel 취소하다

complaint 불평

concern 걱정, 염려; 관련시키다

damaged 손상된

defective 결함 있는(=faulty)

exchange 교환; 교환하다

explain 설명하다

inconvenience 불편

postpone 미루다(=delay)

refund 환불; 환불하다

■ 구매 / 주문

account 계정, 계좌

brochure 소책자(=booklet)

bulk 대량

clarify 명확히 하다

confirm 확인하다

include 포함하다

method 방법

parcel 소포

purchase 구매; 구매하다

receipt 영수증, 수령

respond 응답하다

status 상태, 지위

■ 출장 / 여행

accommodations 숙박 시설

belongings 소지품

destination 목적지

book 예약하다

board 탑승하다

departure 출발

expense 비용

itinerary 여행 일정표

passport 여권

reservation 예약

round trip 왕복 여행

take off 이륙하다

■ 구인 / 구직

application 지원(서)

benefits 복지 혜택

bilingual 두 개 언어를 구사하는

candidate 후보자

certified 공인된

résumé 이력서

cover letter 자기소개서

desirable 바람직한

deadline 마감일 (=due date)

degree 학위

fluent 능숙한

hire 고용하다

Human Resources 인사과

job opening 공석

preference 우대사항

applicant 지원자

perform tasks 업무를 수행하다

permanent 정규직의

primary duty 주요 업무

proficiency 능숙함

qualified 자격을 갖춘

reference 추천서

relevant 관련된 (=related)

replacement 교체, 후임자

required 필수적인

employ 채용하다

headquarters 본사

■ 공사 / 건축

aim 목표; 겨냥하다

annex 부속 건물

commuter 통근자

interrupt 방해하다, 중단시키다

launch 시작하다

plumbing 배관 (작업)

procedure 절차

put into action 조치를 취하다

refurbish 재단장하다

repave 도로를 재포장하다

restoration 복원, 복구

resume 재개하다

■ 부동산

commercial 상업적인; 광고

flat 아파트

floor plan 평면도

fully-furnished 내부가 완비된

landlord 집주인

lease 임대하다

realtor 부동산 중개인

rent 임대료; 임대[임차]하다

residential 거주용의

separate 분리된

located ~에 위치한 (=situated)

studio 원룸 형태의 공간

RC

PART 7

■ 경제

adverse effect 역효과, 부작용

analyze 분석하다

debt 빚

commerce 상업

expenditure 지출

figures 수치

investment 투자

lack 부족(하다)

market share 시장 점유율

quarter 분기

recession 불황 (=downturn)

spokesperson 대변인

■ 경영

aid 원조, 지원; 돕다

aspiring 장차 ~이 되려는

associate 제휴하다, 결합시키다; 사원

boost 북돋우다

competitor 경쟁자

corporation 기업, 법인

entrepreneur 기업가

executive 임원; 행정의

expand 확장하다

founder 설립자

morale 근로 의욕, 사기

motivate 동기를 부여하다

■ 청구 / 결제

amount 양

balance 잔액

billing address 청구 주소

deposit 보증금, 착수금[선불금]

estimate 견적(액); 어림잡다

expedite 신속히 처리하다

invoice 송장

measurement 치수, 측정

overdue 기한이 지난, 늦은

payment 지불(액)

recipient 수령인

reduction 할인, 축소

■ 상품 / 서비스

appliance 전자제품

assemble 조립하다

beverage 음료

browse 둘러보다

custom-made 맞춤식의

diverse 다양한

manufacturer 제조업체

offering 할인, 특가 행사

price tag 가격표

release 출시하다

specification 명세서

state-of-the-art 최신식의